FIGHTING POVERTY
Labour Markets and Inequality in South Africa

Haroon Bhorat
Murray Leibbrandt
Muzi Maziya
Servaas van der Berg
Ingrid Woolard

AERC
CREA

UCT
PRESS

Fighting Poverty — Labour Markets and Inequality in South Africa

First published 2001

© UCT Press
PO Box 24309, Lansdowne 7779

ISBN 1 919713 62 X

Copy editing and proofing by Alfred le Maitre
Typesetting by Zebra Publications, Cape Town
Cover design by The Pumphaus Design Studio cc

Printed and bound in South Africa by Mills Litho
11th Avenue, Maitland, Cape Town

Contents

FOREWORD

In 1997, the African Economic Research Consortium (AERC) initiated a large-scale collaborative research and training programme – Poverty, Income Distribution and Labour Markets. The South African study was the first of a number of country case studies funded under this programme. A key feature of this programme has been 'twinning' between the research teams and a collaborating university. Under this arrangement, three of the authors of this book spent a sabbatical semester at Cornell University in the first half of 1998. During this 'twinning' period, we met with the authors frequently to discuss research ideas, and they also participated fully in the intellectual life of the labour economics and development economics communities at Cornell. Upon returning home, the team completed the initial draft of this work, presented their work widely, both in South Africa and abroad, and then revisited and finalised the manuscript.

This study uses current methods in modern labour economics, deploys them on appropriate South African data sets, and answers questions on which previously we had limited knowledge, or in some cases none at all. In manuscript form, this volume is already regarded as *the* major reference work on labour markets, poverty and inequality in South Africa, and its reputation will surely grow after the book is published and it is circulated more widely. In the larger African context, the South African study sets the standard for other African research teams, and indeed we have consistently referred researchers in other countries to it as a model for formulating and carrying out their own research. We are delighted that the AERC programme has led to a fruitful South Africa–Cornell connection, and look forward to continued work over many years to come.

GARY FIELDS AND ERIK THORBECKE
Ithaca, New York
October 2000

The Contributors

- **Haroon Bhorat** is the Director of the Development Policy Research Unit at the University of Cape Town.
- **Murray Leibbrandt** is a Professor in the Department of Economics at the University of Cape Town.
- **Muzi Maziya** was formerly a Senior Analyst at the Competition Commission, and is now an Independent Researcher on labour markets and socioeconomic issues.
- **Servaas van der Berg** is a Professor in the Department of Economics at the University of Stellenbosch.
- **Ingrid Woolard** is a Senior Lecturer in the Department of Economics and Economic History at the University of Port Elizabeth.

Acknowledgements

This study was jointly funded by the African Economic Research Consortium (AERC) and the South African Department of Labour. It had its genesis at the AERC's Training Workshop on Poverty, Inequality and Labour Markets which was held in Kampala in August 1997. We have incurred many debts over the full cycle of this project. Although the members of the research team take full responsibility for the output, we gratefully acknowledge all of the input and help we have received.

The South African team arrived at the 1997 workshop with long-standing interests in labour markets, poverty and inequality. However, the training offered at this workshop was instrumental in illustrating the shortcomings of the existing South African literature, and therefore strongly indicated the areas of work that would require special attention in the new project.

Since late 1997, the AERC coordinators for this new research theme, Erik Thorbecke, Ali Ali and Germano Mwabu, and the AERC research division under Ibrahim Elbadawi, Augustine Fosu and Dominique Njinkeu have offered constant support for our work. This support included facilitating the presentation of sections of our work at AERC workshops in Cape Town, Accra and Nairobi, organising for the formal refereeing of our work and, most importantly, showing personal interest in our work.

At the 1997 workshop, the South African team decided that it would seek a more formal bridge with the South African policy milieu by asking the South African Department of Labour to partner the AERC in funding the project. From the first, the Department responded positively. Guy Mhone, the Chief Director Labour Market Policy, gave valuable commentary on the proposal and took charge of the formal aspects of the partnership between his Department and the AERC. Upon his departure from the Department, Cynthia Alvillar, the Director Labour Market Policy, took over these roles. She organised for the presentation of aspects of our work in the Department of Labour and broadened the ambit of these fora to include other public-sector and NGO researchers to whom the issues are pertinent.

Part of the AERC approach to the country studies on this theme has been to build in a budget for the twinning of country teams with an international researcher and university. At the 1997 workshop, the South African team met Professor Gary Fields of Cornell University, as well as the strong Cornell contingent that was teaching at the workshop. We were fortunate that Professor Fields agreed to be twinned with our study. He has been doing research at the interface of labour markets, poverty and inequality for many years, and it is hard to think of another academic better suited to facilitate our work. The twinning process has been a most valuable and enjoyable aspect of this project for the South African team. The major reason for this has been the friendly but intensive working relationship that we have enjoyed with Professor Fields – from the preparation of the South African proposal to our time at Cornell and through to the completion of this study.

Three of our team spent time at Cornell in the first half of 1998. This period was unique for us. Cornell University is incredibly well-endowed with high-profile academics in both Labour Economics and Development Economics. The range and quality of teaching enabled each of us to meet specific and different needs. Despite their eminence, many professors showed interest in our work and gave freely of their time. Special mention in this regard should be made of professors Thorbecke, Kanbur, Jakubson, Sahn and Younger.

Aside from presentations at AERC workshops and Department of Labour policy seminars, our work has enjoyed exposure and commentary from a number of other seminars. We thank the seminar participants at Harvard University's Institute for International Development, Associates for International Research and Development of Tufts University, the Economics Department of the University of Massachusetts at Amherst, the Southern African Division of The World Bank, Cornell University's Institute for African Development, the Western Economic Association, the South African Economic Society's Biennial Conference, the Economics Department at the University of the Witwatersrand and the MacArthur Network Workshop on Inequality in South Africa.

Finally, as the project reached its maturity, it was natural that some of the research would find its way into the public domain in the form of working papers and journal articles. In the case of the former, this book is based on a series of nine working papers published under the auspices of the Development Policy Research Unit (DPRU), based at the School of Economics, University of Cape Town. In addition, several of the authors here have published components of these chapters in journals. Specifically, articles were published by:

- Bhorat in the *South African Journal of Economics*, 67(2), June 1999 and *Development Southern Africa*, 16(1), Autumn 1999;
- Leibbrandt and Woolard in *Development Southern Africa*, 16(1), Autumn 1999;
- Leibbrandt, Bhorat and Woolard in *Contemporary Economic Policy*, IXX(1), January 2001;
- Leibbrandt, Woolard and Bhorat in *Studies in Economics and Econometrics*, 24(3), November 2000;
- Van der Berg in *Development Southern Africa*, 14(4), December 1997.

The usual disclaimers apply to all of this work.

With regard to the final processing and publishing of this manuscript, the authors would like to thank Glenda Younge for supporting the researchers and Allison Stevens for her tireless efforts in liaising between the authors and the publishers.

Introduction

Murray Leibbrandt
Servaas van der Berg
Haroon Bhorat

This book focuses on inequality and poverty in contemporary South Africa. It pays particular attention to the interface between the functioning of the labour market and the generation of poverty and inequality at the household level. Although South Africa is an upper middle-income country, the social indicators suggest that living standards are closer to those of lower middle- or even low-income countries. This difference between economic status and social development in South Africa can be ascribed largely to high levels of material inequality that have left inordinately large numbers of people outside the economic mainstream. This implies that society is highly inefficient in converting economic resources into equitable social welfare outcomes.

As is well known, the cause of this malady lies mainly in the long history of segregation and discrimination that has left a legacy of inequality and poverty, and also, in more recent decades, low economic growth. The strong racial bases to this inequality have attracted special prominence. Malfunctioning labour markets have, in turn, been integral to South Africa's racially-based inequality. For most of the 20th century, the labour market was rigged by legislated occupational discrimination by race. In addition, clear racial differences in the quantity and quality of education, health and other social policy provisions reinforced this segmentation by skewing the human capital endowments with which participants entered the labour market.

Table 1 offers a broad-brush reflection of this unfortunate legacy. The table shows estimates of the per capita income of the different race groups since 1917.[1] Due to the variety of income and expenditure concepts used and the data deficiencies inherent in all the surveys, these figures should not be interpreted too finely. Nevertheless, despite this proviso, it is still possible to draw some broad conclusions from these data as to movements in per capita income. In the first place, the mean per capita income of the poorest group – Africans – reached the poverty line around 1970 and has since doubled. But, even today, many members of this group are still in poverty, as will be discussed later. In the high-growth 1960s, the African/white income gap actually increased, because skills scarcity, exacerbated by the industrial colour bar, led to a premium being paid on the wages of relatively skilled white workers. In the early 1970s, the shift in economic power and, to a lesser degree, changing skill profiles, narrowed the wage gap – and thereby the income gap. Thereafter, the impact on the income gap of the continued narrowing of the wage gap was partly counteracted by growing unemployment amongst those with the least

TABLE 1

Compilation of estimates of per capita personal income by race group (1995 rands),
and relative to white levels (1917–95)[a]

Year	White	Coloured	Asian	African	Average
		Per capita income in constant 1995 rands			
1917	R9 369	R2 061	R2 075	R849	R2 829
1924	R9 931	R1 986	R1 931	R788	R2 966
1936	R13 773	R2 151	R3 185	R1 048	R3 842
1946	R18 820	R3 068	R4 328	R1 671	R5 417
1956	R21 861	R3 698	R4 780	R1 883	R6 123
1959	R22 683	R3 568	R3 876	R1 746	R6 061
1960	R22 389	R3 568	R3 828	R1 815	R6 006
1970	R32 799	R5 684	R6 630	R2 246	R7 986
1975	R35 757	R6 945	R9 095	R3 075	R9 102
1980	R34 655	R6 623	R8 821	R2 931	R8 472
1987	R32 854	R6 862	R9 910	R2 781	R7 643
1993	R32 789	R6 877	R14 376	R3 260	R7 265
1995	R28 436	R5 682	R13 766	R3 835	R7 388
		Relative per capita personal incomes (% of white level)			
1917	100	22,0	22,1	9,1	
1924	100	20,0	19,4	7,9	
1936	100	15,6	23,1	7,6	
1946	100	16,3	23,0	8,9	
1956	100	16,9	21,9	8,6	
1959	100	15,7	17,1	7,7	
1960	100	15,9	17,1	8,1	
1970	100	17,3	20,2	6,8	
1975	100	19,4	25,4	8,6	
1980	100	19,1	25,5	8,5	
1987	100	20,9	30,2	8,5	
1993	100	21,0	43,8	9,9	
1995	100	20,0	48,4	13,5	

[a] Own estimates based on McGrath 1983, official national accounts data, 1993 PSLSD and 1995 OHS/IES. Data were proportionally adjusted to be consistent with national accounts.

skills and education. Economic growth best translates into a reduction of the intergroup income gap when the racial wage gap narrows and there is sufficient growth of employment.

The major recent distributional trends have been the gradual narrowing of the African/white income gap concurrent with the widening income gap among Africans – mainly due to differential access to formal employment. While some have benefited from a doubling of their real wages over the past two decades, unemployment, which affects mainly the poorly educated, has also increased. Unemployment, and therefore also income inequality, have strong geographic dimensions, with insiders being largely urban and outsiders rural. A strong rise in the income of Asians has improved their position considerably. However, because of their small numbers, they play a minor role in the broader picture of inequality in South Africa.

As this brief description of Table 1 has highlighted, the operation of the labour market is integral to this aggregate picture. Therefore, it is appropriate to provide a detailed review of the labour market developments that inform the contemporary picture.

The origins of poverty and inequality in the South African labour market

Over the last hundred years, political influences on the South African labour market have been characterised by a plethora of legislation that was instrumental in maintaining, until the early 1970s, a workforce strictly divided on the basis of race. Though particular economic interests provided the incentives for such labour market interventions, economic forces also often highlighted the inappropriateness of a racially constituted labour market. During the early 20th century, the economy seemed to thrive on a divided workforce, but industrialisation and the need for increased skills meant that a segregated labour market would later become a hindrance to economic progress. We start our review with the advent of apartheid in 1948.[2]

1948–1973: The apartheid labour market

Political apartheid became institutionalised after 1948, and eventually operated at three levels. At the macro level, 'grand apartheid' tried to create black nation-states and to give these economic content by development of the homelands and the policy of industrial decentralisation. At the intermediate or meso level, apartheid emphasised separation between race groups ('own community life') through influx control, urban settlement patterns (group areas), population removals, separate schools, etc. At the micro level, 'petty apartheid' emphasised separation between individuals of different race groups through separate amenities (e.g. parks, sports fields, etc.), prohibition of interracial marriages and sexual relations, etc. While macro-level apartheid was the most costly in fiscal terms, meso-level apartheid measures probably had a greater detrimental economic impact through their effects on the labour market. The costs of these measures could be borne with ease as long as the economy was still relatively underdeveloped, inward-looking and expanding rapidly. However, these costs grew with time, especially after the end of the 1960s economic boom.

The government aggressively promoted the employment of whites in state-controlled enterprises and in the burgeoning bureaucracy, revitalised public relief programmes to ensure short-term employment for whites, gave assistance to Afrikaner business, and supported commercial (white) agriculture through a variety of measures.

The onslaught on the black population is now well documented, and it is only necessary here to discuss briefly some of the policies that specifically affected the labour market. One of the first actions of the new government was to overturn the 1946 Fagan Report, which had argued that black urbanisation should be viewed as a natural outcome of industrialisation and should be regulated but not prevented. The Sauer Commission witnessed a reversion to the Stallard principle of spatial separation of races, where blacks had to reside in rural areas and only work in urban areas when required by whites (Lipton 1986:22). Indeed, a striking feature of this period was the energy put into reaffirming and tightening up influx control. Labour bureaux were established, through the 1968 Bantu Labour Regulation Act, to control the movement of such labour. Pass law-related arrests reached 700 000 in 1968 (Lipton 1986:35), which constituted approximately one arrest for every twenty economically active Africans. Although the National Party altered influx control and increased its complexity, it was essentially a reversion to past policies. But as South Africa was by then a much more industrialised country than when Stallardism was first imposed in the 1920s, it was much more in conflict with labour market needs.

The Bantu Labour (Settlements of Disputes) Act of 1953 tightened the exclusion of Africans from the industrial relations system by barring African workers from registered unions and forbidding strikes by African employees (Greenberg 1980:160). Instead, African workers were provided with a separate system of 'works' and 'liaison' committees, within which management and African workers were supposed to negotiate terms of employment (Lipton 1986:27).

The upward mobility of black workers was halted by a series of complementary laws. The Industrial Conciliation Act of 1956, for example, assured the maintenance of the racial division of labour and significantly widened the ambit of the 'civilised labour' policy to all sectors. In reaction to employer resistance, a 1959 amendment to the Act assured that the state could overrule an Industrial Council agreement, thus giving the state almost complete control over the hiring practices of private sector employers. White workers were given preference in the public sector, and in many cases black labour was substituted by white labour (Lipton 1986:24). In government services, for example, African employment fell by 12% between 1946 and 1951.

As an auxiliary to job reservation, the 1953 Bantu Education Act required that African education be largely self-funded, thus tying expenditure on African education to revenue earned in the form of taxes from Africans (Bromberger 1982). In the early years of National Party rule, expenditure on African education fell in per capita terms, declining from 13% of white levels in 1953 to only 10% in 1961 (SAIRR 1961).

Thus African school-leavers entered the labour market at a severe disadvantage. At the point of entry to jobs, further discrimination was evident in the form of the 'civilised labour' policy, which gave first preference to white workers. If Africans were able to gain entry into a job, their mobility was curtailed and their bargaining power reduced through constraints on trade union activity. Thus from pre-employment to employment, African workers faced a battery of laws that sought to undermine their ability to accumulate human capital, to increase their wages, to gather relevant job experience and to negotiate for better wages and working conditions.

While industrial expansion during World War II had improved the relative wages of blacks, the end of the war and the advent of National Party rule shifted economic power back to white workers. By 1960, the African-to-white wage ratio had returned to its pre-war level. During the high-growth era of the 1960s, this ratio deteriorated somewhat (as shown in Table 3), as whites were the main beneficiaries of the expanding need for skills created by the economic boom.

In the midst of these dramatic changes to the labour market, the South African economy was going through a decade of unprecedented growth. Economic growth in the period 1961 to 1970 exceeded 5%. Large capital inflows, a high gold price and abundant cheap labour sustained these golden years of the apartheid economy. The boom period created a greater demand for skilled labour, and the state resorted to encouraging immigration, upgrading the skills of employed whites and also enticing women into the labour market (Lipton 1986: 33–4). It nevertheless became increasingly difficult to rely solely on a small base of white employees. The state responded by allowing the colour bar to become, de facto, a 'floating bar'. This involved the reclassification of jobs to allow blacks to be trained in the less skilled components of 'white jobs'. Racial divisions were still strictly adhered to, as no black worker could supervise a white employee (Lipton 1986:33). In addition, skilled work for blacks was limited, particularly where it competed with whites. The mobility allowed by the government was constrained as it sought to maintain the rigid overlap between race and occupation (Lipton 1986:33).

The windfall economic gains of the 1960s heightened the tension between legislative provisions in the labour market and the economy's need for a wider skills base. The state's response was an attempt to institute concessions within the broader realm of an apartheid labour market, an approach whose bankruptcy was to become apparent in the following two decades.

1973–1990: The origins of the post-apartheid labour market
In 1973, the first oil shock began an era of prolonged recession and a structural crisis from which the South African economy is still trying to recover. Economic growth rates dipped below population growth for most of this period, and per capita income declined by 15% from 1974 to 1993.

Politically, as resistance to apartheid grew during this period, the National Party resorted to increasingly desperate measures to maintain power. Its policy responses vacillated between oppression and reform, as reflected in, for example, the 'total onslaught' strategy, half-hearted attempts at political reform — as encapsulated in the tricameral parliament — and more fundamental labour and urbanisation policy reforms (discussed below). Explosive examples of the clash between oppression and resistance include the 1976 Soweto uprising and the numerous struggles waged by communities during the 1980s. Faced with a chronic crisis, a hostile international community and the obvious anachronism of apartheid, political reforms began in 1990, resulting in a democratically elected government in April 1994.

In the labour market, perhaps the most important events of this period were the 1973 wildcat strikes, which were as spontaneous as they were widespread. The strikes forced both government and employers to rethink their industrial relations strategies. Their responses were embodied in the reports of the Wiehahn and Riekert commissions in 1979.

The Wiehahn Commission recommended the legalisation of black trade unions and the scrapping of job reservation. This led to the Industrial Conciliation Amendment Act of 1979, which widened the definition of an employee to include African workers, although migrant workers initially remained excluded and the Act still barred non-racial trade unions (this provision was to be omitted two years later) (SALDRU 1991). Other notable exclusions from the ambit of the 1979 Act were agricultural and domestic workers. One of the results of these reforms was a more than threefold growth in trade union membership — from 701 758 in 1979 to 2 458 712 in 1990. Thus the upshot of the Wiehahn Commission was a black workforce with greater bargaining power that was increasingly drawn into the regulated labour market, where they were now covered by legislation on minimum conditions of employment.

The Riekert Commission investigated the issue of African labour mobility. It argued for the relaxation of controls on workers who held rights of urban residence or employment, to allow for a freer flow of labour to the cities. Given the mining industry's increased reliance on local labour and pressure from manufacturing industry for a stable workforce, influx control was abolished in 1986. This eliminated one of the last pillars of the apartheid labour market.

Wage and income inequality

The impact of these developments can be seen through wage movements over the period. Between World War II and the late 1960s, African wages across all sectors remained fairly stagnant. However, from the 1970s onwards, wages rose rapidly for all groups but whites. Indeed, this rise in wages is considered to be one of the most important factors explaining the change in income distribution patterns over the last twenty years, and its cause can to a large extent be found in an important shift in relative economic power.

In mining, there was a dramatic turnaround in trends in the racial wage gap, which had widened consistently until the early 1970s, but then began to narrow from both sides as African real wages rose startlingly in the 1970s, while white wages often lagged behind inflation (Table 2). Black wages in mining were only 6% of white wages in 1960, but by 1985 this figure had risen to 19% (Table 3). Indeed, from 1972 to 1980, mean African wages in mining increased almost threefold (by 184%). In manufacturing and construction, too, the wage gap narrowed considerably, if not as spectacularly. The major causes of these changing wage trends of the 1970s and beyond were the increased bargaining power of particularly African workers, their access to higher occupational levels due to the increasing skills scarcity of the 1960s, and rising educational levels.

Econometric investigation confirms that the factors contributing to this rise in black wages during the 1970s were higher levels of education and training amongst blacks, a decline in wage discrimination and the rise of powerful black trade unions (Hofmeyr 1990). As Table 4 and Table 5 illustrate, greater occupational mobility amongst African workers was evident in the labour market. Hence, in all occupations – from managers to semi-skilled manual workers – African workers' representation improved during the period 1969 to 1977. Though definitional differences make Table 4 and Table 5 not strictly comparable, it is also clear that this major shift in the occupational distribution of the African population has continued, as is evident by comparing, for example, the 40% in elementary occupations in 1995 with the 71% in manual unskilled occupations in 1969 and the 62% in 1977.

Thus, from the 1970s onwards the anachronism of a racially divided labour market constructed by specific legislative interventions had become clear. The urgency of promoting economic growth dictated the need to allow for occupational mobility and increased wages for black workers. In a sense, continued economic stagnation provided proof of the limitations of racist labour market provisions. Thus the labour market began to reveal a perceptible alteration from the rigid racial division of labour that had existed in the past. Increasingly, the overlap between race and occupation began to blur.

A segmented labour market

What is clear from the above is that the numerous obstacles faced by black workers in the labour market began to erode during this period. Hence black workers were given the right to organise in trade unions, real wages rose rapidly and occupational mobility became evident. However, these positive developments were countered by growing unemployment in an environment of poor economic growth rates. The corollary of South Africa's economic stagnation has been unemployment. Rising unemployment was a result not only of inadequate economic growth but also of the relative costs of capital and labour. Apart from union action, state policy also

TABLE 2

Real growth of wages of whites and Africans by industry/sector, 1945–93 (% per annum)[a]

Sector	Race	1945–60	1960–72	1972–75	1975–80	1980–85	1985–93
Manufacturing	Whites	3,05	3,35	0,92	1,16	0,08	−0,80
	Africans	0,44	2,57	7,57	3,62	1,59	1,21
Construction	Whites	1,89	4,18	−1,63	1,42	−0,56	−2,68
	Africans	0,07	3,38	6,07	−0,38	2,16	−2,67
Mining[b]	Whites	2,35	2,48	4,44	−1,59	0,36	—
	Africans	0,31	1,32	29,59	5,44	3,12	—
	All races	1,57	1,51	15,74	2,51	1,65	1,17
Formal sector	Whites	—	—	0,83	−0,79	1,79	—
	Africans	—	—	10,47	3,29	2,88	—
	All races	—	—	2,42	0,75	1,75	1,38
Non-primary sectors	Whites	—	—	—	−0,74	1,22	−0,28
	Africans	—	—	—	2,85	2,28	3,12
	All races	—	—	—	0,58	1,76	1,26

[a] Hofmeyr 1999, Table 2.

[b] The 1980–85 period is replaced by 1980–84 for the white and African groups because a racial breakdown was not provided after 1984.

TABLE 3

Real growth rate of black wages and black–white wage gap by industry, 1960–94 (% change per annum)[a]

Period	Mining	Manufacturing	Construction
Growth of real black wages per annum (%)			
1961–0	0,72	2,69	2,96
1971–80	13,18	4,61	2,83
1981–85	−0,14	0,81	1,15
1985–94	—	1,21	−0,29
Black wages as % of white wages			
1960	6	19	18
1970	5	17	15
1980	17	23	19
1985	19	25	21
1994	—	29	30

[a] Fallon 1992; SA Labour Statistics 1995.

TABLE 4

Percentage share of white and African employment by occupation (1969 and 1977)[a, b]

Occupation	White 1969	White 1977	African 1969	African 1977
Managers	8,22	11,28	0,39	0,46
Professional/semi-professional	10,11	11,52	1,89	2,53
Clerical, white collar	42,74	43,29	6,29	9,17
Supervisors	4,71	5,24	0,48	1,15
Skilled manual	22,98	22,72	2,86	4,97
Semi-skilled manual	8,68	4,91	16,73	19,67
Unskilled manual	2,56	1,06	71,37	62,04
Total economically active	100,00	100,00	100,00	100,00

[a] Simkins & Hindson 1979.
[b] Due to rounding, figures may not all add up to exactly 100%.

TABLE 5

Percentage share of white and African employment by occupation (1995)[a, b]

Occupation	Whites	Africans
Legislators, senior officials, managers	14,62	2,91
Professionals	8,41	2,00
Technicians, related professionals	18,51	9,65
Clerks	22,52	7,84
Services, shop and market sales	10,57	11,18
Skilled agriculture and fisheries	3,58	0,65
Craft, related trades	14,97	10,22
Plant, machine operators and assemblers	3,84	14,04
Armed forces	1,64	40,08
Elementary occupations	0,17	0,22
Occupation unspecified, unknown	1,21	1,18
Total economically active	100,00	100,00

[a] South Africa 1996a.
[b] Due to rounding, figures may not all add up to exactly 100%.

9

contributed to making it cheaper to use capital. Such policies included negative real interest rates for a long period, tax concessions on capital equipment and an overvalued exchange rate.

Between 1976 and 1990, the number of those without formal sector jobs increased by 32%. By 1994, about half of the economically active population were unable to find formal sector employment. Indeed, employment growth remained below labour force growth for almost all of the past quarter of a century. As a rule, growing unemployment translates into a higher incidence of poverty and general social degradation amongst the affected groups.

In order to better appreciate the effect of the poor performance of the economy on the composition of employment and its impact on income distribution, it is useful to decompose the South African labour force into three groups according to their access to the modern consumer economy:

- Those employed in the *core consumer economy*, consisting of the dominant high-wage modern sectors of manufacturing, government service, and other industries and services. For present purposes, mining is not included in this sector.

- Those employed in the *marginal modern sectors*. In this group we include the two low-wage sectors of commercial agriculture and domestic service, as well as mining. Although mining is no longer a low-wage sector, many mining workers are only tenuously linked to the modern economy, as the dependants of single migrants residing in mine compounds do not fully participate in modern consumer society.

- The *peripheral labour force*, whose existence signifies substantial job scarcity in the formal sectors. In this group we include subsistence agriculture, the informal sector and the unemployed.

Many households, of course, have more than one earner, and earners may fall into different sectors. Nevertheless, this division is pertinent even for households. The sharp wage rises for Africans in the modern sectors since the early 1970s sharply reduced poverty wages amongst most workers in the core modern sectors and reduced poverty amongst households dependent on their earnings, though there is still much poverty in households mainly dependent on the modern marginal sectors. Poverty in its most extreme form is most widespread in the peripheral sectors, where most potential earners are jobless or underemployed.

By 1994, the core modern economy contained about 35% of the labour force, and the marginal modern economy about 15%, thus leaving about half the labour force (liberally estimated) without formal employment. As can be seen from Table 6, the share of the core is decreasing. Instead of expanding rapidly so as to draw increasing proportions into the mainstream consumer society, employment in the core economy is virtually stagnant. The only growing component in the last decades has been the public sector, whilst all three components of the marginal modern economy are shrinking. The brunt of the increase in the labour force thus falls upon the peripheral sectors, the unemployed, subsistence agriculture and the informal sector – precisely those sectors experiencing the greatest poverty. Growth of employment in the core economy is crucially affected by the overall growth rate in the economy, and the scope for a further reduction in poverty is largely determined by the ability of the core economy to create more jobs.

TABLE 6

Percentage share of the labour force by access to modern consumer economy[a]

Segment	1960	1970	1985	1994
Core economy (manufacturing, government, other industry and services)	29	46	40	35
Modern marginal sectors (commercial agriculture, domestic service, mining)	47	32	20	15
Peripheral labour force (subsistence agriculture, informal sector, unemployed)	24	22	40	50

[a] Calculations based on Van der Berg 1987; South African Labour Statistics (various years). Sadie's relatively high labour force estimates (Sadie 1991) were used, thus leading to a larger peripheral sector than observed by the OHS 95.

Conclusion on labour market roots of poverty and inequality

This section has shown how the South African labour market was forged by the interaction between political agendas and economic needs. As the economy developed, the state insisted on promoting and protecting white workers at the expense both of black workers and longer-term economic interests. This contradiction was most starkly revealed in the period from the 1970s onwards, and only after one and a half decades of abysmal economic performance did the state seek to break with the past. In doing so, it overturned the last vestiges of legislated racism in the labour market, strengthening market forces that had already sharply reduced labour market discrimination despite the effects of legislation. By stubbornly adhering to a race-driven political agenda, however, social and welfare backlogs accumulated at a dramatic rate. The new democratic government would find this legacy its chief challenge in trying to redress the wrongs of the past.

Given the importance of inequalities in remuneration and access to employment, the labour market should be given centre stage in any analysis of the origins of contemporary poverty and inequality in South Africa. However, remuneration is not the only source of income. Non-remuneration income consists of income from the other factors of production (land rent, interest on capital, profits on entrepreneurship) as well as transfer incomes. It is the combination of all the processes driving remuneration income and non-remuneration incomes that has produced the stark per capita racial income distribution picture shown in Table 1. As apartheid strangled opportunities for black South Africans to earn non-remuneration income from land, capital and entrepreneurship – or at least drove such activities underground – little progress could take place through such activities. Transfer incomes, on the other hand, are directly related to the impact of government policy on poverty and income inequality. We will return to these policies at the end of this study. However, it is worthwhile at this point to discuss briefly the relevant historical experiences with regard to the role of the state in fiscal redistribution.

Fiscal incidence and differential social spending

In South Africa, fiscal incidence studies have naturally focused on the racial incidence of taxation and, more particularly, of public spending. Until recently, blacks have paid a small portion of overall taxation, and consequently the focus of fiscal incidence studies fell mainly on determining the extent of racial inequality in public expenditure between race groups. Under apartheid, the division of service delivery into racially-based departments made it relatively easy to determine the financial costs of the services provided for different race groups, though it was not possible to determine how the benefits from a particular service differed among consumers in terms of where they were located and the quality of the service provided. A particularly intractable problem in apartheid South Africa was how to deal with wage differences amongst providers of services. As black teachers and health workers were paid less than their white counterparts, financial costs exaggerated differentials in actual service provision by race. No adjustment was made for this in the incidence studies discussed here.

Trends in expenditure incidence

By combining a number of fiscal incidence studies, it is possible to deduce broad patterns of social expenditure for various years after World War II. The results, summarised in Table 7, show that the narrowing gap was made possible partly by reduced white benefit levels after 1975. The remaining gap is accounted for not so much by differential benefit levels as by differential access to services.

TABLE 7

Estimates of real per capita social spending by race group (1949–93)[a]

Year	White	Black	Coloured	Asian	All groups
1949	R978	R120	R413	R348	R315
1959	R1 250	R152	R511	R457	R391
1969	R1 511	R163	R598	R696	R450
1975	R2 033	R239	R804	R891	R607
1986	R1 792	R375	R969	R1 127	R647
1990	R1 856	R513	R1 074	R1 309	R761
1993	R1 475	R751	R1 022	R1 488	R1 062

[a] Own estimates based on McGrath 1983, Van der Berg 1992a & 1992b, Lachman & Bercuson 1994, and Janisch 1996.

As a result of these shifts, African social expenditure per capita, stagnant at about 12% of white levels until 1975, increased to 51% by 1993. Together with rapidly rising social expenditure ratios, this meant that real social spending for Africans grew at 6,5% per annum from 1975 to 1993 – during a period of sluggish economic growth and before apartheid had been officially abandoned. Thus when the new government assumed power in 1994, the trend of reducing racial disparities in social expenditure was already well established, even though many disparities were still large.

In education – which constitutes half the social budget – educational spending on Africans, admittedly starting from a low base, increased remarkably as more children entered schools, those in school remained there longer and expenditures per pupil rose. As recently as 1982, spending on African education was less than half of that for whites; five years later it had surpassed that for whites for the first time. If educational expenditure is expressed per potential student at all levels of education – taken to be the population aged 5–24 – expenditure on Africans stood at 4% of that for whites in 1975, but increased substantially to 18% by 1991 (De Villiers 1996). This still left a very large gap, not all of it due to continued discrimination in education provision. To a large degree, it also reflected past backlogs, which had prevented many blacks from reaching higher levels of education. But for the new government, the elimination of these backlogs still represents a considerable fiscal challenge.

The redistributory impact of the budget

All studies reviewed agree that the national budget has been an instrument of limited redistribution to Africans – at least from the late 1920s. The high degree of income inequality between races led to whites paying by far the largest share of taxes. Even under apartheid, part of these taxes was used to provide services to Africans. Thus post-fiscal distribution by race has long been more equal than the primary distribution of income, even though the patterns of expenditure were still highly discriminatory and large post-budget racial welfare differentials remained.

Surprisingly, racial redistribution through the budget actually increased even during the apartheid years. Fiscal redistribution before the 1930s seems to have been negligible or even regressive across races, but since then rising social spending on Africans ensured greater redistribution through the budget. Redistribution accelerated particularly during the 1970s, with the growing need for integration into a single economy, as described in the historical overview above.

Table 8 shows the effect of budgetary redistribution on welfare by race group in 1993. Before the redistributive effect of the budget is considered, we must note that the per capita income of Africans (excluding social pensions, which are part of social spending) was only 10,3% of white levels. After the budget, African secondary income per capita was 15,6% of white levels, due to a net gain from fiscal incidence of R895 per African person and a net loss of R3 421 per white person – more than African per capita income before the budget. Thus even though the budget redistributed, the post-budget racial gap remained extremely large. It is rather daunting, therefore, to note that there is limited additional scope to use the budget to meet the high expectations of the newly enfranchised poor. The major fiscal challenge now is to improve the efficiency of public resource use so as to enhance the quality of and access to services. Redistribution, on the other hand, will increasingly have to occur in terms of primary or personal incomes; a precondition for this is the creation of employment to draw the poor into the economic mainstream.

TABLE 8

Racial redistribution through the budget, and limits to such redistribution (1993 rands)[a]

Income breakdown	White	African	Coloured	Asian	Average
Income per capita (excluding social pension)	R26 850	R2 758	R5 088	R10 921	R6 305
% of white level	100,0	10,3	18,9	40,7	23,5
Minus: Income tax per capita	R5 546	R187	R500	R1 320	R941
Disposable income per capita	R21 304	R2 571	R4 588	R9 601	R5 364
Plus: Social spending per capita	R2 125	R1 082	R1 473	R2 144	R1 278
Secondary income per capita:					
Actual 1993	R23 429	R3 653	R6 061	R11 745	R6 642
% of white level	100,0	15,6	25,9	50,1	28,3
Assuming equal social spending of R1 278 per capita	R22 582	R3 849	R5 866	R10 879	R6 642
% of white level	100,0	17,0	26,0	48,2	29,4
Per capita effect of budget:					
Actual 1993	−R3 421	R895	R973	R824	R337
Assuming equal social spending of R1 278 per capita	−R4 268	R1 091	R778	−R42	R337
Scope for redistribution	−R847	+R196	−R195	−R966	R0

[a] Own recalculations based on Janisch (1996).

Anti-poverty policy investigations, past and present

During the 20th century, there were four major investigations into aspects of South African poverty. During the 1930s, the Carnegie Investigation considered the 'poor white' problem (Le Roux 1978); in the 1950s, the Tomlinson Commission looked at the economic situation within what later became known as the homelands; in the 1970s, the Theron Commission investigated poverty amongst coloured people (Terreblanche 1976); and the Second Carnegie Inquiry into Poverty and Development in the early 1980s looked particularly at African poverty (Wilson & Ramphele 1990). The Tomlinson Commission was unique in that its brief was to investigate ways of improving the economic situation within particular areas; for this reason, it is not fully comparable with the other investigations. The other three investigations had some common features:

they all saw an active role for the state in redressing poverty; all placed particular emphasis on education; and all perceived employment creation as necessary, but not sufficient unless accompanied by social upliftment on a large scale and over a substantial time period. But, crucially, all three reports, and the debates that flowed from them, emphasised the importance of political structures in ensuring that the problem of poverty was given priority.

The (first) Carnegie Report's recommendations were largely put into effect, with the result that white poverty was largely eliminated within a generation. In the process, the state reduced economic disparities between Afrikaners and English-speaking whites. The Second Carnegie Inquiry had no direct impact on policy as it had no official standing. Indeed, a major purpose of the inquiry was to debunk all attempts to dress up aspects of apartheid policy in the clothes of development policy by revealing the full gamut of the dire social and economic consequences of apartheid. The evidence was collected in Wilson and Ramphele (1990) and played an indirect role in the formulation of improved anti-poverty policy.

Following South Africa's first democratic elections in 1994, the new government was confronted for the first time with the task of dealing with poverty as an encompassing, national phenomenon. In doing this, it squarely faced the unenviable task of trying to undo the consequences of apartheid. The corpus of work in the Second Carnegie Inquiry then became a daunting benchmark of the mountain that had to be climbed. This was reiterated in the first national sample survey, conducted in late 1993 to provide the government with consistent and reliable information on living standards. Analysis of this data (SALDRU 1994) confirmed the magnitude of South Africa's poverty and inequality problems. From the outset, the new government faced severe fiscal constraints in its attempts to address pervasive poverty.

Despite the scale of the poverty challenge, the post-1994 euphoria was accompanied by optimistic expectations about the possibilities for addressing the distributional and poverty problems in South Africa. In 1994, the principles of the new democracy, as well as the heightened expectations for swift transformation, were captured in the Reconstruction and Development Programme (RDP) of the new government of national unity. However, the programme did not grapple with the harder economic issues confronting the realisation of this vision. The period from 1994 to 1996 can be seen as the learning period during which the magnitude of the South African social project came to be appreciated. In 1996, the government tabled a more formal macroeconomic and growth strategy, known as GEAR (Growth, Employment and Redistribution).

GEAR saw substantial long-term economic growth rates as achievable, given improvements in education, the freeing of international trade and possible long-term capital flows to South Africa in the absence of apartheid. GEAR aimed at sustaining growth by establishing a medium-term growth record that would attract foreign investors and loosen the balance-of-payments constraint. To that end, it essentially involved an export-led policy, following the real exchange rate decline of early 1996. This was regarded as an opportunity to stimulate exports, if the inflationary consequences of depreciation could be staved off by anti-inflationary policies, including fiscal restraint, continued tight monetary policies and wage restraint.

Alongside the tabling of GEAR, a series of reforms to labour legislation were introduced after 1994. These reforms included the Labour Relations Act of 1995, the Basic Conditions of Employment Act of 1997, the Employment Equity Act of 1998 and the Skills Development Act of 1999. This legislation has received support from organised labour, but is perceived in the business and investor communities as being in conflict with the spirit of GEAR because of the increased labour market regulation it embodies.

In the growth-orientated approach of GEAR, employment creation is the key linkage between solid macroeconomic management, growth and social upliftment. Thus, the period from 1996 to the present has witnessed an increasing interrogation of the compatibility between GEAR and the labour legislation and a growing concern with rising unemployment and poverty. This concern led to the Presidential Job Summit at the end of 1998, which brought together government, organised labour and the business sector. The major consensus issues to emerge from the meeting were the needs for occupational training and job creation schemes, but details were vague. Government also used this opportunity to reiterate its position on GEAR as the central part of its economic strategy. Over the last two years, there has been a number of investigations into the impact of labour legislation on employment but, as yet, the new labour market legislation has not been amended.

In sum, then, the enduring nature of South Africa's legacy of inequality and poverty is matched by a heritage of poverty and inequality analysis. Following the advent of the first democratically elected government, there has been a flurry of anti-poverty and labour market policy-making. This study, by a team of researchers who have worked both jointly and separately on these issues, seeks to make a contribution to the analysis of poverty and inequality in South Africa by addressing four major issues that are pertinent to this policy milieu, namely:

- household inequality and poverty;
- vulnerability in the South African labour market;
- labour market participation and household poverty; and
- labour market and social policy interventions.

A profile of household inequality and poverty

Chapters 1 and 2 profile household inequality and poverty, respectively, in South Africa and also present detailed methodological reviews of the measurement issues associated with such profiling. The empirical analysis contained in these chapters and in the study as a whole is based on data from the 1993 Project for Statistics on Living Standards and Development (PSLSD) and the 1995 October Household Survey (OHS) and the accompanying Household Income and

Expenditure Survey (IES). The South African PSLSD data has already been used extensively in describing poverty in South Africa (The Poverty and Inequality Report 1998). Therefore, there was already a base of quantitative and qualitative material to draw on and summarise. In this study, we complement this work by making use of the 1995 IES for the first time. These surveys are not far enough apart to compare changes over time, but comparison is useful in assessing robustness of results to the choice of data.

However, Chapters 1 and 2 seek to do more than replicate existing work with new data. The Poverty and Inequality Report and most existing South African poverty research have been kept simple. The aim in Chapters 1 and 2, and indeed in the whole study, is to complement the available descriptive work with a clear but technically rigorous approach. A general weakness of the existing South African work is that it has not kept up with significant theoretical developments that have taken place in the international poverty and inequality literature over the last decade. In Chapters 1 and 2, two specific gaps are filled. First, there is now a rich literature that enables assessments to be made of the robustness of empirical results to choices of:

- different poverty and inequality measures,
- the choice of individual poverty lines, and
- the aggregation of individual poverty lines into household lines.

Second, there have been a number of recent advances in poverty and inequality decomposition analysis. Chapters 1 and 2 incorporate a consistent and thorough application of these new techniques to the South African data. Such work serves as a bridge between the description of inequality and poverty and the analysis of the processes that generate and perpetuate poverty in South Africa. There is a rich return to this work in determining the priorities for anti-poverty efforts. The study returns to this important enterprise in Chapters 5 and 6. However, these chapters require, as context, a detailed understanding of the incidence and perpetuation of labour market vulnerability in South Africa. It is in this direction that Chapters 3 and 4 of the study are directed.

Understanding vulnerability in the South African labour market

There are a number of reasons why an adequate understanding of the nature and functioning of the labour market serves as a logical follow-on from our detailed analysis of household poverty and inequality. First, the inequality and poverty decompositions by income sources reveal that household wage income is a dominant factor determining the poverty status of the household and the position of a household in the distribution of total income. GEAR's approach to poverty and inequality alleviation gives a central role to private sector employment creation as the major link between growth and the reduction of poverty and inequality. Despite this key linkage, GEAR does not discuss the labour market in any detail. In addition, the GEAR strategy envisages government's major direct intervention to be the creation of employment through training and public works programmes. Once again, the success of such programmes is conditional on a detailed understanding of the labour market, and particularly its rural segments. Finally, the expenditures by the state on education, health and many welfare services can be viewed as human capital investments in South Africa's people. These investments generate ongoing returns only to the extent that the recipients of these services can use these investments to embark on sustainable livelihoods. For most people, this means successful integration into the labour market.

In sum, then, the operation of the labour market is and will be central to the success or failure of anti-poverty policy in South Africa. But there are many ways to look at labour markets. The dictates of this study demanded the delivery of detailed information and understanding about the most vulnerable segments of the labour market. Most of South Africa's large and contested research on the labour market has thus far adopted a focus on formal sector employment and formal sector wage differentials. Such intra-formal-sector dynamics are important, but a much wider definition of the labour market is required as a starting point in order to adequately capture the actual and potential roles played by the labour market in society-wide inequality and poverty. For this study, the determinants of unemployment and labour market participation are at least as important as the determinants of earnings. Indeed, many of the key issues revolve around the links between the formally employed, the self-employed and the unemployed and the overlaying rural–urban household linkages.

This broad approach was best served by focusing, sequentially, on two specific sets of questions:

- What is the current situation and, in particular, in which sectors and segments of the labour market are the most vulnerable participants to be found? These issues are dealt with in Chapter 3.

- What are the key determinants in the process that allocates individuals to different segments of the labour market and then determines their earnings within segments? Is there any evidence regarding the specific processes relegating labour market participants to no-earning and low-earning sections of the labour market? These issues are modelled in Chapter 4.

The above sets of questions, addressed in Chapters 4 and 5, provide a nuanced understanding of the operation of the labour market, with particular attention to its most vulnerable participants. However, poverty measurement and policy are often directed at poor households rather than poor individuals. We therefore conclude the analytic section of this study with two chapters that explore the links between participation in the labour market by *individuals* and the incidence and perpetuation of *household* poverty and inequality.

Labour market participation and household poverty

The poverty and inequality decompositions in Chapters 1 and 2 show that the labour market is an important determinant of household poverty and inequality. For this type of analysis to link to the understanding of labour market participation derived from Chapters 3 and 4, there is a need to ascertain how increases in employment and unemployment of individuals in a household change the poverty and inequality status of that household. In addition, for policy purposes, there is an imperative to discern whether these labour market impacts retain their importance after controlling for the impact of household demographics, race, location and household educational factors. This project is explicitly completed in Chapter 5, in which multivariate models of household poverty and inequality are built.

Chapter 5 provides strong evidence that, even after controlling for a full set of poverty determinants, poor households are poor because they contain clusters of no-earners and low-earners. In addition, these labour market factors are shown to have a significant effect in terms of positioning households within the distribution of household income. Aside from these labour market findings, Chapter 5 also provides interesting evidence on the relative importance of all the markers of household poverty and inequality that were flagged in Chapters 1 and 2.

However, the multivariate models of Chapter 5 do not formally build on the evidence of Chapters 3 and 4, showing that it is unemployed individuals as well as agricultural workers and domestic workers who are the most vulnerable labour market participants. Chapter 6 makes use of existing poverty measurement methodologies to interrogate the poverty status of the *households* of these especially vulnerable workers. By taking the analysis back to the level of the household in this way, this chapter integrates the labour market discussion with the broader poverty and inequality discussion of Chapters 1 and 2. It also offers a bridge to the two policy chapters that conclude the book by showing that labour market policies that have an impact on employment and earnings for these especially vulnerable workers will have a much larger than proportionate impact on household poverty in South Africa.

Two policy discussions

As mentioned in the first part of this introduction, two major implications for anti-poverty policy fell to South Africa's first democratically elected government in 1994. First, the new government found itself with the explicit mandate to address the full ambit of our poverty problem for the first time in our history. Second, the very inequality and poverty generated by previous policies ensured that the miracle of the political transition would not be accompanied by significant increases in fiscal revenues. Since then, it has become clear that anti-poverty resources will always be very limited. Accordingly, anti-poverty efforts need to be tightly focused and aimed at addressing the principal causes of poverty.

Addressing poverty in a context such as South Africa requires attention to employment and wage levels, transfers to the poor and the provision of services and productive resources to the poor. Although the primary focus of this study is the link between poverty and inequality and labour markets, our work contains implications for social security and the provision of social services. In addition, the specifics of social policy hold many implications for the labour market, particularly with regard to the impacts of the quantity and quality of education on access to employment and labour market earnings. Policy analysis therefore starts with social policy in Chapter 7 and follows on to labour market policies in Chapter 8. In both of these concluding chapters, we emphasise possible new policies as well as understanding the impact of present policies and recent policy shifts. These chapters therefore seek to balance policy recommendations derived from the formal work in the study with a perspective on how these recommendations mesh with the direction of current policies. This is, after all, the art of the possible for any pragmatic analyst of policies to fight poverty and inequality.

Notes

1. We use the race classification system whereby the society is divided into four groups, namely African, coloured, Asian and white. African, coloured and Asian individuals are collectively referred to here as blacks.
2. Table 1 makes it clear that the origins of systemic inequality in South Africa preceded the advent of apartheid. For a review that includes earlier labour market developments, see Van der Berg and Bhorat (1999).

1

Understanding Contemporary Household Inequality in South Africa

Murray Leibbrandt
Ingrid Woolard
Haroon Bhorat

The dominant themes of South Africa's economic history are inequality and exclusion. Given this history, a key benchmark against which all contemporary economic planning must be assessed is the role such plans can play in narrowing inequality and breaking down the barriers that exclude people from participating in the economy on the grounds of race, gender or location.

Such planning necessitates an information base detailing the dimensions of inequality and poverty in South Africa in the mid-1990s. This base needs to be nuanced enough to allow for assessment of programmes that are narrowly targeted at different segments of the South African population. For example, with policy focusing predominantly on the upliftment of the African group, an understanding is needed of the economic forces at work within this populace. An accurate information base is also a *sine qua non* for more ambitious social development modelling which sets out to inform the policy selection process.

South Africa's Gini coefficient has always served as the starkest indicator of the country's unequal distribution of income.[1] For a long time, South Africa's Gini was the highest recorded in the world. Table 1.1 presents a comparison of South Africa's Gini coefficient and the income shares of countries with similar income levels. It is clear that Brazil and South Africa are far less egalitarian societies than the other nations presented here,[2] but also that Brazil has a slightly higher level of income inequality than South Africa. Both these Gini values, though, are extremely high, indicating very skewed distributions of income. By comparison, Poland and Thailand have Gini coefficients of 0,27 and 0,46, respectively, showing that these economies have a significantly more equitable distribution of income.

Another way to express the degree of inequality in a country is to examine the income shares of households by decile (a decile is a 10% segment of all households ranked according to income level). From Figure 1.1, it is evident that, using this measure, the degree of inequality is striking. The poorest four deciles (40%) of households — equivalent to 52% of the population — account for less than 10% of total income, while the richest decile (10%) of households — equivalent to just 6% of the population — capture over 40% of total income.[3]

TABLE 1.1

Comparison of selected middle-income countries[a]

Measure	Poland	Thailand	Venezuela	Brazil	SA	Malaysia
GNP per capita US$ (1994)	2 410	2 410	2 760	2 970	3 040	3 480
Gini	0,27	0,46	0,54	0,63	0,60	0,48
% share of income of poorest 20%	9,3	5,6	3,6	2,1	2,8	4,6
% share of income of richest 10%	22,1	37,1	42,7	51,3	41,9	37,9

[a] 1996 *World Development Report* and own calculations (South Africa).

FIGURE 1.1

Inequality in South Africa

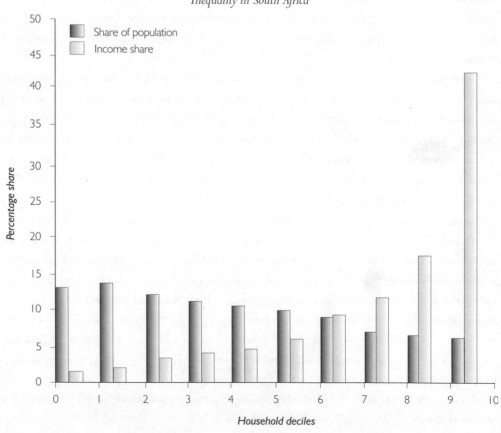

Whiteford and McGrath (1998) have shown that while the Gini coefficient remained static between 1975 and 1991, this masked the fact that the rich got richer while the poor got poorer. They found a similar pattern when looking at each race group separately. In other words, they observed a widening of the gap between the richest Africans and the poorest Africans, the richest whites and the poorest whites. For example, the income share accruing to the poorest 40% of African earners fell by a disquieting 48%, while the share accruing to the richest 10% rose by 43%.[4]

Given this background, this chapter seeks to unpack further the nature of inequality in contemporary South Africa. The intention is to complement the recent historical review provided by Whiteford and McGrath (1998) – especially their between- and within-race analysis – and then to focus more explicitly on the link between the labour market and household inequality.

There are three sections to the chapter. The first section examines the racial fault line in South African inequality through the use of various categorical decomposition techniques. Once the aggregate importance of 'between racial group' versus 'within racial group' inequality has been examined, the second section uses a decomposition analysis of income inequality by income components to immediately focus attention on the key labour market, asset ownership and state welfare processes driving South Africa's inequality. This analysis suggests that the labour market is the key driver of household inequality. In the light of this finding, the final section focuses explicitly on the labour market.

In South African policy debates, there is generally insufficient scrutiny of empirical results. The problem may be divided into two major maladies. First, there is scant recognition of the fact that different measurement techniques will generate different results. In contrast to this, the theoretical literature on inequality has paid a great deal of attention to the fact that different measures of inequality do not define inequality in exactly the same way and therefore will arrive at different estimates of inequality.[5] The importance of this literature lies in its questioning of the extent to which any inequality results are technique-driven rather than neutral representations of the circumstances prevailing in that society. We control for this possibility by using a variety of techniques wherever possible. Conflicting results will then serve as an indication that the situation really is not as clear-cut as any of the techniques would have us believe. Indeed, a detailed discussion of how techniques differ and why these differences should have led to the measured differences, is itself a useful way to start an interrogation of the processes generating inequality in South Africa.[6]

Second, the South African literature gives too little recognition to the fact that different data give different results. In the past, this could be excused because of the shortage of usable data. However, there are now two national data sources available to cover contemporary South Africa; the 1995 Income and Expenditure Survey (IES), conducted by Statistics South Africa and the survey undertaken as part of the Project for Statistics on Living Standards and Development

(PSLSD) by the Southern Africa Labour and Development Research Unit at the University of Cape Town in late 1993. There are clear advantages to using IES data rather than the PSLSD: the data is more recent, the sample was much larger (almost 30 000 households, compared with just under 9 000 in the PSLSD study) and the questionnaire was solely devoted to collecting income and expenditure data – which should point to greater attention to detail and less respondent fatigue. The only disadvantage to using this data is that it does not provide information about small-scale agricultural production and consumption from own production.[7] We therefore focus our textual analysis on the IES data. However we have used the PSLSD data to reproduce all of our tables (see Appendix) and we highlight any discrepancies in results from the two sets of data as part of our discussion.

The importance of race in national inequality

The literature on the decomposition of total inequality by subgroups has a long lineage.[8] If we divide the population into mutually exclusive, exhaustive subgroups then there is a degree of inequality both *within* these subgroups and *between* them. It is desirable that we should be able to decompose a measure of overall inequality into the 'within' and the 'between' portions.[9] The value of decompositions is that 'they gauge the relative importance of various sources and sectors in respect of overall inequality, and thereby direct our attention to potentially fruitful areas of research' (Fields 1980:438). Indeed, South Africa's historical legacy makes a much stronger case than this, in that we are drawn to these tools because they allow for an explicit focus on race in driving inequality. This section concentrates solely on this racial question.

Measures and estimates of income inequality

The most commonly cited additively decomposable measure of inequality is the Theil-T statistic, derived directly from the notion of entropy in information theory (Fields 1980:103).

The Theil-T can be decomposed as follows:

$$T = T_B + \Sigma q_i T_i$$

where:

T_i is the Theil-T inequality measure within the ith group;

q_i is the proportion of income accruing to the ith group; and

T_B is the between-group contribution. T_B is calculated the same way as T, but assumes that all incomes within a group are equal.

The Theil-L decomposes in a similar way to the Theil-T, except that the group statistics are weighted by the proportion of households (not income) in each group, expressed as:

$$L = L_B + \Sigma p_i L_i$$

where p_i is the population share of the ith group.

A second broad class of inequality measures is contained in the Atkinson measure. This starts from an additive social welfare function in order to derive the following inequality index:

$$ 1 = 1 - \left(\frac{1}{N} \sum_{i=1}^{N} (\frac{y_i}{\mu})^{1-\varepsilon} \right)^{\frac{1}{(1-\varepsilon)}} $$

which may he decomposed into between- and within-group inequality, such that

$$ I = I_B + I_W + \text{Residual} $$

The measure can be interpreted as the proportion of the present total income that would be required to achieve the same level of social welfare as at present if incomes were equally distributed (Atkinson 1970:48). Atkinson explicitly introduces distributional objectives through the parameter $\varepsilon \geq 0$, which represents the weight attached to inequality in the distribution. By specifying different values of ε one can vary the importance society attaches to mean living standards versus equality. If society is indifferent about the distribution, we will set ε equal to zero. By increasing ε, we give more weight to inequality at the lower end of the distribution. At ε equal to infinity, society is concerned only with the poorest household.

All three of the above decomposition techniques – the Theil-T, Theil-L and Atkinson's measure – would seem to have obvious relevance for South Africa. Yet, it is only recently that such decompositions have begun to be used in this country.[10] Table 1.2 presents the results of the decomposition of South Africa's total national income by race, using the three decomposition techniques discussed above. We attach the household adult equivalent income to each individual in the household; thus we are comparing inequality amongst individuals, not households.

TABLE 1.2

Comparison of distribution measures[a]

Measure	Between component	Within component	Residual	Total
Theil-T	0,319	0,483		0,802
	(39,7)	(60,3)		
Theil-L	0,254	0,452		0,706
	(36,0)	(64,0)		
Atkinson $\varepsilon = 0,5$	0,091	0,187	0,001	0,278
	(32,8)	(67,0)	(0,2)	
Atkinson $\varepsilon = 1,5$	0,215	0,368	0,001	0,584
	(36,8)	(63,0)	(0,2)	
Atkinson $\varepsilon = 2,5$	0,279	0,445	0,001	0,724
	(38,5)	(61,5)	(0,01)	

[a] The figures in brackets show the percentage contribution to total inequality.

All the indices point in a similar direction; that is that the 'within' and 'between' components are both important contributors to overall inequality, with within-group inequality accounting for more than three-fifths of overall inequality, by all the measures used. In addition, the more highly we value equality – i.e. the larger we set ε in Atkinson's index – the more between-group inequality grows in significance as a contributor to overall inequality. This suggests relatively greater equality amongst African households as we move down the income distribution, and that a key inequality wedge is that between white and African households.

Table 1.3 further decomposes the within-group Theil measures, this time by race. Hence we determine the share of each racial group in explaining aggregate within-group inequality. It is immediately evident that the choice of the Theil-L versus the Theil-T index paints a very different picture of the contribution of different races to overall inequality.

TABLE 1.3

Within-race contribution to overal inequality[a]

Measure	African	Coloured	Asian	White
Theil-T	0,594	0,387	0,400	0,395
	[0,265]	[0,027]	[0,018]	[0,172]
	(33,2)	(3,4)	(2,2)	(21,4)
Theil-L	0,486	0,353	0,350	0,333
	[0,371]	[0,030]	[0,009]	[0,042]
	(52,6)	(4,2)	(1,3)	(5,9)

[a] The first row of figures show the measure when considering only the particular race group. The figures in square brackets show the absolute contribution to total inequality. The figures in round brackets show the percentage contribution to total inequality. Akinson's index is *generally* but not *additively* decomposable, hence we cannot apportion the within contribution amongst the race groups.

The Theil-T suggests that inequality among the white group is almost as large a contributor to overall inequality as inequality amongst the African group, yet the Theil-L suggests that African inequality contributes 52,6% to total inequality *vis-à-vis* a contribution of 5,9% from white inequality. The reason for the different Theil-T and Theil-L results can be found in the use of income as opposed to population weights. This stresses the importance of considering the nature of the decomposition measure before relying on any one statistic.

The results for Table 1.2 and Table 1.3, utilising the PSLSD data set instead, are provided in Table A-1 and Table A-2 in the Appendix. It is evident that a similar general result is found, namely that overall inequality is driven primarily by within-group inequality. However, there are important differences in the figures obtained from the two surveys. Firstly, while the within-group component does drive overall inequality from the PSLSD, its share on average of 55% is much smaller than the corresponding mean of 63% found in the IES. Hence, the IES data has a much stronger contribution from the within-group component to total inequality. Secondly, the Atkinson measure for the IES data showed that the higher the value of ε, the greater the contribution of between-group inequality to the total. For the PSLSD, however, the result is the opposite: the higher the value of ε, the smaller the contribution of between-group inequality. This suggests that since most of the poor are African, inequality at the lower end of the income distribution will tend to be within-group. A third important difference in the data is in the within-race Theil measures. Here, the PSLSD also shows a rising contribution of African inequality, from 22,6% to 48,1%, when the Theil-L is used instead of the Theil-T. However, the Theil-T African and white contributions to overall inequality are almost the same, at 22,6% and 22,1%, respectively, which is very different to the IES figures in which the African and white contributions are much further apart.

One possible explanation for the above trends is that in the PSLSD survey, the variance in income amongst Africans is smaller, given that more poor Africans relative to non-poor Africans were sampled. This would imply that the contribution of the within-group component in PSLSD to overall inequality is not as large as in IES. However, as there are relatively more poor than non-poor Africans in PSLSD, an increased concern about inequality through Atkinson's measure — meaning a move down the income distribution — leads to the within-group share reasserting itself in the measure. Furthermore, this relatively higher number of poor Africans sampled may be reflected in the lower within-race Theil-T value, at 22,6% — as opposed to 33,2% for IES. Ultimately, then, the comparison between the two surveys suggests that the sample income distributions differ, with the distribution in the PSLSD weighted more toward poor African individuals and households.

Despite the difficulties in trying to reconcile results from these two data sets, the racial contribution to inequality in South Africa — within an international perspective — provides for a fairly clear, and indeed very powerful, picture. This can be seen in Table 1.4, which provides Anand's (1983) Theil-T decomposition analysis of Malaysian household income by race. Malaysia offers a good comparative example, as it is also a society with a history of social and economic stratification by race.

At 13%, though, Malaysia's between-group share in inequality is very low compared to South Africa's. When using personal income instead, Anand (1983:96) finds an even lower contribution of 9,2% due to between-group inequality. The baseline value for South Africa — either with IES or PSLSD data — using the Theil-T measure is 36%. In the case of Malaysia, then, between-group inequality is not very helpful in explaining individual income inequality. In South Africa, on the other hand, income inequality between the four racial groups, and particularly between African and white, is a crucial predictor of total income inequality in the society.

A Latin American example, provided by Fiszbein and Psacharopoulos (1995), helps to further illustrate just how important race is in South Africa. This study of seven countries at two

TABLE 1.4

The Theil-T decomposition by race for Malaysia[a]

Race	Per capita household
Malay	0,41
Chinese	0,42
Asian	0,54
Other	0,94
Share	
All (total)	0,52
Within	0,45 (87%)
Between	0,07 (13%)

[a] Anand 1983:95–6.

periods of time finds that the *joint contributions* of age, employment status and education to worker per capita income ranges from 32,6–53%, with a mean of 45,3%. Given that these are the major variables that, conventionally, we look at in explaining individual incomes, this gives a sharp sense of perspective on the magnitude of the between-race numbers in South Africa.

Sources of income and national inequality

The decomposition literature of the previous section is of a much older vintage than the income source analysis of this section. However, over the last decade, a busy international literature has developed around the derivation and refinement of techniques for decomposing inequality measures (in particular the Gini coefficient) by income sources.[11] Such decompositions highlight those income sources that dominate the distribution of income and, as such, offer a bridge between the description of inequality and the key economic processes generating inequality in a society.

Elsewhere (Leibbrandt *et al.* 1996), the Gini coefficient has been decomposed by income sources using the PSLSD survey. These results are reported in the Appendix (Table A-3 and Table A-4). Here, the same methodology is applied to the IES. The application of such work to South Africa provides an immediate addition to the knowledge of South African inequality. The IES data set contains detailed information on all sources of income and, therefore, is an ideal data set to apply such analysis. Clearly, the level of aggregation that is chosen is determined by the context under consideration and the questions that the analysis is addressing. For the purposes of this chapter, the goal is to distinguish between the relative importance of the major foci of policy attention. Total income for each household is therefore divided into five sources:

- *remittances*: from absent family members and marital maintenance (alimony);

- *wage income*: regular and casual employment and value of benefits such as subsidised housing, transport and food;
- *capital income*: dividends, interest, rent income, imputed rent from residing in own dwelling and private and civil (contributory) pensions;
- *state transfers*: social pensions, disability grants, poor relief, unemployment insurance and child maintenance grants; and
- *self-employed*: formal and informal business activities.

Such a breakdown is still at a fairly aggregate level and any number of more disaggregated breakdowns are possible to answer more specific questions.

The key aspects of the decomposition technique can be summarised in the following way: If South African society is represented as n households deriving income from k different sources (i.e. k different income components), then the *Gini coefficient* (G) for the distribution of total income within the group can be derived as follows:

$$G = \sum_{k=1}^{K} R_k G_k S_k$$

where:

S_k is the share of source k of income in total group income (i.e. $S_k = \mu_k/\mu$);

G_k is the Gini coefficient measuring the inequality in the distribution of income component k within the group; and

R_k is the Gini correlation of income from source k with total income.[12]

This equation tells us that the effect of source k income on total income inequality can be broken down into three components:

- the share of income component k in total income (captured by the term S_k);
- the inequality within the sample of income from source k (as measured by G_k); and
- the correlation between source k income and total income (as measured by R_k).

The larger the product of these three components, the greater the contribution of income from source k to total income inequality. However, it must be noted that whilst S_k and G_k are always positive and less than one, R_k can fall anywhere on the interval $[-1,1]$. When R_k is less than zero, income from source k is negatively correlated with total income and thus serves to lower the overall Gini measure for the sample.

Now, suppose that there is an exogenous increase in income from source j, by some factor S_j then it can be shown that the derivative of the Gini coefficient with respect to a change in income source j is:

$$\frac{\partial G}{\partial \sigma_j} = S_j (R_j G_j - G)$$

If $\partial G/\partial\sigma_j$ is negative, then a marginal increase in income component j will lessen income inequality. This will be the case either when:

1. income from component j has either a negative or zero correlation with total income $(-1 \le R_j \le 0)$; or when

2. income from source j is positively correlated with total income $(R_j > 0)$ and $R_j G_j < G$.

Alternatively, in order for a marginal increase in source j income to worsen income inequality it is necessary that $G_j > G$ (i.e. income from source j must be more unevenly distributed than total income). However, this condition alone is not sufficient for a change in income component j to worsen the overall income distribution as the sign of $\partial G/\partial\sigma_j$ will still be influenced by the strength of the Gini correlation between source j income and total income (Stark *et al.* 1986:260).

Table 1.5 presents the results of this decomposition for the total South African sample.[13] A few illustrative features of this table will be highlighted. It can be seen that wage income has a dominant share of income (66%) and makes a similar contribution to inequality (67%). The reason for this is the high R of 0,88, implying that a household's rank in the distribution of wage income is strongly correlated with that household's rank in the distribution of total income. This strong correlation is more than enough to compensate for the fact that the Gini coefficient for wage income (0,67) is the lowest of all income sources.

TABLE 1.5

Decomposition of total national income by income sources[a]

Income source	Proportion of households receiving income source	Mean income from source	Share in total income	Gini for income source for households receiving such income	Gini for income source for all households	Gini correlation with total income rankings	Contribution to Gini coefficient of total income	Percentage share in overall Gini	Effect on overall Gini of a 1% change in income component
	(P_k)		(S_k)	(G_A)	(G_k)	(R_k)	$(S_k G_k R_k)$		
Remittances	0,13	R64,81	0,02	0,48	0,93	−0,07	−0,001	0,25	−0,015
Wage income	0,70	R1 815,63	0,66	0,53	0,67	0,88	0,39	66,59	0,002
Capital income	0,18	R251,51	0,09	0,69	0,95	0,69	0,06	10,16	0,006
State transfers	0,33	R155,84	0,06	0,40	0,80	−0,12	−0,006	−0,94	−0,039
Self-employment	0,09	R451,02	0,16	0,71	0,97	0,89	0,14	24,44	0,047
Total		R2 738,82	1,00				0,59	100,00	

[a] G_A is the Gini for the income source when we only consider households with positive income from that source. G_k is for the Gini of the income source when we consider all households. Lerman and Yitzhaki (1994) show that $G_k = P_k \times G_A + (1 - P_k)$.

The Gini coefficient for a particular income source (G_k) is driven by the inequality amongst those earning income from that source (G_A) and the proportion of households who have positive income from that source (P_k) – or, changing the focus, *the proportion of households with no access* to a particular income source ($1 - P_k$). Then we see that, for example:

$$G_{wage} = 0,67 = P_{wage} \, G_A + (1 - P_{wage}) = 0,37 + 0,30.$$

This brings us part of the way to apportioning the 'blame' for Gini inequality between the inequality amongst earners and the inequality between those with some wage income and those with none. It would appear that almost half of what we have termed 'wage inequality' is in fact driven by the 30% of households with zero wage income.

Remittance income has the smallest share of total income (2%) and makes a small, negative contribution to inequality (–0,25%). This negative contribution arises because of the small negative correlation (R = –0,07) between the rank ordering of remittance income and the rank ordering of total income. This negative correlation would seem to imply that the fairly high Gini coefficient for remittances is due to the fact that remittance income is disproportionately distributed to those at the bottom of the total distribution relative to those at the top. In essence, this analysis suggests that the factors which boost remittance income for current recipients would lower overall inequality.

The last column of Table 1.5 shows the effects of a 1% increase in a particular income component. We see that a change in state transfers, remittances or income from self-employment will have the greatest effect on the overall Gini. In the last case, the Gini increases, but in the other two cases it decreases. The components which increase inequality correlate highly with total income rankings (i.e. R_k is high), which implies that an increase in these sources will primarily benefit the better-off and thus aggravate the Gini. The sum of the absolute changes in the Gini coefficient is zero. This follows because increasing all components of income by 1% has no effect on the income distribution and therefore no effect on the Gini.

From the point of view of government policy, state transfers are of special interest. A well-targeted, redistributionist state expenditure programme would be evidenced by a strongly negative R. The value of R at –0,12 suggests that state transfers serve to decrease the value of the overall Gini. Moreover, we see that an increase in state transfers of 1% will reduce the Gini by 0,04 (7%).

While G_k is the coefficient needed to calculate the contribution to inequality, a closer look at G_A is instructive. G_A is the Gini coefficient used when considering only those households actually receiving income from that particular source. We see that there are large disparities in the incomes earned from self-employment, capital income and wage income. This points to the dichotomous nature of the South African economy, in which immense gaps exist between those engaged in high- and low-wage employment, formal versus informal self-employment and those earning income from interest and dividends versus those accruing a small capital benefit as a result of owning their dwelling.

A comparison with the PSLSD shows fairly similar patterns in the data. These include, for example, a share of wage income in total income at 69% and a contribution to overall inequality of 74% — both figures slightly higher than those in the IES. What is interesting from the wage income data is that the PSLSD reports a G_{wage} decomposition that has a greater share (34%) of households in the sample that earn no wage income. Hence, the greater wage income contribution to overall household inequality (G_k) is a function partly of the PSLSD reporting more households with no wage-earners.

In terms of remittances, the PSLSD captures a larger proportion of households receiving this type of income. This is an accepted difference between the two data sets, given that the PSLSD was more diligent in tracking down remittance-recipient households. Given the relative homogeneity of these households in terms of income levels, the percentage share in the overall Gini is stronger at −0,40 rather than the −0,25 found using the IES. The IES yields a stronger result on the impact of state transfers, as the PSLSD reports a zero, rather than a negative, contribution to inequality for these transfers. An interesting result in comparing the two data sets is the effect on the Gini of a 1% change in the different income components. While the IES reports the strongest impact on the Gini from a 1% increase in an income source to emanate from self-employment income (0,047), the PSLSD is far less sensitive, with self-employment only increasing the Gini by 0,006. This may be partly due to the more structured and consistent efforts made in the IES to uncover individuals involved in self-employment across the entire income distribution.

A central point to note from Table 1.5, though, is that while wage incomes on their own are very important, remittances and self-employment are also incomes derivative of the labour market. If the cumulative impact of all three of these sources is considered, it can be seen that the labour market dominates South African income and income inequality. This is in line with comparisons of such studies in other countries. A quotation from Fields (1980:114) will suffice:

> Individually and together, the results for Taiwan, Pakistan and Colombia give a common impression about the contribution of various income sources to overall inequality. The bulk of income inequality is attributable to labour income. The high factor inequality weights for labour incomes suggest that the principal inequality-producing factor is some people receiving a great deal more income for their work than do others. This has important implications both for the research (researchers should study the labour market) and for policy (policy makers should create more well-paying jobs). The intuitively prior notion that the most unequally distributed factors (property, gifts, etc) contribute the most to total inequality is found to be false in each case.

However, while the analysis of any of the income sources presented in the table is usefully indicative, it does not really reveal enough about what is going on at the lower end of the distribution relative to the top end. So, for example, it is quite possible for the same aggregate outcomes to result from an income source that contributes exclusively to the very poor and very rich or exclusively to the middle of the distribution. This points to the need for some complementary sensitivity analysis. A particularly useful exercise would seem to be one that splits the population by a poverty line. This was done for the South African case and the results are presented in Table 1.6.

TABLE 1.6

Decomposition of total national income by income sources, below and above the poverty line

Income source	Proportion of households receiving income source	Mean income from source	Share in total income	Gini for source for households receiving such income	Gini for income source for all households	Gini correlation with total income rankings	Contribution to Gini coefficient of total income	Percentage share in overall Gini	Effect on overall Gini of a 1% change in income source
	(P_k)		(S_k)	(G_A)	(G_k)	(R_k)	$(S_k G_k R_k)$		
Below the poverty line									
Remittances	0,23	R78,02	0,12	0,38	0,86	0,16	0,02	5,64	−0,020
Wage income	0,50	R308,00	0,49	0,31	0,65	0,60	0,19	63,0	0,044
Capital income	0,09	R23,65	0,04	0,59	0,96	0,47	0,02	5,51	0,005
State transfers	0,49	R206,81	0,33	0,33	0,67	0,31	0,07	22,03	−0,032
Self-employment	0,04	R17,24	0,03	0,42	0,98	0,44	0,01	3,86	0,003
Total		R633,72	1,00				0,30	100,00	
Above the poverty line									
Remittances	0,09	R58,81	0,02	0,50	0,95	−0,09	−0,001	−0,27	−0,01
Wage income	0,79	R2501,56	0,68	0,47	0,58	0,84	0,33	63,3	−0,02
Capital income	0,21	R355,19	0,10	0,67	0,93	0,58	0,05	9,9	0,002
State transfers	0,26	R132,65	0,04	0,45	0,85	−0,15	−0,005	−0,91	−0,02
Self-employment	0,11	R648,39	0,18	0,68	0,97	0,86	0,15	27,98	0,05
Total		R3 696,60	1,00				0,52	100,00	

Inspection of this table shows that the data from Table 1.5 is only a rough average of very different processes taking place above and below the poverty line.[14] As agriculture is a consistently low contributor to average income and to inequality in both the above and the below group, it will not be discussed further.

We will consider wage income first. In the above group, this income source makes a large and stable contribution to average income (68%) and to the distribution of income (63%). This distributional effect is the result of a low Gini coefficient (0,58) being offset by a high R of 0,84. For the below group, the share of wage income in total income is far lower (49%) but, even within the poor, higher wage income is strongly correlated with higher total income (R = 0,60) and this income source therefore still makes a high contribution to inequality (63%). It is clear from this breakdown of above and below groups that access to wage income is central to determining which households are able to avoid poverty and even the depth to which poor households sink below the poverty line. This reasserts the importance of the labour market in understanding poverty: that the formal earnings capacities of households will either reinforce or shed their poverty status.

On the other hand, it is encouraging to see that state transfers make up a much smaller part of the total income for the above group (4%) than the below group (33%). Moreover, R = −0,15 in the above group reveals that this income is not going to the higher-income households in society. However, the fairly high Gini coefficient for state transfers in the below group (0,67) and rank correlation (R = 0,31) implies that it is the relatively better-off within the poor who are receiving state transfers.

There are two possible explanations for such an outcome. The first is that the targeting of state assistance is not that successful. The second is that the depth of poverty in South African society is so acute that access even to some state assistance is sufficient to move a household away from the bottom of the poverty ranking. Apartheid-derived racial biases in welfare allocations are certainly a cause of inefficient allocation.[15] However, there is also some recent econometric evidence (Case & Deaton 1996) indicating that state pensions are not badly targeted. In addition, studies of rural poverty (see May *et al.* 1995) have made it clear that 'claims against the state' are central to rural livelihoods. Thus, on balance, the second explanation is more likely to be true.[16] What can be said with greater certainty is that the analysis of wage income and state transfers serves to confirm that, in South Africa, the poorest of the poor are those households that lack access to either wage income or state transfers.

The low share of remittances in total income (2%) and the negative correlation for remittances (R = −0,09) in the above group along with the very much higher share of remittances (12%) in the income of the below group indicate that remittances are much more important on average in the below group. In South Africa, remittances generally flow from urban to rural areas; to a large extent, this result merely confirms that a large component of South Africa's poor are located in rural areas (Whiteford *et al.* 1995). However, there is additional information to be gleaned as well. The low, positive rank correlation (R = 0,16) in the below group results in a small contribution to inequality (5,6%). This implies that remittance income is well disbursed within the poor. So, while remittances are not important enough to be a major discriminator of who lies above or below the poverty line, factors which might cause an increase in remittances would have a generalised positive impact on the poor. The converse is true for capital income. This income source is far more important to the above group than the below group, both as an average share (10% and 4%, respectively) and as a contributor to inequality (9,9% and 5,5%, respectively).

When considering only those households actually receiving such income, a look at the 'actual' Gini (G_A) for the components reveals much the same picture as the analysis for the total population. We would, perhaps, have anticipated lower Ginis in the below group, which might be expected to be fairly homogenous since everyone is, after all, technically 'poor'. This is, however, not the case. There are considerable deviations in the incomes earned from capital income and self-employment both in the above and below groups. Self-employment in the below group, however, produces less inequality amongst those engaged in these activities than in the above group. This is to be expected, since all those in the below group are likely to be involved in marginal, informal activities.

The comparison with the PSLSD yields some interesting results. Within the below group, for example, the percentage share of wage income in total inequality is smaller, at 51,6% as opposed to 63% for IES. This is due to a larger contribution from state transfers to total inequality, of 28,4% rather than 22% in the IES. More interestingly, the effect on the Gini of a 1% change in the income source shows different-signed answers within the below group for capital income, state transfers and self-employment. While IES predicts an increase in the Gini by 0,005 with capital income, the PSLSD survey predicts a decrease of 0,005. This may be due in part to the fact that imputed rent, as part of capital income, was more carefully collected in the PSLSD. In this case, more poor households were allocated this income, and hence the decline in inequality from an increase in this source. Likewise, state transfers were shown to increase rather than decrease the Gini, while self-employment was predicted to decrease the Gini. The figure for state transfers makes a claim that while state pensions may be well targeted at the poor, there is a smaller share of the poor receiving these transfers than not. Hence, a rise in the value of pension payouts to poor households, as in the PSLSD survey, will exacerbate inequality. The self-employment numbers suggest that the returns to the poor through working for themselves may be more evenly distributed than the IES predicts. Using PSLSD, one may be more confident of the equity-generating impact of increased self-employment income to poor households.

For the above group, the percentage share of wage income in the Gini is higher (70,7%) than in the IES (63,3%). Further, the contribution of capital income to the overall Gini is much higher (16,6%), while self-employment income is far less important in explaining the Gini (7,82%) than in the IES (27,98%). The impact of a 1% change in the income sources on the Gini reveals all the same-signed answers for the two data sets. Using the PSLSD, then, we may be confident that the key drivers of total inequality for the above group were wage income, followed by capital income and self-employment income. Using the IES however, we would predict that wage income, income from self-employment and then capital income determine inequality in the above group. For households above the poverty line, the PSLSD places more importance on capital income than income from self-employment in generating inequality. It is true, however, that in its concerted efforts to uncover those individuals working for themselves, the IES may be a more accurate predictor of the dynamics of self-employment in the above group – and indeed the below group as well.

Irrespective of the data set used, this sensitivity analysis serves to reinforce the finding that, within both the above and below groups, wage income is the key determinant of income inequality in the society. In earlier work, Leibbrandt, Woolard and Woolard (1996) decomposed within African income using identical methods. This within-African analysis generated a picture that is quite different from the total income picture for the above and below groups. This illustrates some of the complexity of South Africa's income dynamics. However, despite these differences, wages have a more dominant influence on South Africa's inequality (79,44% in the IES and 82,25% in the PSLSD) in this group than in any of the other cuts. Thus, the importance of wage income and, by direct implication, the labour market is very clear across all cuts of South African households.

A closer look at inequality, poverty and the labour market

The overriding message of the previous section was the dominance of wage income in driving household inequality in South Africa. The decomposition analysis also robustly suggested that the role of wage income is significantly influenced both by the fact that many households have no access to it and by the fact that wage income is very unequally distributed across those households that do have access to it. When similar results were presented in the past (Leibbrandt, Woolard & Woolard 1996; Bhorat, Leibbrandt & Woolard 1995), such a picture was taken to imply empirical support for an insider–outsider model of the labour market in South Africa. While these empirics certainly do not preclude this possibility, such an implication is premature. As stated in the introduction, this chapter focuses on inequality at the household level. In contrast, individuals are usually the focus of attention in labour market studies. There is, therefore, an aggregation problem and an uneasy relationship between this inequality analysis and any labour market analysis. The non-wage-earning households are particularly problematic, as such households do not constitute a tight labour market category. For example, a household with two pensioners would be a non-wage-earning household. A household containing a mother taking care of her children would also be a non-wage-earning household. Neither of these households contain *any* labour market participants and they therefore do not imply anything about the operation of the labour market.

This mapping between individuals in the labour market and household-level poverty and inequality outcomes has proved to be problematic in all international studies, including this one.[17] In this concluding section, we present a tighter exploration of the labour market implications of the earlier decomposition work by focusing directly on the unemployed and their attachments to different households in the society. Table 1.7 seeks to highlight the differences between households when classified by the number of unemployed members resident in the household. The expanded definition of unemployment is utilised here, while figures based on the narrow definition are included in the Appendix.

From Table 1.7 it can be seen that over two-thirds of households (72%) have no unemployed members. This figure falls to 64% among African households. Amongst households with unemployed members, most contain only one unemployed person. Nevertheless, a significant number of households (approximately 800 000) contain two or more unemployed persons. Urban households are more likely to have no unemployed members, despite higher participation rates in urban areas.

The demographic section of the table (sections A and B) is striking. Households where no-one is unemployed are typically smaller and the members are significantly older. This has been explained (Klasen & Woolard 1998) by the fact that the young unemployed generally remain with their parents or attach themselves to the households of other relatives. Once employment is found, they are able to form separate (and thus smaller) households. Not surprisingly, households with no unemployed persons are slightly better educated.

It can be seen from the next section of the table (section C) that more than half of the unemployed are in households with two or more unemployed persons. The situation of these households is clearly particularly grim when one considers the average employment (or, conversely, unemployment) rates in households with two or more unemployed persons. While 47% of labour force participants in households with one unemployed member are formally employed or own-account workers, this figure falls to 27% in households with two unemployed members, and to a dismal 17% in households with three or more unemployed.

The average household unemployment rate controls for household size, or, more specifically, for the number of labour market participants in households. It is therefore a tighter measure of the severity of unemployment at the household level. This row in the table shows that such average unemployment rates are higher than the more conventional unemployment rates that are discussed above. Using these average household rates as a guide, over half of the labour market participants are unemployed in all households with any unemployed members.

Not surprisingly, income levels fall as the number of unemployed in the household increases. Incomes in households with no unemployed are almost twice those in households with one unemployed person, before taking account of the fact that households with unemployed members are significantly larger. If one compares the Theil-T contributions (section D of Table 1.7) to inequality to the population shares (shown in the first line of Table 1.7), we can see that households where no-one is unemployed are the major contributors to inequality. Thus, most of the household-level inequality in South Africa is driven by income dynamics within households with no unemployed members. Thus labour market earnings – rather than unemployment – need to be highlighted when looking at the labour market factors driving household income

TABLE 1.7

Expanded definition of unemployment[a]

Household type	0	1	2	3+	Total	Column shares
A General						
ALL	71,8	19,1	5,9	3,2	8 801 992	100,0
African	64,0	23,8	7,7	4,4	5 950 904	67,6
Coloured	73,4	18,6	5,7	2,3	747 530	8,5
Asian	81,6	14,8	2,7	0,8	245 661	2,8
White	94,7	4,8	0,4	0,1	1 857 897	21,1
Rural	68,1	20,8	7,2	3,9	3 483 220	
Urban	74,2	18,0	5,0	2,8	5 318 772	
B Other demographics						
Average age	31,8	26,3	27,1	27,8	30,4	
Average size	3,8	5,1	6,4	8,1	4,3	
Average number of children under 15	1,3	1,9	2,2	2,3	1,5	
Average number of adults	2,5	3,1	4,2	5,8	2,8	
Average number of labour market participants	1,3	1,9	2,7	4,3	1,6	
Average adult years of education	7,0	6,0	5,6	5,6	6,7	
C Labour market						
% of total unemployment	0	43,4	28,0	28,5	100	
% of total self-employment	78,1	14,7	4,6	2,6	100	
% of total formal employment	78,2	15,6	4,0	2,3	100	
Average household unemployment rate	0	65,6	80,9	85,7	24,7	
Average unemployment rate	0	53,1	73,4	83,0	28,6	
Average self-employment rate	14,5	6,5	4,4	2,7	10,3	
Average formal employment rate	85,3	40,6	22,3	14,4	61,0	
D Poverty and inequality						
Average household income per annum (standard deviation)	42 094 (75 493)	22 886 (48 283)	17 929 (21 675)	17 970 (18 559)	35 770 (67 662)	
Average household expenditure per annum (standard deviation)	40 564 (73 687)	22 848 (47 611)	17 209 (20 968)	18 197 (19 812)	34 658 (66 073)	
Theil-T (% contributions to overall inequality)[a]	79,9	11,5	1,9	0,9	94,1	
Poverty shares:						
$FGT(P_0)$	51,9	28,0	12,2	7,9	100,0	
$FGT(P_1)$	48,1	28,7	13,9	9,3	100,0	
$FGT(P_2)$	45,6	29,0	15,1	10,3	100,0	

[a] The figures sum to 94,1%. The remaining 5,9% is the 'between group' inequality.

inequality. However, this does not imply that unemployment is unimportant. Indeed, one of the major reasons for this finding is that households with unemployed members are uniformly bunched in the low-income sections of the household income distribution. This is confirmed by the poverty decomposition analysis.

The incidence of poverty (measured by the Foster–Greer–Thorbecke P_0 measure, more commonly known as the head-count index) clearly increases as the number of unemployed household members grows. While 72% of households have no unemployed members, they only make up 52% of the poor. Similarly, while only 3% of households have three or more unemployed members, they account for 8% of poor households. In addition to being more *likely* to be poor, poor households are also *more poor.* We see from the FGT P_1 and P_2 measures (which can be considered to measure the depth and severity of poverty, respectively) that households with unemployed persons make up even higher proportions of poverty than when measured by the head-count index.

Conclusion

The oblique references to the differences generated by using two different data sets, or indeed even alternative inequality measures, do not detract from a few simple yet powerful observations made here about income inequality in South Africa. Firstly, income inequality between different races, although smaller than the within-race contribution, is amongst the highest in the world – if not the highest. Secondly, the largest within-race contributor to inequality is amongst African households. Greater inequality exists amongst African households than any other race group. Thirdly, it is evident that the most important determinant of the Gini coefficient in South Africa is wage income, while self-employment income appears as a highly relevant inequality measure as well. Finally, the material presented in this chapter reinforces the fact that the labour market is central to our understanding of poverty in the society. Specifically, most household-level inequality is driven by income dynamics within households with no unemployed members, because households with unemployed members tend to be crowded below the poverty line at the lower end of the household income distribution.

Notes

1. The Gini coefficient always has a value between zero and one. The bigger the number, the more inequality exists.
2. Note that because of variability in the date of data collection and differing methodologies, these figures should be taken as indicative only.
3. As the average household size is larger for the lower deciles, the inequality is worse than it would have been if no attention had been given to household size. However, in our calculations household incomes were ranked according to adult equivalent incomes rather than per capita incomes. These

adult equivalents give explicit cognisance to the fact that children require less income than adults and that there are certain economies of scale associated with larger households. Following May (1995), we used an adult equivalence scale here and later in the chapter, of the form:

$$E = (A + 0,5K)^{0,9}$$

where E = number of adult equivalents, A = number of adults, and K = number of children.

4. These figures are questioned by the Centre for Development and Enterprise (1995) who suggest that the distribution among black households is 'more equal' than Whiteford and McGrath suggest. CDE Research No. 1, September 1995: 'Post-Apartheid Population & Income Trends: A New Analysis'.

5. See Deaton (1997) and Cowell (1995) for recent reviews of this literature.

6. To bring out such points requires that we spend a lot of time unpacking the details of the various techniques. We have done this in the chapter partly in the hope that access to such information will be valuable to South African readers.

7. While the questionnaire asked for considerable detail about these activities, Statistics South Africa (SSA) failed to place a value on them.

8. See Fields (1980) for a review.

9. A *generally decomposable or aggregative* index is defined as one where the overall inequality level can be expressed as some general function of the subgroup means, population sizes and inequality measures. The most useful type of decomposability is *additive decomposability*. A measure is additively decomposable if it can be tidily expressed as the sum of a 'between-group' term and a 'within-group' term. The between-group component is the value of the measure were every member assigned the group mean (i.e. there is assumed to be no inequality within the group). Similarly, the within-group component is the value of the inequality measure when all the between-group inequalities are suppressed.

10. See McGrath and Whiteford (1994) and Moll (1998).

11. The literature starts with Shorrocks (1983) and is most recently extended by Lerman and Yitzhaki (1994).

12. R_k is a form of rank correlation coefficient, as it measures the extent to which the relationship between Y_k and the cumulative rank distribution of total income coincides with the relationship between Y_k and its own cumulative rank distribution.

13. It should be noted that the overall Gini coefficient in the table is 0,60 as opposed to the 0,65 of McGrath and Whiteford (1994) from the same data. McGrath and Whiteford reweighted the sample to coincide with 1991 census population shares, thereby giving more weight to white incomes and accentuating inequality. In our calculations, we used the survey enumeration weights and used a slightly refined data set taking account of the errors in the social pensions data discovered by Pieter le Roux (University of the Western Cape).

14. For ease of expression, we will refer to those above the poverty line as the above group and those below the poverty line as the below group.

15. See Bhorat (1995) for the historical details of racial biases in pension allocations.

16. The one clear contribution made by this analysis of state transfers is to illustrate how careful we have to be in adding interpretation to the empirics of the income decomposition analysis.

17. The furore over the poverty impacts of a minimum wage in the United States is a good example. See Card and Krueger (1994) versus Neumark and Washer (1997).

2

Measuring Poverty in South Africa

Ingrid Woolard
Murray Leibbrandt[1]

The debate about the meaning of poverty continues. In spite of this, certain basic steps in the analysis of poverty have become quite standard (Hentschel & Lanjouw 1996:1). Firstly, households or individuals are ranked on the basis of a welfare indicator – usually income or consumption expenditures. Secondly, a poverty line is selected which separates the poor from the non-poor. Finally the poor, identified in this way, are examined more closely through the construction of a poverty profile.

The first two sections of this chapter deal with, in Sen's (1976:219) terminology, the 'identification problem' of distinguishing which individuals are poor. The third section deals with the 'aggregation problem' of constructing an index of poverty using the available information on the poor. While most of the more recent theoretical literature is concerned with the aggregation problem (Foster & Shorrocks 1988:173), the issue of identification has great bearing on applied work and needs to be carefully examined.

Therefore, we begin by focusing on the critical issue of how to identify 'the poor'. We review the main methods that have been proposed for the derivation of a poverty line and touch on a range of issues which arise in practice. These include: the choice of recipient unit, the welfare concept used and the difficulties associated with comparisons across households that differ in size and age structure.

Identifying the poor

Chambers (1988) distinguishes five dimensions of poverty:

- *'poverty proper'*, being a lack of adequate income or assets to generate income;
- *physical weakness* due to undernutrition, sickness or disability;
- physical or social *isolation* due to peripheral location, lack of access to goods and services, ignorance or illiteracy;

- *vulnerability* to crisis and the risk of becoming even poorer; and

- *powerlessness* within existing social, economic, political and cultural structures.

It must be stressed at the outset that this chapter is concerned only with 'poverty proper'. While money-metric poverty measures probably provide the best single 'objective' proxy for poverty status, there are other important ways of assessing poverty. The poor are *not* concerned exclusively with adequate incomes and consumption. Achieving other goals, such as security, independence and societal participation, may be just as important as having the means to purchase basic goods and services.

Measuring 'wellbeing'

Most empirical work on the distribution of welfare is done using either expenditure or income data recorded in household surveys (Glewwe 1988:3). This is intuitively appealing and it is not necessary to review here the theoretical framework that allows us to make the link between the distribution of income/expenditure and the distribution of welfare.

The concept of 'standard of living' can be either welfarist or non-welfarist. The welfarist approach typically emphasises expenditure on all goods and services consumed, including consumption of home production valued at appropriate prices. By contrast, a common non-welfarist approach emphasises specific commodity forms of deprivation (Ravallion 1992:7), usually inadequate food consumption.

Either way, a person's standard of living is generally taken to depend only on the consumption of *market* goods. While the limitations of this approach are well documented (Deaton & Muellbauer 1980:223), the problems involved in valuing access to public goods are enormous. It is thus to a large extent for pragmatic reasons that current consumption or current income is used as the indicator of wellbeing.

Consumption as a measure of poverty

This work conforms to the international norm of using material wellbeing or 'standard of living' as the welfare indicator (Hentschel & Lanjouw 1996:1). The lead of the World Bank is followed in defining poverty as 'the inability to attain a minimal standard of living' measured in terms of basic consumption needs (World Bank 1990).

To measure material welfare, it is necessary to measure what and how much individuals consume (Deaton & Case 1988:1). This chapter follows the conventional approach of ignoring the consumption of public goods and the value of leisure time (Ravallion 1992:7). Thus a person's standard of living is taken to depend on the current consumption of privately supplied goods, goods (e.g. crops) from own production and the imputed rents from owner-occupied housing.

Empirical work on the distribution of welfare is sometimes done using income data (Glewwe1988:3). There are several conceptual and pragmatic reasons for preferring private consumption expenditure over income as a measure of wellbeing. The most important of these reasons is that expenditure is usually more reliably reported and more stable than income, especially among the poor (Ravallion 1992:13).

Alternative measures of poverty

The choice of private consumption expenditure (PCE) per adult equivalent as an appropriate welfare measure has a strong theoretical basis as well as intuitive appeal. The question arises whether other popular poverty definitions would select the same individuals as poor. As we do not yet wish to turn to the issue of the equivalence scale, we use *per capita* PCE as our referent. The following poverty definitions were tested:

- per capita consumption;
- household consumption;
- per capita income;
- per capita food expenditure;
- per capita caloric intake;
- budget share of food expenditure (food ratio); and
- average educational level of adult household members.

We compare the characteristics of the poor selected under each definition. In order to make the comparisons meaningful, we define 40% of households as poor using each definition.

Tables 2.1 and 2.2 show the results. It is immediately apparent that the face of poverty is radically altered when we use per capita caloric intake as the poverty definition. On the basis of caloric intake, poverty amongst the coloured population appears to be a more severe problem than amongst Africans – clearly an absurd result. In general, however, the seven definitions of poverty give broadly consistent results.

Tables 2.3 and 2.4 show the correlation between poverty as defined by per capita consumption and the alternative definitions of poverty suggested above. The first two columns give the total number of households who are classified by both definitions as poor and non-poor, respectively. (Thus, if the two definitions were perfectly correlated these numbers would be 40% and 60%, respectively.) The tables indicate that some definitions of poverty are much more strongly correlated with per capita PCE than others. The poorest measures are adult school attainment and caloric intake. As shown in later chapters of this book, school attainment of less-than-completed secondary education is a poor predictor of finding employment and thus correlates poorly with standard of living. The difficulties associated with caloric intake as a measure of wellbeing are discussed below.

Information sources

If the government is to address poverty and inequality, it requires reliable data on the extent and nature of the problem. The new government faces the problem that the previous regime had little interest in collecting information of this nature. Between 1970 and 1994, official statistics excluded the so-called 'independent states' of Transkei, Bophutatswana, Venda and Ciskei, thus automatically excluding a large proportion of the poor from official statistics.

In 1993, Statistics South Africa (SSA) ran the first *October Household Survey* and has continued to do so annually, although only the 1994 and 1995 surveys were available for use in this study. The survey collects a variety of household information, such as housing types and access to services, as well as person-level data about, for example, education, health and work status. A substantial part of past questionnaires has been dedicated to collecting information needed for labour statistics. Birth and death data are also recorded for demographic purposes. Unfortunately, it was only in 1995 that the survey was accompanied by a detailed Income and Expenditure Survey (IES), which collected information about income from sources other than employment and about expenditure. The 1993 and 1994 surveys are thus of little use in analysing income poverty or inequality. The analysis in this chapter thus relies largely on the 1995 OHS/IES.

This chapter also makes use of the Project for Statistics on Living Standards and Development (PSLSD) survey conducted in 1993 by the Southern Africa Labour and Development Research Unit (SALDRU) at the University of Cape Town with technical assistance from the World Bank. This survey collected a wider range of indicators of standard of living, including food intake and anthropometric data for children under six.

Ismail Serageldin aptly describes poverty statistics as 'people with the tears wiped off' (quoted in Moser 1996). While objective measures are undoubtedly useful, the textured data obtained from exercises such as the South African Participatory Poverty Assessment (SA-PPA), conducted in 1995 (May 1998), offer useful insights. Qualitative data restores the reality that lies hidden behind the rates and averages of poverty statistics. The SA-PPA was undertaken at the request of the RDP office. The purpose of the exercise was to provide a fuller and more integrated understanding of poverty from the perspective of those who are poor and to fill the gaps that the PSLSD could not readily explain.

TABLE 2.1

Incidence of poverty amongst selected groups, by poverty measure (1993 data)[a, b]

Measure	% Africans in poverty	% Coloureds in poverty	Incidence of rural poverty	Incidence of urban poverty	Incidence of poverty amongst female-headed households
Per capita consumption	51,4	25,3	60,5	20,3	53,4
Total household consumption	51,8	21,1	58,2	22,5	52,1
Per capita income	51,6	19,2	59,5	21,3	52,4
Per capita food expenditure	49,6	35,2	56,3	24,4	49,9
Per capita caloric intake	42,5	57,2	42,4	38,0	44,2
Food ratio	50,9	20,5	57,8	22,0	51,9
Average adult education	49,9	27,8	56,5	24,1	43,8

[a] Assuming that the poorest 40% of households are poor.
[b] PSLSD 1993.

TABLE 2.2

Incidence of poverty amongst selected groups, by poverty measure (1995 data)[a, b]

Measure	% Africans in poverty	% Coloureds in poverty	Incidence of rural poverty	Incidence of urban poverty	Incidence of poverty amongst female-headed households
Per capita consumption	53,6	35,8	60,6	24,1	52,2
Total household consumption	52,1	36,0	59,2	25,2	52,2
Per capita income	53,4	36,2	59,1	25,3	53,0
Per capita food expenditure	53,2	33,3	56,7	27,2	48,8
Food ratio	49,0	45,3	54,4	28,9	53,0
Average adult education	50,8	46,6	59,3	25,2	44,0

[a] Assuming that the poorest 40% of households are poor.
[b] IES & OHS, SSA 1995.

TABLE 2.3

Correlation of alternative definitions of poverty with the per capita consumption definition (1993 data)[a]

Definition	Percentage of population 'correctly' identified		
	Poor	Non-poor	Total
Household consumption	70,5	80,3	76,4
Per capita income	77,0	84,7	81,6
Per capita food expenditure	85,8	90,5	88,6
Per capita caloric intake	62,3	74,8	69,8
Food ratio	65,8	77,2	72,6
Adult school attainment	60,5	73,7	68,4

[a] PSLSD 1993.

TABLE 2.4

Correlation of alternative definitions of poverty with the per capita consumption definition (1995 data)[a]

Definition	Percentage of population 'correctly' identified		
	Poor	Non-poor	Total
Household consumption	75,8	83,8	80,6
Per capita income	90,8	93,8	92,6
Per capita food expenditure	79,3	86,2	83,4
Food ratio	69,0	79,3	75,2
Adult school attainment	64,8	76,5	71,8

[a] IES & OHS, SSA 1995.

Deriving a poverty line

Modern interest in poverty can be traced to the concern of social observers such as Booth and Rowntree in Britain during the late 19th century. From those times, social policy analysts have found it useful to focus debate through reference to a minimum desirable level of income, or a *poverty line* (Johnson 1996:110).

A poverty line divides the population into two groups on the basis of some measure: below the line, a household/individual is considered to be poor, and above the line it is considered non-poor. Clearly, poverty lines are extremely useful for descriptions of poverty. By defining a line that is regarded as some kind of minimum living level, we are able to ascertain the number of poor people, as well as the depth and severity of poverty.

However, the point at which we draw the line is always somewhat arbitrary and often highly contentious. After all, it is clearly rather crude to assume that a household earning R999 per month is in poverty, while the household earning R1 000 is not. A poverty line will always be an imperfect measure, but for purposes of analysis we need to draw the line *somewhere* in order to go forward in understanding the nature of poverty.

Many approaches to identifying the poor begin with the specification of a set of basic needs. This can be termed the 'direct approach' (Callan & Nolan 1991:244). If one specifies minimum levels for certain consumption items (e.g. food, clothing, housing), then an individual who does not meet these minimum levels for *each* commodity is clearly poor. The difficulty that arises is that a person may be, for example, 'food-poor' but not 'energy-poor', making this a cumbersome measurement to use in practice.

An alternative to the direct approach is to work out the cost of a minimum basket of goods and use the required expenditure level as the poverty line. This is what Sen (1976:219) terms the 'income approach'. A variant on this approach is to build in a factor for waste and inefficient expenditure — for example, if it costs Rx to purchase the minimum set of commodities, the poverty line could be set at $Rx(1 + y)$ where y represents the proportion in excess of the strict minimum cost budget.

The conceptual distinction between the direct and income approaches is significant. While the direct approach identifies those individuals or households who *fail* to meet some minimum standard of living, the latter approach identifies those that are *unable* to do so. Out of respect for individual choice and in accordance with convention, we rely on the 'income approach'.

Absolute versus relative poverty lines

The literature distinguishes between *absolute* and *relative* poverty lines. An absolute poverty line is not meant to change with the standard of living in society. People are defined as poor when they lack the command over resources to meet some absolute needs. A relative poverty line, on the other hand, will move with standards of living (as represented by, say, median income): the poor are then taken to be those persons that are suffering *relative* deprivation.

The question of whether poverty should be seen as a state of absolute or relative deprivation has dominated the literature on the construction of a poverty line (Ravallion 1995:24). The distinction is important because it affects the way we perceive poverty-reduction policies. For example, economic growth will generally result in a reduction in the number of people in absolute poverty, but only a change in the distribution of income will reduce the number of people in relative poverty. As we are only looking at a single survey, these dynamic effects are not relevant to our work. However, we will derive and use an absolute poverty line.

Deriving an absolute poverty line

It is undeniable that there exist levels of consumption of food, clothing and shelter below which survival is threatened (Ravallion 1992:25). But in most societies the notion of what constitutes the 'minimum' living level is quite a bit higher than what is *essential* to survival. After all, as Beckerman (1984:6) has observed, it does not really make sense to define poverty at some minimum level when people continue to survive below it.

The most common approach in defining an absolute poverty line is to estimate the cost of a bundle of goods deemed to assure that 'basic needs' (as determined by the analyst) are met. In developing countries, where food expenditure will make up a large part of the basic needs bundle, a poverty line based on the amount of money needed to buy enough food to obtain the minimum intake of kilojoules and a modest allowance for non-food goods is often advocated.

Choosing the food energy requirement is, however, fraught with difficulties. Firstly, the number of kilojoules required is highly variable from one person to another, since people have different metabolisms and activity levels. Secondly, the household's consumption behaviour is not taken into account. The minimum cost for attaining the necessary energy intake may be less than the expenditure level at which a household normally attains that kilojoule intake. People do not simply consume food in order to stay alive. They have preferences for particular types of food: a diet of maize meal and beans may provide all the necessary nutrients at very low cost, but it may be loathsome to the individual.

There are also problems with determining the allowance for non-food consumption. The 'food energy approach' (Ravallion 1992:27) fixes a food energy intake in kilojoules and then finds the total consumption expenditure or income level at which a person typically attains that food energy intake. This has the appeal that it yields a poverty line which is consistent with local tastes and prices.

A variation on this method is first to find the minimum cost of a minimum-kilojoule food bundle and then divide this by the share of food in total expenditure of some group of households deemed likely to be poor. The immediate difficulty with the method is that it requires a prejudgement of who is 'poor' in order to determine who is poor, thus making the exercise somewhat circular.

Relative poverty lines

The view that poverty has to been seen in the context of the standard of living of the society in question enjoys wide popularity (Callan & Nolan 1991:252). This has led to the derivation of poverty lines that are explicitly based on relative wellbeing. The rationale of this is that those falling more than a certain distance below the average welfare level in a particular society are unlikely to be able to participate fully in the community.

The crudest definition of a relative poverty line is that income level which cuts off the poorest p percentage of the population in the national income distribution. The choice of p will always be somewhat arbitrary, but 40% is often chosen.[2] There are two objections to this method. First, the method prejudges the extent of poverty — it is p per cent by definition. Second, it requires us to accept the fact that 'the poor are always with us'. Even in the event of a massive shift in living standards, the proportion of people in poverty remains unchanged.

Another method is to define poverty in relation to contemporary living standards. For example, many studies for developed countries have used a poverty line that is set at a particular percentage of mean or median consumption. Typically, the poverty line is set at 50% of the national mean income. Thus, while the poverty line shifts upwards as the general standard of living rises, it is still possible to eliminate poverty (Atkinson 1977:189).

For South Africa, the per capita household income level which cuts off the poorest 40% of households in 1993 was R228 per month. The percentage of individuals who fall below this poverty line is 54,3%, however, because the poor have larger households on average than the non-poor.

The estimated per capita income in South Africa in 1993 was R472, so a relative poverty line set at 50% of per capita income would be R236 per month, which is very close to the figure of R228 obtained above.

Dual poverty lines

Ravallion (1992:34) advocates always considering at least two (and preferably multiple) poverty lines. This has the appeal of testing the sensitivity of measures to small changes in the setting of the poverty line. He further advocates the use of an absolute and a relative poverty line on the same data sets.

Selecting a poverty line for South Africa

The two most widely used South African poverty lines are the Household Subsistence Level (HSL) calculated by the Institute for Planning Research (Potgieter 1993), and the Minimum

Living Level (MLL), determined by the Bureau for Market Research. Both organisations calculate their poverty lines biannually for the major urban centres of South Africa and irregularly in rural areas.

Table 2.5 shows several possible definitions of a poverty line, including lines based on both absolute and relative poverty definitions. These lines yield results which show a range from about 24 to 57% in the proportion of the population who are poor. We use the 1993 data for this comparison, as its inclusion of caloric consumption allows for a greater variety of poverty lines to be derived.

TABLE 2.5

Comparison of selected poverty lines for South Africa (1993)[a]

Type of poverty line	Rands per month cut-off	Percentage of individuals below the poverty line
1. Population cut-off at 40th percentile of households ranked by adult equivalent expenditure	R301,70 per adult equivalent	52,8
2. Population cut-off at 50% of national per capita expenditure	R201,80 per capita	46,9
3. Amount of money required to achieve a per capita caloric intake of 8 500 kJ per day[b]	R149,50 per capita	40,4
4. Minimum and supplemental living levels per capita set by the Bureau of Market Research, University of South Africa[c]		
Supplemental Living Level (SLL)	R220,10 per capita	56,7
Minimum Living Level (MLL)	R164,20 per capita	44,7
5. Per adult equivalent household subsistence level (HSL) set by The Institute for Development Planning Research, University of Port Elizabeth[d]	R251,10 per adult equivalent	45,7
6. International poverty line of US$1 (1985 prices) per capita per day[e]	R105,00 per capita	25,6

[a] PSLSD 1993.

[b] Derived through regression analysis, using the Food Energy Intake Method (Ravallion 1998), which relates food expenditure per adult equivalent (X) and energy intake per adult equivalent (C) by means of a function of the form $ln\ X = a + bC + \mu$.

[c] For the minimum and supplemental living level, the values given are based on a family of five, converted to an adult equivalence scale.

[d] The HSL is calculated separately for various combinations of geographical location and household composition. The line used here is the average for the metropolitan centres where the minimum level of welfare required by a family of two adults and three children was set at R825,10 per month in September 1993.

[e] Deaton (1997:157).

The wide divergence of the poverty lines suggested above is the rationale for employing a 'poverty critical range' in place of a single poverty line. In the rest of our analysis we select a wide poverty critical range in order to establish whether our poverty rankings are robust.

Adjusting for household size and structure

Households differ in size and demographic make-up. Consequently, a straightforward comparison of household consumption may be deceptive. It is thus common practice to use some form of normalisation. The simplest normalisation is simply to divide household consumption by household size and then to compare households on the basis of household per capita consumption. More complex forms of normalisation, in which household consumption is converted to consumption per 'equivalent adult males', have become fashionable. A household of given size and demographic composition is taken to have the equivalent needs of a given number of adult males.

There exists a vast literature regarding the aggregation of individual living standards into household living standards (Sen 1987; Nelson 1993; Lanjouw & Ravallion 1995). Two broad issues arise in this literature. First, there is the issue of household size. Larger households require more expenditures than smaller households in order to achieve the same level of consumption. Clearly, this is not a linear relationship, as larger households may benefit from economies of scale in consumption of household public goods. The second class of issues relates to household composition. A three-adult household is unlikely to have equivalent consumption requirements to a household with one adult and two young children. A household has to be aggregated into a number of adult equivalents. In sum, then, in order to account for differences in household size and composition, total household consumption has to be divided by the number of adult equivalents and adjusted to take into account economies of scale (Deaton & Muellbauer 1980).

Children impose financial costs on the households in which they reside, but it is generally agreed that the cost of a child is smaller than the cost of an additional adult. One standard and widely used procedure is to define children as a fraction of an adult according to nutritional needs. Based on the caloric requirements set down by the World Health Organisation (e.g. a child aged 7–8 requires 64% of the calories required by an adult male), it is possible to calculate the number of equivalent males in the household. The difficulty with this approach is that children (and adults) consume non-food items as well, and there is no good reason to believe that non-food expenditure is in proportion to caloric needs. Furthermore, the empirical evidence suggests that even individuals who have the means to purchase 'sufficient' calories do not necessarily do so, making the link between nutrition and welfare very tenuous.

Engel's procedure is the best-known method of measuring child costs and economies of scale. Engel observed that amongst households of similar size and composition the budget share devoted to food declined as total consumption increased. Secondly, for households with the same total expenditure, he observed that the larger the household the larger the budget share devoted to food. Finally, he argued that households with the same budget share have the same level of welfare, regardless of the demographic make-up of the household.

We used the Working (1943)–Leser (1963) form of the Engel curve to estimate equivalence scales for African households. A demand model was constructed in which the budget share devoted to food consumption (the food ratio) was regressed on the log of per capita expenditure and the numbers of persons in various demographic categories living in the household. If we accept that the food ratio is a valid indicator of welfare, then by fixing the referent welfare level (and hence the food ratio), the regression equation tells us by how much total consumption must differ in order that a household be exactly compensated for its different composition relative to another household.

The prime objection to the use of this technique is that it assumes that the food share is a valid indicator of wellbeing. Ravallion points out that, at the very least, food share is a 'noisy' indicator because the relationship between food share and consumption differs across households since their tastes will differ (Ravallion 1992:21). A further problem is that the income elasticity of demand for food can be close to 1 for poor households, making the food ratio an unreliable indicator.

We then fitted an equivalence scale of the form $(A + \alpha K)^\theta$ to the data using (weighted) non-linear least squares. When the food ratio is fixed at 50%, we obtain estimates of α and θ of 0,997 and 0,68, respectively. When the food ratio is fixed at 40%, we obtain estimates of α and θ of 0,812 and 0,62, respectively.

Nicholson (1976) argues that Engel's procedure overstates the cost of children. He reasons as follows. Assume that a couple have a child, who brings with her an endowment that exactly compensates the household for the costs associated with the child. By assumption, the parents are as well-off as before and are able to continue to consume in the same pattern as before. However, the consumption patterns of the child are likely to differ: specifically, we expect that a higher percentage of the child's total consumption will be on food. Consequently, the food share of the household as a whole has increased, despite perfect compensation. Therefore, had the household been compensated according to the Engel procedure, they would have been given sufficient money to drive the food share down to the level it was at before the birth of the child. Thus, the household would be overcompensated.

In the past, South Africans have followed the lead of May et al. (1995) in choosing to set $\alpha = 0,5$ and $\theta = 0,9$. These values were suggested by Angus Deaton in a lecture given in South Africa in 1994, but were simply suggested as plausible values for the purposes of explaining the principle of the equivalence scale.

The only other source of implicit equivalence scales for South Africa can be found in the methodology of the Household Subsistence Level (Potgieter 1995). First, we note that the amount of money needed to feed and clothe a 10-year-old child is 0,68 that of providing for a (male) adult. Then, by comparing the HSLs for 5- and 6-person households, where the additional person is assumed to be a child, we find that the implicit value of θ is 0,72.

Of course, if our poverty profile is insensitive to changes in the values of α and θ, then it is unimportant where we fix the equivalence scale parameters. We tested the robustness of the poverty profile to a variety of values of α and θ, namely $\alpha = 0,5, 0,75$ and 1 and $\theta = 0,6, 0,75$ and $0,9$. We kept the share of individuals in poverty fixed at 40%.

TABLE 2.6

Incidence of poverty among selected groups, using a variety of equivalence scales[a]

Equivalence scale		% Africans in poverty	% Coloureds in poverty	% Rural residents in poverty	% Urban residents in poverty	% Female-headed households in poverty	% Elderly in poverty	% Children in poverty	Adult equivalent poverty line (annual)	Annual transfer required to eliminate poverty
$\alpha = 0,5$	$\theta = 0,6$	51,1	29,8	58,4	24,6	52,5	41,3	45,5	R5 089	R14,1 bn
$\alpha = 0,5$	$\theta = 0,75$	51,1	29,6	58,4	24,5	52,3	40,0	45,7	R4 069	R14,2 bn
$\alpha = 0,5$	$\theta = 0,9$	51,0	29,8	58,2	24,5	52,0	38,9	45,9	R3 238	R14,4 bn
$\alpha = 0,75$	$\theta = 0,6$	51,0	29,9	58,5	24,4	52,9	40,1	46,6	R4 740	R14,1 bn
$\alpha = 0,75$	$\theta = 0,75$	51,1	29,5	58,6	24,2	52,7	38,5	47,0	R3 719	R14,1 bn
$\alpha = 0,75$	$\theta = 0,9$	51,0	29,5	58,5	24,1	52,6	37,3	47,4	R2 911	R14,5 bn
$\alpha = 1,6$	$\theta = 0,6$	51,0	29,6	58,7	24,1	53,1	39,1	47,3	R4 471	R14,2 bn
$\alpha = 1$	$\theta = 0,75$	51,0	29,5	58,7	24,0	52,9	37,6	48,0	R3 455	R14,4 bn
$\alpha = 1$	$\theta = 0,9$	51,0	29,5	58,6	23,9	52,9	36,1	48,6	R2 665	R15,0 bn

[a] IES & OHS, SSA 1995.

The results in Table 2.6 are encouraging, for they show that the poverty profile changes very little even when we make large adjustments to the scale parameters. The poverty rate amongst Africans, coloureds and rural and urban dwellers remains astonishingly unchanged.

When we consider particular age categories, the impact of the parameters is more noticeable. By definition, the higher the value of α, the more children are in poverty. Nevertheless, the changes are not dramatic, with the percentage of poor children varying from 45,5 to 48,6%. The flip side of this is that the more heavily we weight children, the fewer elderly are in poverty. The incidence of poverty amongst the elderly varies slightly more, with between 36,1 and 41,3% of the elderly being defined as poor. In addition, the greater the economies of scale, the more elderly are in poverty (because the elderly tend to live in smaller households), while the reverse is true for children.

This does not mean, however, that the *same* households are identified as poor using different assumptions about child costs and economies of scale. If we take the May scales of $\alpha = 0,5$ and $\theta = 0,9$ as our reference points, Table 2.7 shows the percentage of households that are 'correctly' identified as poor when using the other scales.

TABLE 2.7

Percentage of poor households 'correctly' identified as poor,
taking α = 0,5 *and* θ = 0,9 *as the reference scale*[a]

Equivalence scale		% of households identified as poor under both scales
α = 0,5	θ = 0,6	96,1
α = 0,5	θ = 0,75	98,2
α = 0,75	θ = 0,6	95,6
α = 0,75	θ = 0,75	97,1
α = 0,75	θ = 0,9	95,9
α = 1	θ = 0,6	94,9
α = 1	θ = 0,75	95,1
α = 1	θ = 0,9	93,6

[a] IES & OHS, SSA 1995.

It is evident that the choice of equivalence scale makes a small difference to the identification of poor households. From a policy perspective, however, the robustness of the poverty profile is more important, since government is more likely to identify vulnerable groups than specific households. We also need to consider whether the choice of equivalence scale will alter the picture we paint of inequality, and this is undertaken in Table 2.8.

TABLE 2.8

Measures of inequality using different equivalence scales[a]

Equivalence scale		Gini coefficient (household income)	Theil-T	Contribution of between-group inequality (%)	Theil-L	Contribution of between-group inequality (%)
α = 0,5	θ = 0,6	0,60	0,75	36,7	0,68	35,5
α = 0,5	θ = 0,75	0,61	0,77	37,5	0,70	35,9
α = 0,5	θ = 0,9	0,62	0,80	37,9	0,74	36,0
α = 0,75	θ = 0,6	0,61	0,75	37,2	0,69	35,7
α = 0,75	θ = 0,75	0,62	0,78	38,0	0,72	36,2
α = 0,75	θ = 0,9	0,63	0,81	38,2	0,76	36,0
α = 1	θ = 0,6	0,61	0,76	37,5	0,70	35,9
α = 1	θ = 0,75	0,62	0,79	38,2	0,73	36,2
α = 1	θ = 0,9	0,63	0,83	38,4	0,78	35,9

[a] IES & OHS, SSA 1995.

We see that the Gini, the Theil-T and the Theil-L all increase as α or θ increases. In other words, as α or θ increases we 'observe' more inequality. The reason for this is not hard to see. When child costs are low or there are substantial economies of scale, we 'compress' the income distribution by weighting large households less heavily. Consequently, our measures of inequality will be smaller.

Clearly, we need to select an equivalence scale for consequent empirical work here. Happily, we see that, within a reasonable range, our choice will not have a significant distorting influence on the results. Because the scales of May *et al.* (1995) are widely accepted in South Africa, we choose to follow their example of setting the child cost ratio at 0,5 and the economies of scale parameter at 0,9. The small contribution that we have made is to justify such a choice of parameters prior to use.

Limitations of the approach

Temporary and chronic poverty

Poverty may be chronic (long-term) or temporary (short-term). Chronic poverty is usually the more difficult to address, and is often associated with persistent intergenerational poverty. Temporary poverty may result from a one-time decline in living standards (e.g. following the loss of a job), from which a household gradually emerges. Or it may show itself in fluctuations in well-being which result in frequent declines in living standards. For example, external shocks in the form of policy changes or natural disasters may plunge a household into poverty. In contrast, seasonal variations in food security may result in some households periodically falling in and out of poverty, sometimes quite regularly, over time. Poverty indicators based on cross-sectional household survey data cannot generally differentiate between short- and long-term poverty.

Poverty and vulnerability

Although poverty and vulnerability are often related, they are not synonymous. Some groups may be at risk of becoming poor because of inherent vulnerabilities (e.g. different types of discrimination based on class, gender or ethnicity, or factors such as disability or region of residence). Certain combinations of vulnerability may be strongly correlated with poverty, such as female-headed households or families living in deep rural areas. But not all members of a particular *vulnerable* group are necessarily *poor*.

This is an important distinction. In short, poverty relates to deprivation, while vulnerability is a function of external risks, shocks and stresses (Streeten 1994:17). However, creating measures that reflect vulnerability is beyond the scope of the present study.

Households as units of co-residence and consumption

The best source of information about living standards comes from household surveys. The first problem that arises in analysing these surveys is: what do we mean when we speak of a 'household'? For the purposes of surveys, households are generally defined as a group of people living under the same roof, eating together and sharing their resources.

That sounds simpler than it really is. People may move easily in and out of households at different times and under different circumstances. Moreover, the concept of a household presupposes that resources, food and incomes are somehow shared amongst household members. But we need to be aware that who lives with whom, who provides consumption needs and who consumes what are all aspects which impact on the *individual's* experience of poverty.

Since a household survey collects information principally at the *household* level, it cannot tell us much about the inequalities in resource allocation *within* households. When we talk about poor children, for example, we are talking about those children who are living in poor households. In reality, there may be many children who, although they live in non-poor households, should be counted as poor because of the inequalities in intra-household allocations. To truly assess individual wellbeing, we would require information on the specific consumption of each individual household member. Regrettably, this information is rarely available (Haddad & Kanbur 1990).

South Africa's history of influx control and migrant labour has meant that many households are relatively fluid units in terms of who actually lives with whom at any one time. It is not only adult members who may come and go. Children may move, or be moved, between different familial households, especially when there is financial or physical disruption. According to findings based on the PSLSD survey, in 1993 only one-third of African children were growing up with both parents present in the household (Le Roux 1994).

While temporary migration may be a part of economic survival strategies, it has an effect on how households are organised. In many instances, women become the *de facto* heads of households, responsible for most aspects of household maintenance. Another aspect of fragmented households is the living arrangements of migrant workers. Here too analysis is made more complicated by the fact that migrants living together in hostels are not households constituted by partnerships derived from choice.

These limitations of the data need to be borne in mind. While household surveys are one of the most valuable instruments for telling us about income poverty and inequality, they cannot provide all the answers.

A profile of poverty in South Africa

In the preceding discussion, we recognised the many dimensions of poverty but then restricted discussion to one dimension: private consumption expenditure (PCE). We then selected an appropriate equivalence scale with which to normalise PCE so as to take account of differences in household size and demographic structure. We also discussed the issue of selecting a poverty line. This choice has a bearing on consequent empirical results but is essentially arbitrary. We therefore recommended that at least two, and preferably multiple, poverty lines always be considered. In this section, we employ a *poverty critical range* in place of a single poverty line. This reduces concern regarding the arbitrariness of the poverty line, since it requires that results hold within a band of welfare levels. At the same time, descriptions of poverty become extremely cumbersome within this framework. Consequently, we tabulate the poverty statistics at two poverty lines as well as graphically presenting the statistics within a range of values. We have selected as our two poverty lines the Household Subsistence Level and the 'dollar a day' international poverty line. The former line is set at R3 509 per adult equivalent per annum, and the latter (which can be thought of as an 'ultra-poverty' line) is set at R2 200 per adult equivalent per annum in 1995 prices.[3]

There is one more theoretical concern that we need to deal with before we profile poverty in South Africa. The preceding discussion has focused on the identification of the poor. Having identified the poor, we need to be clear about the issues involved in aggregating all of the poor into a national poverty statistic. It is important to focus not only on the number of poor households but also on the depth and severity of the poverty which they experience. Consequently, we employ *distribution-sensitive* decomposable poverty measures, which reflect the depth of poverty through sensitivity to the income distribution among the poor.

The following four axioms (Sen 1976) form the basis of what has become a widely accepted consensus concerning the basic requirements of a good poverty measure:

- *monotonicity*: if the income of a poor individual falls (rises), the index must rise (fall);
- *transfer*: if a poor individual transfers income to someone less poor than herself (whether poor or non-poor), the index must rise;
- *population symmetry*: if two or more identical populations are pooled, the index must not change; and
- *proportion of poor*: if the proportion of the population that is poor grows (diminishes), the index must rise (fall).

The most commonly quoted measures of poverty are the head-count index and the poverty gap index. The head-count index (H) is simply the proportion of the population that is poor. The poverty gap index (PG) measures the average distance that a poor person is from the poverty line. PG can be considered to reflect the depth of poverty amongst the poor.

The head-count index, while popular, has some flaws. Watts (1968:325), for example, points out that poverty should not be seen as a 'discrete condition. One does not immediately acquire or shed the afflictions we associate with the notion of poverty by crossing any particular income line.'

The poverty gap index has a number of advantages over the head-count ratio. Because the head-count ratio is discontinuous at the poverty line, it violates the principle of transfers. It is possible to increase social welfare by taking money from the very poor to lift some of the just-poor out of poverty. The poverty gap index, on the other hand, is continuous and concave. Thus, transfers from the poor to the just-poor in order that they become non-poor will increase PG. PG nevertheless neglects inequality *among* the poor. These two measures are special cases of the generic class of decomposable measures proposed by Foster, Greer and Thorbecke (1984). The Foster–Greer–Thorbecke (FGT) class of poverty measures can be expressed as follows:

$$P_\alpha = \frac{1}{n}\sum_{i=1}^{q}\left[\frac{z-y_i}{z}\right]^\alpha \quad \text{for } \alpha \geq 0$$

where:

z is the poverty line;

y_i is the standard of living indicator (e.g. PCE) of the ith household; and

α is the 'aversion to poverty' parameter.[4]

The head-count index is obtained by setting $\alpha = 0$, and the poverty gap by setting $\alpha = 1$. P_2 is often calculated as a measure of the severity of poverty, and can be thought of as the sum of two components: an amount due to the poverty gap, and an amount due to inequality amongst the poor (Ravallion 1992:39). Thus, P_2 can be expressed as follows:

$$P_2 = \frac{PG^2}{H} + \frac{(H-PG)^2}{H}CV_p^2$$

$\qquad\qquad\quad\uparrow\qquad\qquad\quad\uparrow$

$\qquad$ (contribution of $\qquad$ (contribution of inequality
$\qquad$ the poverty gap) $\qquad$ amongst the poor)

where CV_p^2 denotes the squared coefficient of variation of income among the poor. While this breakdown goes part of the way towards explaining the meaning of P_2, it remains difficult to interpret. In any event, the magnitude of P_2 tells us very little when taken on its own. The value of P_2 lies in allowing us to make comparisons over time or space or between different policy options.

The FGT class of measures has several desirable properties. For example, both the poverty gap and P_2 are strictly decreasing in the living standards of the poor (the lower your standard of living, the poorer you are deemed to be). P_2 has the further desirable property that the increase in your measured poverty due to a fall in standard of living will be deemed greater the poorer you are.

In this chapter, we consider P_0, P_1 and P_2 in order to obtain measures of the *incidence*, the *depth* and the *severity* of poverty. One of the most useful properties of the FGT class of measures is that total poverty can be decomposed into additive subgroup poverty shares. If we split the population into m (mutually exclusive and exhaustive) subgroups containing n_i individuals, then we can derive intragroup FGT measures such that:

$$P_\alpha = \sum_{i=1}^{m} \frac{P_{\alpha i} n_i}{n}$$

where:

$$P_{\alpha i} = \frac{1}{n_i} \sum_{j=1}^{q_i} (1 - \frac{y_{ij}}{z})^\alpha$$

Poverty critical range and partial poverty ordering

As discussed earlier, there is great uncertainty about the setting of an appropriate poverty line. It is easy to construct a theoretical example of two distributions of PCE, A and B, for any poverty measure $P(z,h)$, in which $P_A(z_0,h) < P_B(z_0,h)$ at one poverty line z_0 and $P_A(z_1,h) > P_B(z_1,h)$ at some other reasonable poverty line z_1 (Cushing & Zheng 1996:5).[5] We regard the poverty levels in these two distributions as non-comparable. If, however, the poverty ordering of two distributions holds at every poverty line within a reasonable range, then there is less question over the ordering.

This consideration led to the development of *partial poverty ordering,* in contrast to conventional complete ordering at one poverty line (Atkinson 1987; Foster & Shorrocks 1988). The relationship between the partial poverty ordering of certain measures and stochastic dominance was established. The poverty critical range that was used was either the whole income range $[0, \infty]$ or a narrower range $[0, a]$ where $0 < a < \infty$. In practice, it is not necessary to specify very wide poverty critical ranges, since the range of income levels that we would consider reasonable for establishing a poverty line is limited.

If Z is the set of poverty lines, then $P(z, h)$ becomes a curve that we refer to as a *poverty value curve*. Partial poverty ordering is the ranking of different poverty value curves. If the poverty value curve of income distribution A lies below that of B, then we say that A dominates B in poverty level.

(Weak) poverty dominance: For two income distributions A and B, we say that A has a lower poverty level than B (i.e. A poverty dominates B), *iff*:

$$P_A(z,h) \geq P_B(z,h) \quad \text{for all } z \in Z \tag{1}$$

and

$$P_A(z,h) > P_B(z,h) \quad \text{for at least one } z \tag{2}$$

Thus, after specifying the poverty critical range Z, we simply have to determine whether conditions (1) and (2) are satisfied. There are three possibilities:

- The poverty measures of the two income distributions are identical for all $z \in Z$.
- One poverty curve dominates the other.
- The poverty value curves cross, i.e. the poverty measures of one income distribution are greater than those of the other at some poverty lines but smaller at some other poverty lines.

In the first two cases, we have no doubt about the poverty ordering, while in the third case we cannot draw any conclusions about the comparison unless we narrow the poverty critical range.

Ravallion and Sen (1996:776) point out that if we trace out two poverty value curves based on the P_0 measure and one curve dominates the other, then this result automatically holds for the poverty value curves associated with a broad range of poverty measures. Thus, if we obtain an unambiguous poverty ordering based on the head-count index, the result will be the same when we map P_1 or P_2.

Where are the poor?

The poverty value curves in Figure 2.1 show the great disparities between rural and urban areas. We divide the urban sample into small towns, secondary cities and metropolitan areas in order to show that there is also differentiation within urban settlement types. For a very wide range of poverty lines, the incidence, depth and severity of poverty are unambiguously highest in rural areas, followed by small towns and secondary cities, and considerably lower in metropolitan areas. Since the results are unambiguous, we do not present the curves representing the P_1 and P_2 FGT measures.

At a poverty line of R3 509 per adult equivalent per annum, the poverty *rate* in rural areas (i.e. the percentage of individuals classified as poor) is 63%, compared with 22% in urban areas taken together. If we consider those who expend half this amount, we find that 27% of rural dwellers fall below this line, in contrast to only 7% of those in urban areas.

Table 2.9 summarises the results of the analysis at the two selected poverty lines. The *poverty share* of rural areas (i.e. the percentage of poor individuals that live in rural areas) at the higher poverty line is 73%. Moreover, the combination of a high poverty rate and deep poverty among the poor in rural areas means that 75% of the total poverty gap is accounted for by poverty in rural households, although they only make up 49% of the population.

Poverty is distributed very unevenly among South Africa's nine provinces. Figure 2.2 shows the values of the head-count ratio over the poverty critical range. We find that the incidence of poverty is highest in the Eastern Cape and Free State and lowest in Gauteng and the Western Cape. Surprisingly, the poverty incidence curve for KwaZulu-Natal does not cross any other line, and we are able to conclude that KwaZulu-Natal has the third-lowest incidence of poverty.

TABLE 2.9

Distribution of poor individuals by locational classification[a]

Location	Population shares (%)	Poverty line = R2 200 per adult equivalent per annum			Poverty shares			Poverty line = R3 509 per adult equivalent per annum			Poverty shares		
		P_0	P_1	P_2	P_0	P_1	P_2	P_0	P_1	P_2	P_0	P_1	P_2
Rural	48,8	39,3	0,083	0,002	77,9	80,1	81,5	6,3	0,28	0,02	71,4	74,7	76,7
Small towns	20,9	16,8	0,028	0,035	14,7	13,3	12,5	32,5	0,13	0,15	18,1	16,6	15,5
Secondary cities	7,0	12,8	0,026	0,011	3,6	3,6	3,7	24,1	0,10	0,06	3,9	3,8	3,7
Metropolitan	23,9	5,1	0,007	0,011	3,8	3,0	2,3	13,8	0,04	0,05	6,7	4,9	4,1
All	100				100,0	100,0					100,0	100,0	100,0

[a] IES & OHS, SSA 1995.

FIGURE 2.1

Incidence of poverty by locational classification[a]

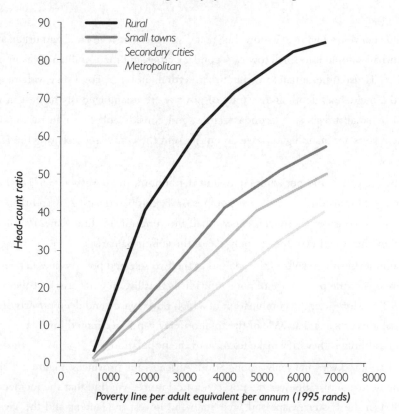

[a] *Sources:* IES & OHS, SSA 1995.

FIGURE 2.2

Incidence of poverty by province[a]

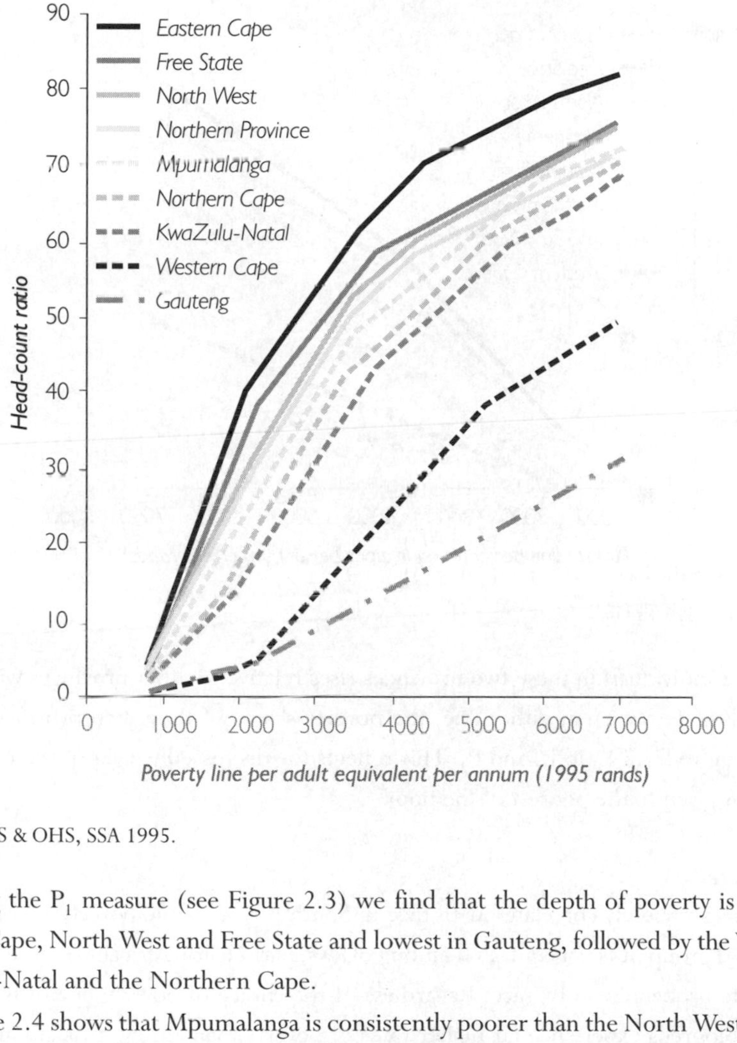

Poverty line per adult equivalent per annum (1995 rands)

[a] *Sources:* IES & OHS, SSA 1995.

Using the P_1 measure (see Figure 2.3) we find that the depth of poverty is highest in the Eastern Cape, North West and Free State and lowest in Gauteng, followed by the Western Cape, KwaZulu-Natal and the Northern Cape.

Figure 2.4 shows that Mpumalanga is consistently poorer than the North West when poverty is measured by the FGT P_2 index. This is easily explained by the fact that Mpumalanga has a higher incidence of poverty at lower poverty lines; thus when we weight the poorest of the poor more heavily, this part of the distribution dominates.

The poverty share analysis of Table 2.10 complements and extends the graphical analysis of Figure 2.2, Figure 2.3 and Figure 2.4 by showing the provincial distribution of poverty at two poverty lines and for all three FGT measures. In these share decompositions, any reversal in poverty shares could be due to the change in poverty line or the change in poverty measure. With regard to the former, it can be seen that the Western Cape and Gauteng increase their shares of poverty with a move from the lower poverty line to the higher line. This reflects the fact that the

FIGURE 2.3

Depth of poverty by province[a]

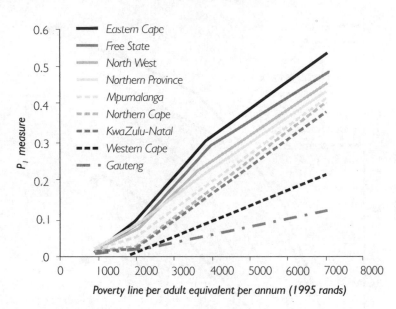

P_I measure

Eastern Cape
Free State
North West
Northern Province
Mpumalanga
Northern Cape
KwaZulu-Natal
Western Cape
Gauteng

Poverty line per adult equivalent per annum (1995 rands)

[a] *Sources*: IES & OHS, SSA 1995

number of poor individuals in these two provinces rises relative to other provinces with a move to the higher line. However, at either line, the poverty shares of these two provinces still fall sharply with a move from P_0 to P_1 and P_2. This reflects the decreased weight of these provinces when priority is given to the poorest of the poor.

Poverty and race

Living standards are closely correlated with race in South Africa. While poverty is not confined to any one racial group, it is concentrated among blacks, particularly Africans. Figure 2.5 shows the poverty rate broken down by race. Regardless of the choice of poverty line, it is clear that Africans and coloureds experience far higher rates of poverty than amongst Asians and whites. Table 2.11 shows that, for either of the choice of poverty lines and any of the poverty measures, Africans totally dominate the poverty shares.

Poverty and gender

Because a household survey collects information principally at the *household* level, it cannot tell us much about the inequalities in resource allocations within households. When we talk about poor women, for example, we are talking about those women who are living in poor households.

FIGURE 2.4

Severity of poverty by province[a]

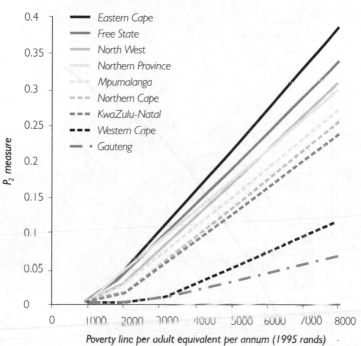

[a] *Sources*: IES & OHS, SSA 1995

TABLE 2.10

Distribution of poor individuals by province[a]

Location	Population shares (%)	Poverty line = R2 200 per adult equivalent per annum						Poverty line = R3 509 per adult equivalent per annum					
		P_0	P_1	P_2	Poverty shares			P_0	P_1	P_2	Poverty shares		
					P_0	P_1	P_2				P_0	P_1	P_2
Eastern Cape	15,87	42,17	0,145	0,067	27,11	28,22	28,48	64,05	0,295	0,165	24,02	26,28	27,29
Free State	6,72	38,03	0,135	0,063	10,35	11,05	11,46	57,51	0,267	0,152	9,13	10,08	10,60
North West	8,03	34,02	0,111	0,048	11,07	10,87	10,46	54,34	0,238	0,129	10,31	10,71	10,79
Northern Province	13,17	31,37	0,115	0,056	16,93	18,53	19,87	50,77	0,230	0,130	15,80	16,98	17,85
Mpumalanga	7,29	2,8	0,090	0,041	8,27	8,05	7,96	49,21	0,200	0,107	8,48	8,19	8,09
Northern Cape	1,79	26,13	0,072	0,029	1,90	1,58	1,40	45,97	0,178	0,090	19,4	1,78	1,67
KwaZulu-Natal	2,11	22,12	0,068	0,030	18,91	17,46	16,91	42,39	0,164	0,084	21,14	19,40	18,43
Western Cape	9,02	5,74	0,013	0,004	2,10	1,42	1,02	19,08	0,054	0,022	4,07	2,75	2,04
Gauteng	17,02	4,87	0,014	0,005	3,36	2,82	2,45	1,27	0,040	0,018	5,11	3,83	3,25
All	100,00				100,00	100,00	100,00				100,00	100,00	100,00

[a] IES & OHS, SSA 1995.

FIGURE 2.5

Incidence of poverty by race[a]

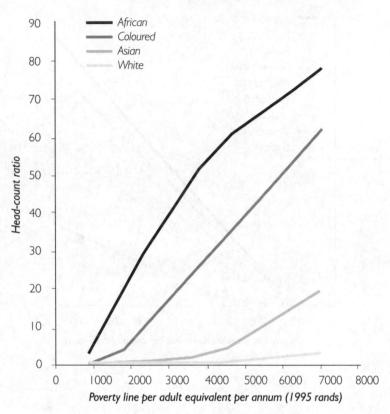

Poverty line per adult equivalent per annum (1995 rands)

[a] *Sources*: IES & OHS, SSA 1995.

TABLE 2.11

Distribution of poor individuals by racial classification

Location	Population shares (%)	Poverty line = R2 200 per adult equivalent per annum						Poverty line = R3 509 per adult equivalent per annum					
		P_0	P_1	P_2	P_0	P_1	P_2	P_0	P_1	P_2	P_0	P_1	P_2
					Poverty shares						Poverty shares		
African	48,8	39,3	0,083	0,002	77,9	80,1	81,5	63,0	0,28	0,02	71,4	74,7	76,7
Coloured	20,9	16,8	0,028	0,035	14,7	13,3	12,5	32,5	0,13	0,15	18,1	16,6	15,5
Asian	7,0	12,8	0,026	0,011	3,6	3,6	3,7	24,1	0,10	0,06	3,9	3,8	3,7
White	23,9	51	0,007	0,011	3,8	3,0	2,3	13,8	0,04	0,05	6,7	4,9	4,1
All	100,0				100,0	100,0	100,0				100,0	100,0	100,0

In reality, there may be many women who, although they live in non-poor households, should be counted as poor because of the inequalities in intra-household allocations.

What emerges clearly from the South African household surveys, however, is that households headed by women are more likely to be poor. For our purposes, we regard female-headed households as those where either the *de jure* or *de facto* head of the household is a woman. (A household where the head of household was specified to be a woman is *de jure* female-headed, while a household where the head of household is in practice female because the designated male head is absent for most of the year is *de facto* female-headed.)

About 65% of households in the PSLSD survey were headed by resident males. In the remaining 35%, the *de jure* or *de facto* head is female. The poverty rate at the higher poverty line was 60% amongst female-headed households, considerably higher than the rate of 31% in male-headed households. There are at least four factors in play here: female-headed households are more likely to be in the rural areas where poverty is concentrated; female-headed households tend to have fewer adults of working age; female unemployment rates are higher; and the wage gap between male and female earnings persists.

Female-headed households tend to be more heavily reliant on remittance and state transfer income (pensions and grants) than male-headed households. The irregular and uncertain nature of remittance income increases the vulnerability of female-headed households. Average wage income in these households is about one-third of average wage income in male-headed households.

The South African Participatory Poverty Assessment (SA-PPA) (May 1998) highlighted the amount of time women spend in unpaid labour. Women are often singly responsible for child care, cleaning the house, fetching and heating water, washing and ironing, shopping, collecting firewood, cooking and washing dishes. The many household activities that women are expected to perform severely restrict the amount of time available for income-earning activities.

Poverty and education

Figure 2.6 shows the relationship between education and poverty. We map the incidence of poverty amongst adults with differing educational attainments. It is clear that there is a very strong correlation between educational attainment and standard of living. It is interesting to note, however, that there is not a large difference in poverty rates between those individuals who have no education and those who have less than seven years of (primary) education. These two groups together are notably more prone to poverty. However, the poverty share analysis of Table 2.12 shows that the 'no education' group increases its share of poverty with a move from P_0 to P_2. The severity of poverty is therefore seen to be worse for this group. The incidence of poverty amongst those with some tertiary education is largely accounted for by young adults who are still studying and thus not yet reaping the financial rewards of their education.

FIGURE 2.6

Incidence of adult poverty by educational attainment[a]

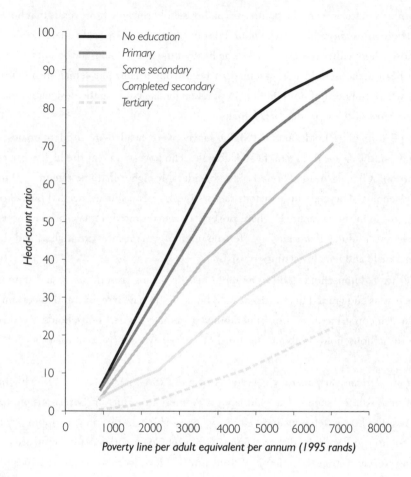

[a] *Sources*: IES & OHS, SSA 1995.

Priority ranking exercises in many of the communities which participated in the studies for the SA-PPA consistently listed education as a priority area for improved access for the poor. There were two dimensions to this: access to basic schooling for children and skills training for adults in order to improve their access to opportunities for employment and income generation. This illustrates that education is judged by the poor in terms of its *relevance* as well as by issues of access and quality – and that relevance is seen primarily in terms of the likelihood of eventual access to employment. The principal asset of the poor is labour time, and education increases the productivity of this asset.

TABLE 2.12

Distribution of poor adults (individuals aged 18+) by educational status

Location	Population shares (%)	P_0	P_1	P_2	P_0	P_1	P_2	P_0	P_1	P_2	P_0	P_1	P_2
					Poverty line = R2 200 per adult equivalent per annum						Poverty line = R3 509 per adult equivalent per annum		
					Poverty shares						Poverty shares		
No education	16,4	0,443	0,156	0,0743	26,3	27,7	28,5	0,681	0,312	0,177	24,2	26,0	26,9
Primary	26,4	0,370	0,125	0,0575	35,5	35,8	35,6	0,605	0,263	0,145	34,7	35,4	35,6
Incomplete secondary	34,5	0,240	0,077	0,035	30,1	28,9	28,4	0,422	0,173	0,092	31,7	30,3	29,6
Completed secondary	15,8	0,125	0,040	0,018	7,1	6,9	6,8	0,234	0,092	0,048	8,0	7,4	7,1
Tertiary	7,0	0,039	0,010	0,004	1,0	0,8	0,6	0,087	0,030	0,014	1,3	1,1	0,9
All	100,0				100,0	100,0	100,0				100,0	100,0	100,0

Poverty and health

Differences in health status are difficult to measure without a physical examination. Reliance on a respondent's own perception of his or her health status often leads to biases, since better-educated individuals are typically more concerned about their health status and will report being sick even if they suffer from comparatively minor ailments. In contrast, health awareness among poorer groups is often lower and leads to a lower reported incidence of ill health, despite objectively worse health indicators (Sen 1992).

This problem was encountered in the 1993 PSLSD survey, in which it was found that the wealthier respondents reported a higher prevalence of ill health than the poor. Despite this, the nature of the health problems listed gave some clues about the true state of health among the poor (Klasen 1996). The health problems listed in Table 2.13 are all related to poverty and demonstrate the higher prevalence of diseases of poverty among lower income groups, including tuberculosis, diarrhoea and fever. In addition, the much higher rates of mental disability among the poor are an indication of poor mental health facilities, as well as the likely influence of violence and trauma on many poor people (Klasen 1996).

TABLE 2.13

Proportion suffering from each illness (%)[a, b]

Illness	Ultra-poor	Poor	Non-poor	All
Tuberculosis	4,4	4,2	2,1	2,9
Diarrhoea	11,5	8,2	4,6	6,0
Fever	10,0	8,5	5,9	6,9
Physical disability	5,2	4,5	3,1	3,6
Mental disability	8,3	6,5	2,5	4,0

[a] PSLSD 1993.
[b] The percentage of individuals *reporting an illness* in the two weeks prior to survey, who complained of a particular symptom.

The PSLSD survey included a physical examination of the heights and weights of a sub-sample of children, which allows a more objective assessment of their health status. It shows that poor children suffer from much higher rates of chronic undernutrition (i.e. stunting). As can be seen from Figure 2.7, 38% of ultra-poor children below the age of five suffer from stunting.

FIGURE 2.7

Stunting rates for children under 5[a, b]

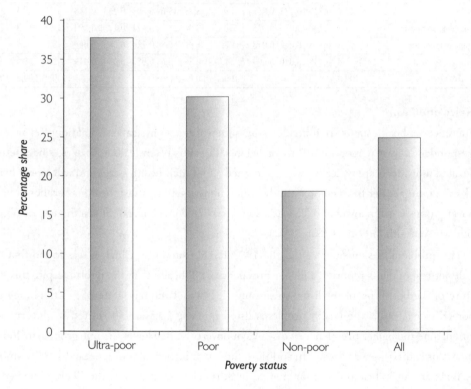

[a] Percentage of children under five whose height for age is below two standard deviations of the reference standard.
[b] *Source*: PSLSD 1993.

Employment and income among the poor

Not surprisingly, poverty and unemployment are closely linked. Table 2.14 shows that the unemployment rate among those from poor households is 52%, in comparison with an overall national rate of 29%. In addition, labour force participation is lower in poor than non-poor households. More than half of the working-age poor are outside the labour market. As a result, the percentage of working-age individuals from households below the poverty line who are actually working is significantly lower than average. Only 29% of individuals aged 16–64 living in households classified as poor are employed, compared with 48% from non-poor households.

TABLE 2.14

Unemployment, participation and sectoral employment by race, gender and location (%)[a]

Unemployment rates	Ultra-poor	Poor	Non-poor	All
(Broad) unemployment rates by:				
Race				
African	59,4	52,7	24,5	36,9
Coloured	46,1	36,7	17,0	21,8
Asian		67,5	12,8	13,7
White		75,0	4,5	4,7
Gender				
Female	65,9	59,1	25,3	37,4
Male	51,6	44,0	12,9	22,4
Location				
Rural	56,3	48,8	22,4	36,7
Urban	65,7	57,5	16,8	24,0
Total broad unemployment rate	58,7	51,5	18,4	29,3
Total narrow unemployment rate	34,9	30,6	11,0	16,4
Labour force participation rate	43,4	45,8	61,6	55,3
Share of adults 16–64 working	17,7	21,9	48,3	37,9

[a] IES & OHS, SSA 1995.

Figure 2.8 shows the differences between the sources of income for poor and non-poor households.[6] (The PSLSD data set is used for this comparison because this survey was more successful in capturing information about small-scale agriculture and remittances.) It is clear that the poor are far more dependent on remittances and state transfers than are the non-poor. What cannot immediately be seen from the graph is that poor households typically rely on multiple sources of income. This reduces risk, making the household less vulnerable should it experience a sudden loss of income from a particular source. Figure 2.8 again highlights the importance of wage income. Poor households are characterised by a lack of wage income, either as a result of unemployment or of low-paid jobs.

Poverty and access to services

Access to water, electricity and sanitation impact directly on quality of life. Access to clean water and sanitation has the most obvious and direct consumption benefits by reducing mortality and poor health and increasing the productive capacity of the poor. For example, the poor (especially females) must commit large shares of their income or time to obtaining water and firewood. This time would be better used in child care or income-generating activities.

FIGURE 2.8

Sources of income among poor and non-poor households[a]

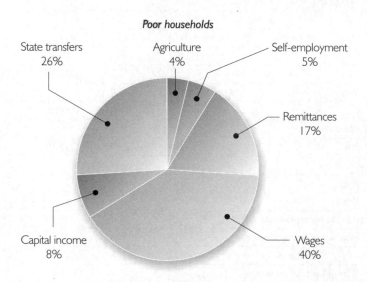

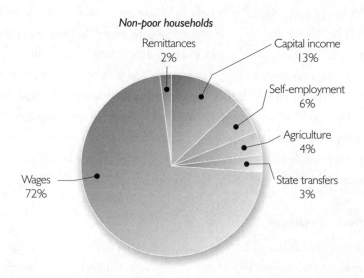

[a] *Source*: PSLSD 1993.

It can be seen from Table 2.15 that lack of access to basic services is closely related to poverty.

TABLE 2.15

Access to basic services[a]

Service	Percentage of households with access		
	Ultra-poor households	Poor households	Non-poor households
Electricity	25,9	32,6	76,5
Toilet inside dwelling	5,7	8,5	52,6
Piped water inside dwelling	13,6	17,6	61,2

[a] IES & OHS, SSA 1995.

Poverty and access to transport

As a result of apartheid policies regarding the spatial segregation of the various racial groups, and the lack of an adequate public transport system, transport has become a major constraint for the poorer population. Consequently, the working poor spend a large amount of time and money on transportation (Table 2.16). This reduces their take-home earnings and increases their cost of living.

TABLE 2.16

Mode of transport used to get to work (%)[a]

Type of transport	Ultra-poor	Poor	Non-poor	All
Bus	10,4	11,9	12,0	11,8
Taxi	8,0	11,9	20,1	19,0
Car/motorcycle	3,3	3,4	30,2	27,7
Foot	68,2	60,9	25,1	29,1
Other[b]	10,1	12,0	12,6	12,4
Total	100,0	100,0	100,0	100,0

[a] IES & OHS, SSA 1995.
[b] 'Other' is largely comprised of people who live on their work premises and thus do not require any form of transport, It also includes those who travel by train or bicycle.

Conclusion

Policy-makers in South Africa regard poverty reduction as one of the most important goals of development policy. However, it is only recently that researchers have begun to look at the issues around collecting suitable data and developing definitions of poverty that will allow for the measurement of poverty, its development over time, intergroup comparisons of poverty, and the identification of poor households or individuals for targeted poverty-alleviation programmes.

In this chapter, we have highlighted the dramatic differences in the poverty levels of the different race groups and different geographical areas. The poor are more likely to be African and to live in rural areas. In addition to these poverty dimensions, we have shown the importance of other cross-cutting correlates. The poor also have low levels of education, lack access to wage employment and are likely to be found in female-headed households. The poor also lack access to basic services and to transport. Given all of the above, it is not surprising that the poor are more vulnerable to illness and to stunted growth. Such physical and human capital deprivations are important in perpetuating the cycle of poverty.

Recent international literature has yielded a number of useful methodological developments in terms of the measurement of poverty. This chapter has attempted to provide a poverty profile that extends the available South African literature by drawing on these recent developments and by explicitly spelling out the assumptions that have to be made in constructing any poverty profile. The key finding of our work is that the defining features of South African poverty are so pronounced that the profile of poverty is robust to changes in the underlying measurement assumptions. This is important because it adds a measure of support to the poverty-measurement exercises that have been used as the basis for policy decisions in recent years. Even though this support is *ex post*, such an assessment has not been undertaken before.

However, within this broadly supportive outcome, we have shown that specific poverty rankings and poverty shares are sensitive to assumptions concerning household structure, the derivation of the poverty line and the choice of aggregate poverty index. For example, in South Africa the assessment of provincial poverty burdens is an important constituent element in deriving needs-based rules for provincial budgets. Our analysis has shown that provincial poverty rankings and shares can change as one makes very reasonable changes in the way poverty is measured. In turn, it is evident that there is still plenty of room for the reassessment of the use of poverty information in the South African policy-making process.

Notes

1. We thank Servaas van der Berg and an anonymous AERC referee for helpful comments. We also thank Chris Woolard for technical assistance in the estimation of the equivalence scales.

2. Anand (1983:113) suggests that the popularity of this particular figure has its origins in Robert McNamara's 1972 exhortation that special policies be initiated to increase the incomes of the lowest 40% in developing countries.

3. To create a poverty line per adult equivalent from the 'dollar a day' per capita line, we assumed that the average household consists of two adults and three children.

4. The higher the value of α, the more sensitive the measure is to the wellbeing of the poorest person. As α approaches infinity, the measure reflects only the poverty of the poorest person.

5. h is the specific poverty value function, such as the head-count ratio.

6. Capital income refers to income from sources such as dividends, interest and imputed rent. Imputed rent is the price attached to the benefit of owning the dwelling in which the household resides. The household is, in effect, renting the dwelling from itself. Thus, imputed rent is regarded as both an income and an expenditure.

3

Correlates of Vulnerability in the South African Labour Market

Haroon Bhorat
Murray Leibbrandt

The purpose of this chapter is to provide an empirical overview of the South African labour market using the OHS 1995 survey data. The focus will be on measuring the nature and extent of low earnings and vulnerability amongst participants in the labour market. We table a descriptive analysis of the level of earnings in the different segments of the labour market. In addition, the various hurdles in the labour participation chain will be presented, in order to better understand the processes through which labour market participants are drawn out of the pool of economically active individuals and, then, how individuals are selected into employment from this pool of labour market participants. The final section concentrates on illustrating and measuring the extent and distribution of low earnings in the labour market. In this section we draw on existing poverty methodologies, which have thus far been applied predominantly to the analysis of poverty at the household level rather than to individuals in the labour market. The conclusion then draws out some of the implications for more formal, econometric work on the labour market, which are examined in Chapter 4.

An overview of labour market poverty

It is very important, yet uncommon in the South African literature, to be clear about the extent to which a description of the labour market is driven by the limitations of available data rather than by judgement calls about its operation. Our selection of individuals in the labour market, and their subsequent categorisation, was constrained in a number of ways by the design of the questionnaire for OHS 95. The first part of this chapter continues this description of the selection process. We then go on to explore earnings and participation in the labour market, using a set of different covariates to facilitate this overview.

The limitations imposed by labour market data

The individuals who formed part of the labour market as a whole were between the ages of 16 and 65, and reported themselves to be working full time, part time or on sick leave at the time of the interview. In addition, those adults claiming to be unemployed, and those not working but looking for a job, were together captured as part of the unemployed. This selection process was quite intricate and careful, given the design of the questionnaire, and the final segmentation was of a labour force made up of employees, self-employed workers, hybrid workers (simultaneously employees and self-employed) and the unemployed. We will briefly describe the derivation of each of these segments.[1]

In attempting to provide a full analysis of the vulnerable in the labour market, a major constraint is the lack of decent information on the informal sector. The construction of the OHS survey was such that the only entry point into the less formal sections of the labour market comes through the subset of workers who were reported as self-employed and owned the business they were operating. It is possible to divide such self-employed into those who registered their business and those who did not, and whether or not the business paid value-added tax. The unregistered, non-tax-paying, self-employed could arguably then be regarded as part of the informal sector. However, as the unregistered self-employed clearly constitute only one portion of the informal sector in South Africa, it would be unwise to refer to this group as 'the informal sector'. For example, the survey did not capture information on individuals who were the employees of the unregistered self-employed.[2] Therefore, in the rest of this chapter we speak directly of the unregistered self-employed and do not use the term 'informal sector' at all.

Another constraint imposed by the survey comes in the analysis of those individuals who listed their status as both formal sector workers and self-employed, thus earning income from two sources. Such persons were included in the sample as a separate category. As these 'hybrid' workers are potentially vulnerable labour market participants, we therefore give them explicit attention (see separate box). However, there was no satisfactory way of deciding on their primary labour market activity, and they were therefore not included in any further tables or analysis.

To estimate the number of unemployed, we made use of a set of criteria that included an individual's willingness to take a job if one was available, and an important 'cleaning' question in which the respondent had to show that he/she had no job for reasons related primarily to the inability to find a job or the lack of adequate skills or qualifications. This allowed for the exclusion of those, for example, who were housewives or students, yet may have regarded themselves as unemployed at the beginning of the questionnaire. In the data set, the latter – who were omitted as unemployed as a result of this question using the weighted sample – numbered 286 293 individuals, or 6,9% of those initially designated as unemployed.[3]

In the light of all of these data considerations, Table 3.1 presents a broad snapshot of the South African labour market. The total population of working age is about 23,9 million, with

The 'hybrid' worker: an overview

According to the OHS 95 survey, formal and unregistered employment totalled 10,3 million individuals, which includes the 148 020 workers who held two types of employment: firstly, as an employee working for a formal sector firm, and secondly as a self-employed individual. These workers drew an income from two sources, and their inclusion in earnings analysis based on the different labour market subgroups would have elicited biased results. The data shows that about 54% of these workers are African and approximately 34% are white. The African share is below that in the formal sector, while a larger share of whites is found in this cohort. The gender distribution is similar to formal employment, with approximately 69% of the sample being male.

Given that the hybrid worker is earning an income from two sources, it is expected that median incomes should be higher than in the formal sector. The table below confirms this, as the median values, by race, are all greater than the corresponding formal sector incomes. The OHS 95 reports these incomes as monthly totals by individuals, and hence it is not possible to decompose them by source. The high standard deviations for whites, and Africans in particular, shows the high dispersion in earnings amongst these workers.

The gap between African and white earnings amongst these workers is marginally higher, as the median earnings of Africans are 33% of white earnings, compared to 36% in the formal sector.

The sectoral distribution of these workers shows that, as with the formal and unregistered sectors, the majority (33%) are employed in community services, followed by wholesale and retail trade (21%) and then manufacturing (18%). The largest share within community services is civil servants (employees coded as central, provincial or local government employees) and public servants working in both education and health. Government employees therefore are a relatively large component of this hybrid worker category. In wholesale and retail trade, the largest component is those workers in the retail trade. The largest occupational category is labourers, at 28 218 or 19%, signalling that it is predominantly workers who are supplementing their formal income with income from self-employment. The next two dominant occupations are labourers (23 488) craft and clerks (17 479). The clerks pick up those employees in the various tiers of government. The shares of the highest two occupations, managers and professionals, yield figures above those in the formal sector.

Relative to the formal sector, therefore, these hybrid workers are disproportionately composed of employees in the mid- to upper levels of the occupational ladder. It could thus be argued that hybrid workers are formal sector workers with steady long-term employment contracts who are generating additional income through self-employment activities.

Median and standard deviation, monthly income (rands)

	African	Coloured	Asian	White
Median	2 146	2 736	3 300	5 510
Mean	3 515	5 547	5 249	10 557
Standard deviation	4 582	9 847	4 919	16 993

more females than males in every race group, except for whites. By race, it is clear that a greater share of white (78%) than African (47%) male workers is in employment. It is also evident that, across all race groups, formal employment (designated as 'employee') dominates as the main form of work activity. The share of African males in unemployment is 18%, much higher than the 2% of white male workers without jobs. Coloured male workers are not far below the figure for African males, with 13% of these workers in unemployment. The figures for those out of the labour force are telling. Amongst males across all race groups, the primary reason for being economically inactive is given as enrolment in education. The figure for African males of 24%, however, is exceptionally high, and in part reflects long periods spent within the education system.

TABLE 3.1

Employment status of adults by race and gender

Employment status	Male				Female				Total
	African	White	Coloured	Asian	African	White	Coloured	Asian	
Total number	8 424 476	1 796 299	1 098 972	343 145	9 016 475	1 748 318	1 161 714	352 004	23 941 403
Employed %									
Employee	43	63	60	59	17	45	36	30	35
Self-employed									
Business registered	0	11	1	8	0	3	0	1	1
Business not registered	2	2	2	5	8	2	8	2	5
Both ('hybrid' employee)	0	1	0	0	0	0	0	0	0
Business registered	1	1	0	0	0	0	0	0	0
Business not registered		1	1	1	1	1	0	0	1
Total	47	78	64	73	26	52	44	34	43
Unemployed %									
Searching for work	9	2	10	6	9	2	9	5	8
Not searching for work	9	0	4	1	12	1	6	3	8
Total	18	2	13	7	21	3	15	7	16
Out of labour force %									
Enrolled in education	24	10	11	11	22	9	9	11	20
Keeping house	0	0	0	0	13	21	16	34	8
Retired	3	8	3	3	5	8	4	4	4
Disabled	3	2	7	3	2	1	4	3	3
Other	6	1	3	2	11	6	8	7	7
Total	36	20	24	20	53	45	41	59	42
Unemployment rate							26		27
Broad	28	3	17	9	45	6	16	18	13
Narrow	13	2	12	8	19	4		18	

The gender differences in the labour market are stark. Hence, while 43% of all African male workers are in formal employment, only 17% of African female workers are in the same position. This can be explained in three different ways. Firstly, there are more African females in non-registered businesses than African males. This picks up the large number of domestic workers amongst African female workers, a point we develop further in the chapter. Secondly, the share of African females in unemployment is also higher. Thirdly, a larger proportion of African females are out of the labour force, with the majority being enrolled in education or involved in house-hold duties. It is interesting to note that the education figures are almost replicated across the genders, indicating that this variable is more differentiated according to race than gender.[4] How-ever, there are also differences amongst female workers. While only 17% of African females are in formal employment, 45% of white females and 36% of coloured females have formal jobs.

Note also that 8% of coloured women are also in unregistered self-employment, again reflecting their involvement in domestic services. The upshot is that African women are the least likely amongst female, and indeed male, workers of all races to have employment.

The unemployment rates in Table 3.1 are presented according to both the strict and expanded definitions. However, it is important to elucidate how these two concepts were derived from the survey. Table 3.2 reflects the results of a specific question in the survey, which was used as the decision rule for whether individuals reported themselves as unemployed according to the narrow or strict definition. Table 3.2 shows that the unemployed number approximately 3,9 million, and of these the majority reported they were doing nothing to find work, but still had the desire to find a job (Code 1). The second-largest category of search was that of the unemployed who had made enquiries at different workplaces for work. This suggests a relatively informal search method, compared to, for example, Codes 3 and 5. Note also that these formal mechanisms of search only account for under 10% of all search behaviour.

The decision rule that ultimately derived the unemployment rates in Table 3.1 was to con-sider those individuals who were unemployed – according to the narrow definition – as those captured in Codes 2 through 9.[5] This captures only individuals who have actively searched for a job in the last four weeks. These unemployed number about 1,9 million, or just under half of the total sample of unemployed. The expanded definition, in trying to capture the discouraged work-seeker as well, therefore includes all individuals coded from 1 through 9. Those workers who have not looked for work in the last four weeks, but who would like to work, are thus included as unemployed. As these numbers suggest, the unemployment rates derived are very sensitive to the choice of definition.[6] Hence, Table 3.1 shows that the total unemployment rate based on the expanded definition is 27%, while it is 13% using the narrow definition.

Examining these unemployment rates more closely, it is evident that African unemployment rates are higher than all other race groups. By the broad definition, the African male unemploy-ment rate is 28%, compared with 3% for whites. The coloured broad unemployment rate is

TABLE 3.2

Method of search in previous 4 weeks

Code	Search method	Number	%
1	Nothing, but still wants work	2 012 592	51,97
2	Nothing: wants work but already has job to start at a definite date in the future	119 502	3,09
3	Waited/registered at employment agency/trade union	279 379	7,21
4	Enquired at workplaces, farms, factories or called on other possible employers	1 215 389	31,38
5	Placed/answered advertisement(s)	72 930	1,88
6	Sought assistance of relatives or friends	132 916	3,43
7	Looked for land, building, equipment or applied for permit to start own business or farming	9 532	0,25
8	Sought/underwent training	7 593	0,20
9	Other	22 874	0,59
	Total	3 872 707	100,00

fairly high as well, at 17%. The gender effect, though, is very strong: the African female broad unemployment rate is 45%, and for coloured females 26%. Noticeably, Asian and white female unemployment rates are double those of their male counterparts, at 18% and 6%, respectively. We therefore reach the familiar labour market outcome: that race and gender are very important determinants of unemployment in the society.

The unemployment rates here, based on the OHS 95, are different to those that have been derived from the SALDRU data. From the analysis here, the narrow rate is higher and the broad rate lower than the SALDRU estimates of 12,3% and 29,8%, respectively (SALDRU 1994). The OHS 94 results, in turn, report a narrow rate of 20,3%, and an expanded rate of 32,6% (SSA 1994). The lower broad unemployment rate reached in the analysis here is in all probability a function of the careful screening that occurred when questioning those individuals who regarded themselves as unemployed. Relative to the unemployment questions in the previous surveys, it is probably fair to regard the OHS 95 unemployment rates as the closest to the true values.

Earnings and participation in the labour market

The earnings data presented here is all in standard monthly figures. The figures were thus not adjusted to derive earnings per month controlled for by hours worked. The reasons for this were that, firstly, 92% of the employed worked 35 hours or more in the week preceding the interview.[7] Hence the overwhelming majority of the sample did in fact work full time. In addition, of those individuals who worked part time or less than 35 hours, the median hours worked was 25 per week. This means that, even for those employed on a part-time basis, the number of hours worked was quite high. Not surprisingly, the data showed that it was those in the labourer categories who predominated amongst the part-timers. Yet, even here, the median hours worked was high, at 21 hours per week. Therefore, given the overwhelming predominance of full-time work amongst the employed, the decision was to present all earnings data as monthly, without recourse to their hourly equivalents.

Tables 3.2 and 3.4 consider the earnings of employees and the self-employed by occupation. The occupational categories are those based on the SSA definitions. Further divisions of this data by gender are provided in the Appendix (Table A-6 and Table A-7). The tables present the value of median earnings in 1995 rands, by location and also in relation to a predetermined low-earnings line. The line used here is R293 per month, which corresponds to a single adult equivalent income used in deriving 1995 household poverty lines.[8] There can be very little contention that this is indeed a low labour market income. The fact that R293 per month is so much lower than any of the median incomes certainly illustrates this point.

It is evident that there is a fairly standard differentiation in earnings by occupation, with managers, for example, earning more than clerks, and the latter in turn being better remunerated than labourers.[9] Amongst labourers, the worst paid are agricultural labourers, with a median income of R428 per month. Hence, the median wage gap between the highest and lowest paid occupation is about 80%. After farm labourers, the worst paid are mining labourers and

TABLE 3.3

Earnings profile by occupation, all employees (1995 rands)

Location	Overall		Urban		Rural	
Occupation	*Median*	H Index (%)	*Median*	H Index (%)	*Median*	H Index (%)
Armed forces	2 177	0	2 663	0	na	na
Managers	5 200	0	5 566	0	3 250	1
Professionals	4 670	0	4 670	0	3 349	0
Technicians	3 133	0	3 379	0	2 646	0
Clerks	2 000	1	2 000	0	1 500	1
Service and shop workers	1 400	3	1 500	2	1 071	5
Skilled agricultural workers	1 115	11	1 346	10	840	12
Craft workers	1 600	2	1 800	1	1 200	4
Machine operators	1 300	2	1 500	0	875	6
Domestic helpers	942	6	1 000	5	754	10
Agricultural labourers	428	26	500	17	410	28
Mining/construction labourers	900	3	908	3	894	4
Manufacturing labourers	1	4	1 115	2	628	9
Transport labourers	1 115	3	1 115	2	1 041	3
Other labourers	1 143	3	1 250	1	900	8

TABLE 3.4

Earnings profile by occupation, self-employed (1995 rands)

Location	Overall		Urban		Rural	
	Median	H Index (%)	Median	H Index (%)	Median	H Index (%)
Registered activities						
Managers	11 249	0	11 000	0	13 000	2
Professionals	16 000	0	16 535	0	na	na
Technicians	8 000	0	8 000	0	na	na
Service and shop workers	2 800	0	3 000	0	na	na
Skilled agricultural workers	9 364	0	5 000	0	11 249	0
Craft workers	5 000	0	5 000	0	2 970	0
Other labourers	3 784	2	3 222	2	na	na
Various 'informal' occupations	3 784	2	3 300	3	4 392	0
Unregistered activities						
Managers	4 167	3	4 649	3	1 600	0
Technicians	1 539	5	2 000	4	1 098	5
Service and shop workers	1 500	0	1 377	0	na	na
Skilled agricultural workers	1 000	21	na	na	1 000	23
Craft workers	1 098	6	1 200	3	909	10
Domestic workers	387	38	431	27	300	46
Other labourers	990	11	1 083	9	750	15
Various 'informal' occupations	2 000	4	2 500	2	1 500	8

domestic helpers. Domestic helpers, in the language of the survey, refer to domestic helpers and cleaners, helpers and cleaners in offices, hotels and other establishments and hand launderers and pressers. In other words, domestic helpers do not encapsulate domestic workers in private households, as these individuals are coded elsewhere in the questionnaire. This would explain the relatively high overall median incomes for domestic helpers. Despite this fact, note that 10% of domestic helpers in rural areas live in poverty. Agricultural labourers are the most poverty-stricken amongst employees, as over one quarter nationally earn less than R293 per month. Categories of labourers outside domestic helpers and those in agriculture all contain fewer working poor.

A category that does not seem to make much sense, in the light of the results obtained, is that of skilled agricultural workers. Here, the median income is below that of a machine operator, and 11% of these individuals live below the low-earnings line, despite the suggestion that these individuals are not in an unskilled occupation. The reason would seem to be in the classification of this occupation. Individuals involved in subsistence agriculture and fishing were included, in addition to gardeners and crop growers and hunters and trappers. The inclusion of these workers would clearly lower the median earnings in this occupation. More detailed examination of the data suggests that the biggest contributor to high poverty levels in this occupation comes from market gardeners and crop growers. Excluding this sub-occupation leads to a fall in poverty incidence from 11 to 2,5%, meaning that the contribution of poverty in the group of gardeners and crop growers is about 8,2%. To avoid erroneous assumptions about occupational earnings, then, it would seem that the label of 'independent farm and fishery workers' would be more apt in describing this occupation.

We turn now to the description of earnings amongst the self-employed, broken down by those involved in registered businesses and those in unregistered enterprises. Again, the data by gender is provided in the Appendix. Table 3.4 confirms that registration status is an important income discriminator. Hence, for those self-employed individuals with a registered business, all except two categories earn a living above the low-earnings line. Even for these two occupation groups – other labourers and various informal occupations – the median monthly wage is R3 784.[10] For those self-employed in unregistered businesses, poverty incidence is higher, particularly in the case of domestic workers and skilled agricultural workers. 'Domestic workers' here refers primarily to domestic workers in private households. For these workers, the median wage is R387 per month, placing 38% of these workers below the low-earnings line. For those in rural areas, 46% work below this line. While the median wage for skilled agricultural workers is higher at R1 000, 21% of these workers earn less than R293 per month.

It is interesting to note that the manager category, in both registered and unregistered activities, yields very different income levels. For the latter, median earnings are just over a third of the income earned by managers in registered enterprises. Clearly the segmentation of the labour market along registration status has a direct impact on understanding the income differentials amongst the self-employed.

Table 3.5 represents the results of segmenting the labour market on the basis of a wider set of covariates, such as years of schooling, location, occupation and sector. The data is presented by labour force, and then for the employed only. We have chosen to segment the sample in this way, and not according to informal and formal sector participants, given the difficulties in the survey of dividing the sample in this manner. These survey problems are highlighted in the box on page 86. All shares are within-group estimates. The gender shares within the labour force show again that males dominate across all race groups. However, the ratios for the employed show a larger share of males, indicating that unemployed females are disproportionately represented in the labour force.

The location distributions are fairly constant when comparing the labour force with the employed. Urbanisation rates for Africans, though, are much lower than for the other three

TABLE 3.5

The labour force and employed, by individual characteristics

Race	African	Coloured	Asian	White	Total
Labour force (number)	9 633 389	1 522 443	419 450	2 393 213	13 968 495
Percentage share	68,97	10,90	3,00	17,13	100,00
Male	55,98	55,19	65,62	59,89	56,85
Female	44,02	44,81	34,38	40,11	43,15
No schooling	11,56	5,90	0,50	0,05	8,64
Primary	30,47	29,38	6,47	0,37	24,47
Incomplete secondary	33,70	41,84	36,03	21,06	32,50
Complete secondary	15,50	15,93	41,09	45,58	21,47
Tertiary	8,78	6,94	15,92	32,94	12,93
Urban	50,31	81,29	93,65	90,27	61,83
Secondary urban	2,38	0,29	2,09	1,02	1,91
Rural	47,10	18,41	4,26	8,71	36,11
Median earnings	450	800	2000	3 799	848
Employed (number)	6 227 236	1 203 899	369 532	2 295 121	10 095 788
Percentage share	61,68	11,92	3,66	22,73	100,00
Male	62,46	57,83	67,86	60,73	61,71
Female	37,54	42,17	32,14	39,27	38,29
No schooling	11,85	6,36	0,56	0,03	8,09
Primary	29,78	29,74	6,29	0,35	22,22
Incomplete secondary	32,17	39,73	34,91	19,97	30,40
Complete secondary	14,34	16,06	41,11	45,80	22,68
Tertiary	11,86	8,12	17,13	33,86	16,61
Urban	52,97	78,17	93,28	90,22	65,92
Secondary urban	2,51	0,31	2,31	1,02	1,90
Rural	44,45	21,53	4,41	8,77	32,14
Union	67,79	73,70	74,09	79,59	71,41
Non-union	32,21	26,30	25,91	20,41	28,59
Agriculture	15,20	18,54	1,32	4,39	12,63
Mining	5,67	1,06	1,00	4,36	4,65
Manufacturing	13,78	19,65	26,67	14,40	15,09
Electrical	0,78	0,61	0,30	1,62	0,93
Construction	4,37	7,46	3,80	4,62	4,78
Wholesale trade	15,48	17,91	32,67	20,09	17,45
Transport	4,56	3,82	5,41	7,38	5,14
Finance	3,27	3,96	8,47	16,05	6,45
Community services	36,89	26,99	20,37	27,09	32,88
Managers	2,89	2,03	10,76	14,56	5,73
Craft workers	10,31	14,53	15,83	15,00	12,08
Labourers	19,03	17,37	6,87	2,53	14,63
agricultural	12,12	15,50	0,03	0,16	9,36
domestic	9,94	6,78	0,12	0,09	6,97
Median earnings (rands)	1 082	1 083	2 333	4 000	1 400

groups. Hence, while close to 80% or more of non-Africans live in urban areas, the corresponding figure for Africans is just over 50%. Clearly, rural labour markets are far more important for the African workforce compared with the other race groups. It must be remembered that, in these rural labour markets, not only is labour demand lower in terms of quantity and quality, but mobility is also severely restricted given existing indigence amongst individuals and their linkages to already poor households.

The dominance of rural labour markets for Africans is replicated somewhat in the sectoral shares for the employed, as 15% of African employees work in agriculture, compared to less than 5% for Asians and whites.

Note, however, that the figure for coloureds is also high. The finance sector presents an interesting contrast, as the figures show that while the share of coloureds and Africans is relatively small, it is considerably higher for Asians and whites. Within finance, the mean skill levels are considerably higher than those found in agriculture. This sectoral-cum-skills division between the two sets of race groups points to a very different labour market for Asians and whites on the one hand, and for Africans and coloureds on the other. This is borne out further in the occupational divisions, where only about 2% of Africans and coloureds are managers, while the figure for Asians and whites is over 10%. The labourer category shows a reversal in these shares, with 17% or more of all Africans and coloureds working in elementary occupations. Amongst labourers, the two most indigent groups are farm workers and household domestic workers. Here, the different labour market shares of the two race groups are much more pronounced, and strongly display the differential between those at the top end and those at the bottom end of the internal labour market.

The median earnings data by race again point to the difference in the quality of employment between the two race groups. Amongst the employed, the median monthly earnings for Africans and coloureds are about R1 000, while for Asians the figure is over R2 000 and for whites R4 000. Even though white median earnings are twice those of Asians, it is clear that for these two racial cohorts the returns to labour are considerable greater than for coloureds and Africans. Notice that when examining these figures for the labour force as a whole, the much higher unemployment rates in this cohort show up as a large reduction in the median income. Correspondingly, the Asian and white incomes fall only marginally.

The education splines presented in the table broadly confirm the trend observed above, namely that, by race, two separate labour market processes seem to be at work. We see that while between 35 and 42% of Africans and coloureds have primary schooling or less, the figures for whites and Asians are only between 0,38 and 7%. Though the incomplete secondary schooling rates for Asians are similar to those of coloureds and Africans, the completed secondary schooling variable yields the familiar pattern. Completed secondary education, as will be shown later, is a key schooling attainment in terms of improved labour market opportunities. What is interesting to note, though, albeit on the basis of descriptive statistics, is that the share of the lower education categories is not much larger for the labour force as a whole than for the employed only. This suggests that education is more important in determining the income from employment, rather than whether an individual gets a job or not.

Given the focus on differing labour participation processes, it is necessary to grasp in more detail the nature of the decision-making sequence for individuals in the labour market. Table 3.6 attempts to do this by dividing the labour participation decision into three broad categories, namely: to participate or not; then, for those who do participate, whether they are employed or unemployed; and, finally, if they are employed, what form of employment is taken up. Beginning with the last row, it is evident that a larger portion of adult females in rural areas are out of the labour force compared to those in urban areas. However, it is also true that a smaller share of rural females is in the labour force than for urban females. Of those rural females in the labour force, only 53% will have a job, with the remainder unemployed, compared to about 70% of urban females with a job. Note that amongst those with a job, the level of unregistered businesses is high for both rural and urban areas. This reflects the high share of domestic workers in private households, as suggested in the box on the informal sector and the OHS 95. Indeed, these high figures for unregistered business are repeated throughout the table, for all the different covariates chosen. In comparison for adult males, for whom the figures are produced in the Appendix (Table A-8), the level of unregistered business activity is much lower. This is important because it implies that all unregistered businesses are dominated by females. In terms of the location results for males, Table A-8 in the Appendix shows that there are larger shares of males in both urban and rural areas who are in the labour force. In addition, shares of those employed in both locations are greater for males than females.

Table 3.6 shows that there is a positive relationship between years of potential experience and the share of those in the labour force, as well as the share of those in employment. Potential experience is calculated as the age of the individual subtracted from their years of education and six years. Hence, as individuals accumulate more experience, so their likelihood increases of being in the labour force and in employment.

The age distribution of labour supply decisions is very interesting. It shows that 71% of females younger than 25 are out of the labour force. These individuals are more than likely to be students. However, note that a greater share of females (80%) over the age of 55 are out of the labour force. This would represent females who are likely to be involved in regular household duties. Of the 29% of under-25 women in the labour force, however, over half are unemployed, unlike the over-55 cohort, in which only 12% are without jobs. Interestingly for the over-55 age group, more females than in any other age cohort are in unregistered enterprises. This suggests that the age distribution of domestic workers is predominantly composed of older individuals. Note, however, that for the employed, wage employment represents the largest share – a trend observed across all covariates in the table.

The misnomer of the 'informal sector' in the OHS 95

As a starting point to capturing individuals in the informal sector, the survey asks a question about the employment *status* of the worker, providing three options for the respondent, namely are they:

- Working for somebody else?
- Working for themselves?
- Working for themselves and somebody else?

Those individuals coded as 1 are automatically captured as part of the formal sector. This means that the employees of those in the informal sector cannot be explicitly identified in the survey. By adopting this approach in the survey questionnaire, the first problem therefore is that a significant part of the informal sector is lost. We are unable to provide an accurate and direct estimate of the informal sector using this data set. A second-best solution would be to impute the size of the informal sector through another question in the survey, although this is of course not ideal.

The individuals who code themselves as 2 can, of course, be either in the formal or informal sector. Loosely put, both doctors and street sellers would belong in the group. Hence, the manner in which the survey differentiates between these two sectors, is to ask these individuals two questions:

- Is/was the business registered?
- Do you have a VAT number?

Specifically, each of the individuals coded as 2 is asked whether the business they own is registered, and then furthermore whether they are registered to pay VAT. If individuals answer 'yes' ('no') to both questions, they are regarded as part of the formal (informal) sector. On the face of it, the only problem is that the size of the informal sector is not explicitly defined and measured. It appears that the categorisation of informal sector individuals through a registration and VAT question is tenable, and not at odds with approaches elsewhere. The problem with this approach, or with the actual survey design, is evident, though, when deriving data for the informal sector. The baseline data is provided below, and it shows that there are about 1,2 million individuals in this sector, of whom close to 80% are Africans.

This data is seemingly congruent with previous estimates, such as the SALDRU 1993 household survey, in which the estimate was about 1,1 million (Bhorat & Leibbrandt 1998). However, closer inspection of the data illustrates a gross bias. Occupational data on this sample of individuals illustrate that the overwhelming majority are household domestic workers. As the table below illustrates, the overwhelming majority of African and coloured workers who are coded as part of the informal sector are actually employed as domestic workers

While the shares for whites and Asians are of course much smaller, the large absolute numbers for Africans and coloureds ensures a distorted aggregate picture of the sector. Hence, the national figures show that of the 1,2 million in the informal sector, over half are in fact domestic workers. Now, given that these workers cannot be readily conceived of as part of the informal sector, we are left with a grossly inadequate description of this sector. Indeed, if we exclude domestic workers, the survey suggests that the informal sector is made up of about 569 000 participants. This figure, it would appear, is a significant underestimate of the number of informally employed.

The upshot of the above is that, for analytical purposes, we cannot use this data set to make a credible distinction between the formal and informal sectors. More broadly, this problem adds to the South African dilemma that very poor data exists on a part of the labour market that is essential to a thorough understanding of poverty and inequality

Informal sector individuals, by race

	African	Coloured	Asian	White	Total
Number	1 014 822	121 427	27 846	126 908	1 291 003
Share	78,61	9,41	2,16	9,83	100

Informal sector individuals who are domestic workers, by race

	African	Coloured	Asian	White	Total
Number	633 756	85 897	437	1 866	721 957
Share	62,45	70,74	1,57	1,47	55,92

TABLE 3.6

The participation patterns of female adults

	Participation		In labour force			Employed	Self-employed		Hybrid	
	% In labour force	% Out of labour force	% Employed	% Unemployed, searching	% Unemployed, not searching	% Wage employee	% Registered business	% Unregistered business	% Registered business	% Unregistered business
Education										
None	40	60	55	15	30	44	1	58	0	1
Literate (more than 8 years)	48	52	57	18	25	57	0	46	0	1
Incomplete secondary (8–10 years)	39	61	57	21	22	83	1	19	0	1
Matriculated (10 years)	61	39	70	17	13	93	3	5	0	1
Diploma (11–12 years)	74	26	92	5	3	94	3	2	0	2
Degree (more than 12 years)	69	31	89	4	7	85	7	7	1	?
Presence of young children										
Mean number of young children	0,68	0,71	0,56	0,85	0,91	0,55	0,29	0,64	0,33	0,51
1 or more children under 6 years	49	51	56	20	24	75	1	27	0	1
No children under 6 years	49	51	71	14	16	77	?	22	0	1
Age of individual										
16–25	29	71	45	28	27	87	1	15		1
25–55	63	37	67	14	18	75	2	25	0	1
55–65	20	80	88	4	8	64	3	35	0	1
Potential experience										
5 or less years	17	83	53	27	20	96	2	7	0	1
6–10 years	43	57	53	24	24	92	1	8	0	1
11–20 years	68	32	61	19	21	83	2	17	0	1
20+ years	51	49	71	12	17	67	2	33	0	1
Location										
Urban	57	43	71	16	13	82	2	17	0	1
Rural	40	60	53	18	30	62	1	40	0	1

The number of dependants in the form of young children that an individual has, seems to have no influence on whether females remain in or out of the labour force. However, those females with no children younger than six to care for are more likely to be employed than those with one or more young children. For males, the experience effect is much stronger in the 11–20 years and 20+ years categories, as a substantially larger (smaller) share of males compared to females are in (out) of the labour force. In the age distribution, across all cohorts, more males are in the labour force, with the overwhelming majority of those younger than 55 being wage employees.

The education data is also extremely interesting. Firstly, the percentage of females in the labour force is related closely to the level of education achieved. Hence, females with no education, less than eight years of schooling or those with some secondary schooling, are all more likely to be out of the labour force. This suggests that a dominant share of females between the ages of 16 and 65 in these education categories are either furthering their schooling or have remained as housewives. The first labour market snapshot above would tend to corroborate this claim. The attainment of a matric certificate or more, though, tends to result in a greater share of females in the labour force than out of it. Secondly, once in the labour force females with higher levels of education are more likely to be employed. Hence there is also a negative correlation between the share of unemployed females in the labour force and the level of education. Thirdly, of the females who are employed, those with no education are predominantly in unregistered businesses, again picking up the domestic services effect. Of those with primary schooling, close to 50% are self-employed in unregistered businesses. Finally, we again pick up an indirect registration status and income link, where as the years of education falls, the number of females with unregistered businesses increases. For males, once again the shares in the labour force across all education categories are greater. One interesting difference here is that while matric attainment resulted in a larger share of women in the labour force than out, for males the share in the labour force is greater for all education categories.

An application of a class of poverty measures to the labour market

The following section focuses on providing a richer description of the distribution of earnings in the labour market. We pay particular attention to identifying the working poor within the labour market. To do so, we apply the tools and framework of poverty dominance analysis to individuals in the labour market. These tools are usually applied at the household level but, given the specific focus of our work here, it is wholly appropriate to use these tools to focus on individuals in the formal and unregistered self-employed sectors as well as the unemployed where applicable. A major strength of the methodology is the fact that it is capable of integrating the unemployed into the analysis. The aim of this section is to derive cumulative distribution functions by predefined labour market categories, in order that we may better understand earnings, segmentation and the nature of job allocation decisions in the labour market. By specifying a low-earnings line, we are also able to highlight the incidence of working poor in different subgroups within the labour market and to derive the shares of working poor within these subgroups. The design of the multivariate modelling of labour market earnings in Chapter 4 will flow from the picture of the labour market that we distil in this section.

The FGT poverty approach

The most widely used approach that captures both the depth and severity of poverty is the generic class of measures found in Foster, Greer and Thorbecke (1984). This FGT class of poverty measures can be expressed in general form as:

$$P\alpha(z) = \int_0^z (1 - \frac{Y}{z})^\alpha f(Y) dY \qquad (1)$$

where α is a non-negative parameter. It is clear from (2) that when $\alpha = 0$, a head-count index (H or P_0) is calculated. The depth of poverty – measured as the poverty gap index (PG) – is calculated when $\alpha = 1$.[11] The severity of poverty, a measure that is sensitive to the distribution of income among the poor, is found when $\alpha = 2$.

The choice of a poverty line is open to much debate, and is probably the most contentious issue surrounding the measurement of poverty. In recent literature, considerable progress has been made in overcoming the restrictions implicit in basing a poverty analysis on one poverty line. The FGT methodology has been extended to a graphical consideration of the widest possible range of poverty lines, from 0 to z^{max} (Ravallion 1994:126). The values taken by this cumulative distribution function over the defined interval will yield the Poverty Incidence Curve. Given that the distribution function is F(Y), it is also true that the poverty deficit curve can be traced as follows:

$$D(z) = \int_0^{z^{max}} F(Y) dY \qquad (2)$$

Hence the area under the Poverty Incidence Curve represents the poverty deficit function. The former traces the values of the head-count index (P_0) for all poverty lines (z) from 0 to z^{max}, while the latter traces the measure for the poverty gap (P_1) for all z from 0 to z^{max}. The poverty severity curve is derived in turn, from the deficit function as follows:

$$S(z) = \int_0^{z^{max}} D(Y) dY \qquad (3)$$

and points on S(z) represent the results for P_2, at any poverty line between 0 and z^{max}.

Given the fact that these three functions are nested within each other, the interlinkages elicit important poverty comparisons (Ravallion 1994:129). Should $F_A(z)$ lie above $F_B(z)$ for all z, then this is true for both distributions on D(z) and S(z). The opposite, though, is not true. Hence, should $S_A(z)$ lie above $S_B(z)$ for all z, it would not necessarily be true that $D_A(z) > D_B(z)$ for all z. These are the axioms of dominance testing, which make it possible to do useful poverty comparisons and rankings, based on the magnitude, depth and severity of poverty for different distributions and subgroups in the population.

The extension of the graphical representations of dominance testing to the description of individual earnings in the labour market is especially useful and illuminating. Using predetermined labour market categories — for example, of all formal sector workers defined by their sector — it is possible to construct a set of curves which will fully describe the distribution of individual earnings within any given sector of the economy. Dominance testing therefore becomes a crucial tool in understanding the difference in earnings status amongst individuals in the labour market. It allows us to provide powerful and very useful information about the magnitude, depth and severity of low earnings amongst individuals in the labour force. In providing such an analysis, we extend our analysis of earnings beyond the somewhat crude median incomes provided in Table 3.1 above.

Cumulative distribution functions for the South African labour market

The cumulative distribution functions (CDFs) that follow are derived for all three major labour market segments, namely the formally employed, unregistered self-employed and unemployed. The intention is to derive different cumulative distributions by a set of relevant markers of low earnings in the labour market. These include race, gender, location and education. In addition, certain other markers were included, namely union status, sector and occupation. It should be clear from the preceding analysis that some of these variables will be relevant predictors of the earnings profile of workers. Therefore, the distribution functions will be important, not only in providing graphical representations of poverty in the labour market, but also in informing any earnings equation estimation. Hence, a crucial input of the functions is to inform how individuals are selected into different segments of the labour market, and what the important set of determinants of participation and earnings are. Dealing correctly and exhaustively with this selection process will go a long way towards increasing the robustness of any earnings equation results.

The difficulty in constructing the distribution functions lies in the choice of cuts to make on the data. The one clear trend is that strong first-order dominance holds almost across all of our selected cuts. Almost no second-order dominance testing was required. The functions that follow are an overview of the most important results found for labour market participants.

Figures 3.1 and 3.2 present the labour force as a whole, and include all employees, the registered and unregistered self-employed and the unemployed. The vertical axis cumulates individuals in the sample and varies from 0 to 1 as the sample increases. To avoid graphical interference from outliers in the sample, income was kept at a maximum of R5 000 per month for all the CDFs presented here. The values on the vertical axis will confirm the percentage of the sample captured in each case. The positive value of the intercepts in Figures 3.1 and 3.2 represent the share of unemployed individuals in the selected subsamples. Hence, the higher-value intercept for the African workforce simply indicates a larger pool of unemployed compared to white workers. The figures below illustrate that for any chosen poverty line between 0 and 5 000 rands, the fraction of all African workers in poverty is significantly greater than the fraction of African employed in poverty, and the share of this sample in poverty is in turn larger than that of the white employed or white workers.

The inclusion of zero-earners, therefore, generates a greater fraction of individuals living in poverty when compared with the sample of employed only. It is clear, though, that race is a crucial predictor of zero and low labour market earnings, with the dominance of Africans over whites being quite stark.

FIGURE 3.1

Earnings distribution of African and white workers

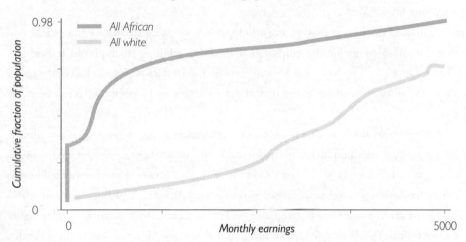

FIGURE 3.2

Earnings distribution of African employed and African workers

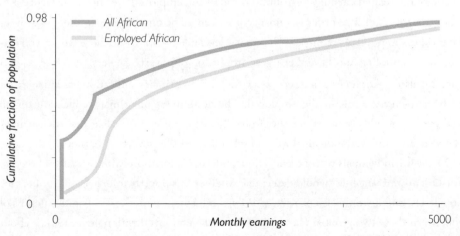

Another and equally important way to interrogate the data presented here is, of course, to determine a poverty line and then estimate the share of individuals falling below that line — the head-count index (H). The individual poverty line calculated is R293 per month.[12] Hence Figure 3.1, for example, shows that at the poverty line the proportion of the white labour force in poverty is only 4,2%, while the H for the African labour force stands at 41,6% — almost thirteen times greater. This is a vivid illustration of the differing poverty status amongst African and white labour market participants. When the unemployed are excluded, the P_0 values drop considerably for Africans to 10,1%, while the decline for white workers is to 0,2%. Labour market poverty in the aggregate, then, is very different for the white workforce compared to that experienced by African workers — in large part a function of the very high unemployment numbers amongst African workers.

Having examined the labour market as a whole, it is interesting to analyse the gender and race distribution of earnings for the employed only, thus excluding unemployed individuals. Figure 3.3 attempts to do this. Note that because the unemployed have been excluded, the intercepts are zero for all the functions. There is clearly both a race and a gender effect in terms of earnings.

Figure 3.3 illustrates that the lowest proportion of earners living in poverty, at any chosen poverty line, are white male employees in the formal sector or white male self-employed informal sector workers, followed by white females in the same two forms of employment. There is robust first-order earnings dominance between whites and Africans, and this dominance also holds for all low-earnings lines when comparing male and female African workers. The higher degree of poverty amongst African females is illustrated also in the H index, where their H value is 16,6%, while for African males it is only 6,2%. What is interesting is that while the male and female CDFs are closer together for Africans, for white workers the vertical differences are, on average, much greater between the genders.

The education-related earnings distributions for all the employed are shown in Figure 3.4. Again, the strong level of first-order dominance is evident. The employed with the lowest fraction of individuals in poverty are those with tertiary-level education, while those with no education or primary schooling only have the largest proportion of poverty earners.

Figure 3.4 also makes it clear that secondary, rather than primary, education has a significant impact on the poverty status of the employed. The attainment of primary education for an employed person is unlikely to reduce the probability of earning more than the low-earnings line, relative to an employed individual with no schooling. At the poverty line, though, the value for H is 23,1% for individuals with no education, and 16,7% for those with primary schooling. A second-order dominance test would determine whether this poverty information is robust for all income levels, and it would also provide additional information on the comparative depths of poverty between these two groups. The value of H for the employed with no education is about

FIGURE 3.3

Earnings distribution of African and white, male and female employed

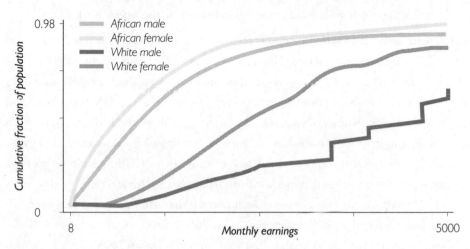

FIGURE 3.4

Earnings distribution by education levels

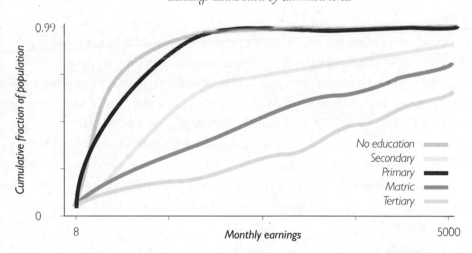

35% higher than for those with tertiary education whose H value is 0,7%. This reinforces the fact that education is a key variable in predicting earnings, relative to poverty, of employed individuals in the labour market.

Another very robust result of first-order dominance is for the employed by region. Again, as with the full labour force, the proportion of individuals in poverty is lower for those in urban areas relative to those in semi-urban and rural areas, irrespective of the low-earnings line that is specified.[13] Given that the demand for labour is strongly correlated with location and wage levels, this result is not surprising. It is evident that in terms of the earnings of labour market individuals, the five education categories chosen, together with the three location variables, are very clear predictors of the earnings status of employed individuals in the labour market.

The following three distribution functions refer to those employed individuals by a preselected subset of sectors and occupations. The survey contains a far larger number of sectors and occupations,[14] and it is convenient to aggregate these into categories that may yield interesting comparative information about labour-market poverty. Figure 3.5, therefore, examines those individuals in four sectors, namely mining, manufacturing, agriculture and finance.[15] Mining was chosen because of its obvious historical importance in output and employment terms to the economy, while manufacturing remains the largest contributor to GDP. Agriculture, together with mining, represents an industry in decline, with relatively high labour–capital ratios, while the finance sector, as the core of the new services industry, is the fastest-growing in the economy. It is evident from the distribution functions that individuals in these sectors also have differing earnings profiles. Hence the largest and smallest fraction of individuals below any chosen low-earnings line are those in agriculture and finance, respectively. The latter is indicative of a high-skill, capital-intensive sector, while individuals in farming are disproportionately labourers with low skill levels.

Applying our low-earnings line reveals that the value of H for workers in agriculture in poverty is about 23%, while for finance it is 0,4%. The close association between the employed in manufacturing and mining is a result of the high level of unionisation in these two sectors, combined with similar mean skill levels. It would appear, though, that the share of manufacturing workers in poverty is higher (H = 1,46%) than the fraction of mining workers (H = 0,45%), for any poverty line. The percentage of unionised manufacturing workers is lower (42,1%) than the share of mining workers who are union members (67,7%), and this may be an explanation for the first-order dominance. The distributions for union and non-union members, which are not shown here, yield first-order dominance of non-union workers over union workers that is robust for any poverty line.

Figure 3.6 and Figure 3.7 derive earnings distributions by selected occupations. Figure 3.6 compares three broad occupations that span the entire job ladder, from managers to those in elementary occupations. We have chosen managers, craft and trade workers and labourers in agriculture to represent this distribution across the job ladder. It is evident that first-order dominance holds, irrespective of the poverty line. Given the relative wages found in most societies, this distribution is not unexpected. It is clear, though, that the level of individual poverty amongst labourers in agriculture is extremely high. For example, a poverty line of R650 would place over 72% of these workers in poverty, while the comparative figure for craft and trade workers and managers would be 13,6% and 4,5%, respectively.[16] Using the study's individual poverty line, the

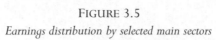

FIGURE 3.5

Earnings distribution by selected main sectors

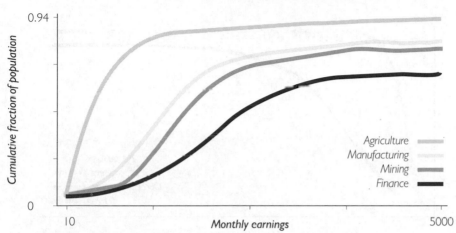

FIGURE 3.6

Earnings distribution of managers, craft and trade workers and agricultural labourers

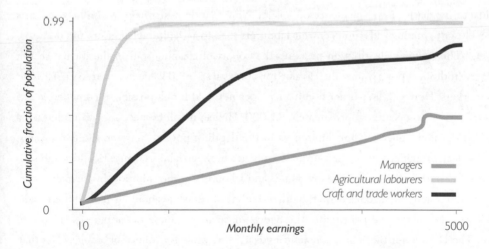

figures for craft workers and managers are close to zero, while the H value for all agriculture labourers is 26,78%.

While Figure 3.6 shows the expected poverty information – that labourers are the lowest earners compared to other occupations in the labour market – Figure 3.7 attempts to provide more detail on the earnings status of those individuals captured broadly as labourers. The survey was very helpful in identifying workers by their occupation and sector together. Hence, it was possible to look at labourers in, say, mining and agriculture compared to domestic services. Figure 3.7, then, shows that the two occupations with the lowest earnings, and with the highest

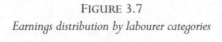

FIGURE 3.7

Earnings distribution by labourer categories

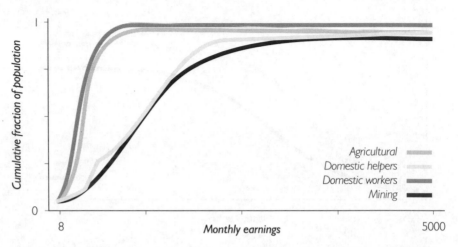

fraction of individuals in poverty, are self-employed domestic workers and agricultural labourers – a result alluded to in the previous figure. Labourers in the formal sector, such as mining and manufacturing, have a lower incidence of poverty. Note that domestic helpers also have a distribution closer to mining and manufacturing labourers than to agricultural labourers and domestic workers. This earnings distribution picks up the cohort of cleaning staff in the formal sector. Using the individual poverty line, the H value for domestics is 38,03%, compared to 26,78% for farm workers. However, first-order dominance does not hold for all possible income levels as a crossover seems to occur at approximately R1 000. Hence, it will be necessary to undertake a second-order dominance test for differences in the depth of poverty between the two groups. There is clearly, though, a strong first-order dominance between labourers in agriculture and self-employed domestic services on the one hand, and labourers in the traditionally formal sectors such as mining and manufacturing on the other. For example, while about 70% of all these individuals earn below R1 250 per month, the figure for farm and domestic employees is close to 100%. The H value for those in manufacturing is 1,54%, while for mine workers it is less than 1%.

In sum, it is clear that agriculture and household domestic workers present the highest levels of earnings vulnerability in the South African labour market, irrespective of the choice of individual poverty line. The constellation of covariates identified in the previous distribution functions, namely race, gender, education, union status and location, are all informative in seeking to locate and explain employment that is both unskilled and very poorly paid. While mean skill levels, as identified by broad occupational classification, may be similar in other sectors, different endowments serve to generate lower individual poverty rates. More specific results on the contributions of these covariates to earnings and poverty status will be generated through the earnings function analysis in the next chapter.

Table 3.5 alluded very strongly to the earnings differences between formal participants and the unregistered self-employed. Within this, it was also noted that African and coloured females represented the lowest earners and the most marginalised within the unregistered self-employed group. By way of further contrast between the formal and unregistered self-employed sectors, Figure 3.8 shows that first-order dominance holds across all income levels. This is indicative of the difference in quality of employment between the two labour markets. Clearly the dominance – in pure numerical terms – of domestic workers within the unregistered self-employed dictates this outcome.

FIGURE 3.8

Formal sector and unregistered self-employed earnings distributions

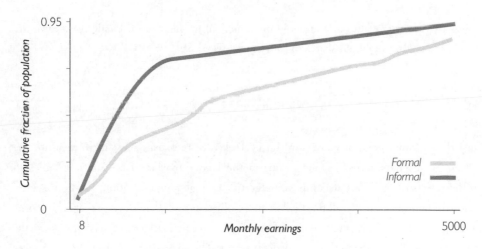

Shares of the working poor in the South African labour market

The second part of this chapter presented a diagrammatic understanding of poverty in the labour market, as embedded in the CDFs. These diagrams are very useful and user-friendly, and are a powerful way in which to present earnings dominance over the entire income range. Of course, the CDFs can impart information about the actual values for the head-count index, and these were also illustrated. We used the head-count index to derive the percentage of labour force participants and/or employed workers in different subgroups of the labour market who earn less than a poverty line of R293 per month.

As discussed in our earlier review of the FGT measures, the head-count is only one of the three poverty measures. We restricted the discussion to the head-count as it offered the most intuitive picture of the incidence of working poor within any subgroup. However, we have derived specific values for all three poverty measures: P_0, P_1 and P_2. This is done in order to utilise one of the key advantages of the FGT measures: namely, in each instance total measured poverty can be fully and consistently distributed between the chosen subgroups. In short, total poverty can be decomposed into poverty shares.[17]

More precisely, we split the labour market population into a relevant set of m subgroups with each subpopulation of n_i, so that the total population is simply:

$$n = \sum_{i=1}^{m} n_i \qquad (4)$$

We then derive intragroup FGT measures for different subgroups in the population. The intragroup FGT measure is best captured as follows:

$$P_{\alpha i} = \frac{1}{n_i} \sum_{j=1}^{q_i} \left(1 - \frac{Y_{ij}}{z} \right)^{\alpha} \qquad (5)$$

where Y_{ij} is the income of the jth household or individual in subgroup i. Finally, we derive the formula for calculating weighted shares of subgroup poverty as:

$$P_{\alpha} = \frac{\sum_{i=1}^{m} P_{\alpha i}\, n_i}{n} \qquad (6)$$

Thus, the decomposable properties of the FGT class of measures allow us to measure the share of all low-earners across key subgroups in the labour market. Table 3.6 and Table 3.8 present the results of this share decomposition across race, gender, education, location, sector, occupation and union status. In all but the last three of these cases, the poverty shares are computed for the full labour force and also for the employed. In calculating these shares, it is worthwhile to do the calculation for all three poverty measures. The changes in the shares as one moves from P_0 to P_1 and then P_2 provide us with a sense of how the poverty shares change as we use measures that give greater weight to the depth of poverty and the poorest of the working poor.

Before discussing the results, there is one final sensitivity issue that we need to address. This is the choice of low-earnings line. Up to this point, we have made use of a R293 per month low-earnings line. The strong first-order dominance illustrated by the CDFs earlier in this chapter imply that the poverty rankings will not change as we change the low-earnings line. However, although the CDFs do not cross, their slopes and relative positions do change, and the actual poverty shares will change based on the actual low-earnings line that is selected.

As stated at the beginning of this chapter, the justification for the R293 line is that this is the monthly adult equivalent income that underlies our household poverty line. However, there is no doubt that this is an extremely low labour market income. For one thing, an adult earning

Selecting a low-earnings line: defining the working poor

- Per capita adult equivalent: R293 per month and R3 516 per year

- Per capita expenditure level: R594 per month and R7 128 per year

- The wage required to meet the household poverty line, given the mean number of employed workers in a household: R814 per month and R9 768 per year

- The wage required to meet the household poverty line, given the mean number of employed plus unemployed workers in a household: R650 per month and R7 800 per year

- The 40th percentile of all wages of employed workers: R1 200 per month and R14 400 per year

- The 25th percentile of all wages of employed workers: R800 per month and R9 600 per year

- The 40th percentile of all workers, presuming a zero wage for the unemployed: R800 per month and R9 600 per year

- 50% of the mean wage of those employed: R1 107 per month and R13 287 per year

such an income would be poverty-neutral in the household in the sense that they pay their own way but make no additional contribution to lifting that household out of poverty.

Ultimately, there is really no rigorous way to choose a low-earnings line. The best that can be done is to be transparent and to explore sensitivity to the chosen line. The box below presents the annual and monthly values for a number of possibilities. We selected the fourth option (R650 per month) for the sensitivity analysis, and Table 3.8 repeats all the share decompositions at this wage. The amount would enable a household of average size with the average numbers of employed and unemployed to earn the relevant household poverty income. Thus, there is a positive household contribution built into this wage, but it is still clearly a low income. For example, it is well below the R800 mark that is the 25th percentile of actual wages or the 40th percentile of wages if we include the unemployed as zero-earners.

The total figures (shown in bold) in Tables 3.7 and 3.8 offer a good starting point for discussing the results. Obviously, the total labour force (13,8 million workers) and the total number of employed workers (9,9 million) are the same in both tables. Of these, 45,6% of the labour force and 25% of the employed are poor when the low-earnings line is set at R650 per month. The respective figures fall to 32,56 % and 7,25% when the line is set at R293 per month. Thus, at this lower line most of the poor are unemployed. In terms of a straight head-count, 86,03% are unemployed. This same number of unemployed participants only form 61% of the working poor at the higher line. As these unemployed are, by definition, the poorest of all the participants, it is no surprise that the poverty share of the unemployed rises sharply in both tables when P_1 and P_2 are used as bases for the shares calculation.

For the labour force as a whole (employed and unemployed), the decomposition in Table 3.8 shows that 88% of the low-earners are African and under 9% are coloured. When the analysis is restricted to the employed alone, these shares are 86% and 12%, respectively. This picture is robust across all poverty measures and across both tables. The dominant racial angle to labour market vulnerability could not have been more clearly revealed. Within the African group, 10% of earners lie below the R293 benchmark, compared to 7% of coloureds. Within this group of working poor, the Africans are clearly the lowest earners, as their share of poverty rises to 100% when P_1 and P_2 shares are calculated. Table 3.8 shows that coloureds retain their share at the higher line.

Thus, we now know that we are predominantly looking at within-African breakdowns as we move away from race to the other cross-cutting factors. A comparison of the total male/female and African male/female breakdowns in Table 3.7 reveals a very stable picture across the measures. Females make up 57% of poor labour market participants and African females alone constitute 50% of this total. This is not only because of the much higher incidence of unemployment. When we focus only on the employed, African females make up 53% of the working poor by straight head-count and 68% when the depth of poverty is considered. Given that African women make up 30,5% of the labour force and 23,3% of the employed, their poverty 'contributions' are seen to be far in excess of their representation. This is a stark illustration of the special vulnerability of this section of the labour force. However, Table 3.8 shows that, amongst the employed, the African male poverty contribution rises sharply relative to African females at the higher low-earnings line. This signals the fact that there are a significant group of African males earning between R293 and R650 per month. Yet, even at this higher poverty line, African female earners constitute between 40 and 46% of the working poor.

Tables 3.6 and 3.7 illustrate a number of important variables that cut across racial and gender divides. The importance of low levels of education in terms of the incidence of low-earnings has already been flagged. The share analysis adds to this by showing that, amongst the employed, 75% of low-earners have primary schooling or less. As such individuals constitute only 31% of the employed, the burden of low levels of education is clearly revealed. When comparing the blocks for all participants versus the employed, it can be seen that secondary schooling and matric have a larger poverty share for all participants. This would seem to imply that these upper levels of education do not necessarily guarantee a person a job but do offer better earnings to those with employment. Underlying this rather anomalous finding is the fact that South Africa's unemployment problem has become far more severe in the last fifteen years and therefore has a strong youth dimension to it. At the same time, the exit levels of South Africans from school have risen sharply. Thus, it is very important to keep the age cohort differences in mind when interpreting these education effects.

TABLE 3.7

FGT measures for individuals in the South African labour market, R293 per month

Variable/measure	Number/share	P_{0i}	P_0	P_1	P_2
Labour force					
Total	13 817 522	32,56	100,00	100,00	100,00
African	69,12	41,58	88,27	88,73	88,19
Coloured	10,92	25,15	8,44	8,23	8,29
Asian	3,00	11,98	1,10	1,01	1,14
White	16,95	4,23	2,20	2,01	2,34
Unemployed	28,01	100,00	86,03	93,37	96,59
Male	56,72	24,62	42,89	42,59	42,60
Female	43,28	42,98	57,13	56,91	56,90
African male	38,61	32,07	38,03	38,87	38,52
African female	30,51	53,62	50,24	49,86	49,67
No education	8,68	47,46	12,65	10,58	10,56
Primary education	24,56	44,75	33,75	30,98	30,05
Secondary	32,50	34,75	34,68	36,56	36,99
Grade 8	21,50	24,08	15,90	17,98	18,44
Tertiary	12,77	7,71	3,02	3,48	3,48
Urban	61,73	24,63	46,69	51,80	52,41
Semi-urban	1,91	30,88	1,81	1,98	2,21
Rural	36,22	46,00	51,17	45,41	45,33
Employed					
Total	9 947 208	7,25	100,00	100,00	100,00
African	61,79	10,14	86,42	100,00	100,00
Coloured	11,97	7,07	11,59	0,00	0,00
Asian	3,67	0,53	0,25	0,00	0,00
White	22,57	0,56	1,74	0,00	0,00
Male	61,60	4,39	37,30	33,33	34,00
Female	38,40	11,85	62,77	66,67	66,00
African male	38,53	6,22	33,06	31,84	31,85
African female	23,26	16,62	53,32	68,16	68,15
No education	8,15	23,10	25,98	24,46	24,56
Primary education	22,31	16,72	51,46	52,07	52,08
Secondary	30,37	4,35	18,22	20,24	20,11
Grade 8	22,74	0,93	2,92	3,23	3,25
Tertiary	16,43	0,67	1,52	0,00	0,00

TABLE 3.7 (CONTINUED . . .)

Variable/measure	Number/share	P_{0i}	P_0	P_1	P_2
Urban	65,81	2,79	25,33	35,10	34,90
Semi-urban	1,90	5,31	1,34	1,58	1,48
Rural	32,24	16,49	73,33	63,32	62,75
Agriculture	12,73	22,82	40,07	26,58	23,34
Manufacturing	15,05	1,46	3,03	3,09	3,80
Mining	4,66	0,45	0,29	0,00	0,00
Finance	6,47	0,39	0,35	0,00	0,00
Wholesale and retail	17,40	3,93	9,43	10,47	10,63
Community	32,88	9,89	44,86	51,26	52,98
Other	10,81	1,32	1,97	8,60	9,25
Manager	5,74	1,27	1,01	1,91	2,87
Craft and trade	12,18	2,15	3,61	4,06	5,09
Agricultural labourer	9,50	26,78	35,07	25,32	26,99
Domestic worker	7,17	38,03	37,60	38,79	39,00
Union	29,02	0,58	2,32	1,96	1,00
Non-union	72,48	9,79	97,87	98,33	99,00

TABLE 3.8

FGT measures for individuals in the South African labour market, R650 per month

Variable/measure	Number/share	P_{0i}	P_0	P_1	P_2
		Labour force			
Total	**13 817 522**	**45,65**	**100**	**100,00**	**100,00**
African	69,12	56,83	86,04	87,32	88,61
Coloured	10,92	44,19	10,58	9,37	8,50
Asian	3,00	16,68	1,10	1,01	0,76
White	16,95	6,13	2,28	2,30	2,13
Unemployed	28,01	100	61,36	76,00	85,45
Male	56,72	37,58	46,70	43,90	42,87
Female	43,28	56,22	53,30	54,89	55,82
African male	38,61	47,73	40,37	39,32	38,70
African female	30,51	68,36	45,69	47,36	48,64
No education	8,68	72,52	13,79	11,99	11,17
Primary education	24,56	67,82	36,48	33,53	32,21
Secondary	32,50	47,04	33,49	34,51	35,47
Grade 8	21,50	28,5	13,42	15,61	16,97

TABLE 3.8 (CONTINUED . . .)

Variable/measure	Number/share	P_{oi}	P_0	P_1	P_2
Tertiary	12,77	10,08	2,82	3,03	3,37
Urban	61,73	32,62	44,05	51,26	52,02
Semi-urban	1,91	49,8	2,89	2,01	2,01
Rural	36,22	67,48	53,06	46,73	45,97
Employed					
Total	9 947 208	25,01	100,00	100,00	100,00
African	61,79	33,36	82,42	83,55	84,48
Coloured	11,97	30,41	14,56	13,44	12,53
Asian	3,67	5,69	0,83	0,64	0,56
White	22,57	2,4	2,19	2,37	2,43
Male	61,60	20,64	50,85	46,34	46,17
Female	38,40	32,01	49,15	52,57	53,83
African male	38,53	27,66	42,61	40,67	40,26
African female	23,26	42,81	39,81	42,88	42,22
No education	8,15	59,9	19,53	19,73	21,27
Primary education	22,31	51,21	45,69	46,12	47,39
Secondary	30,37	22,12	26,86	25,75	23,90
Grade 8	22,74	6,39	5,81	5,63	4,94
Tertiary	16,43	3,2	2,10	2,05	2,07
Urban	65,81	12,79	33,66	33,15	33,50
Semi-urban	1,90	31,01	2,36	2,30	2,35
Rural	32,24	49,58	63,91	62,77	64,15
Agriculture	12,73	72,27	36,78	31,58	31,62
Manufacturing	15,05	12,37	7,44	5,93	5,95
Mining	4,66	7,97	1,49	0,87	0,87
Finance	6,47	4,88	1,26	0,93	0,94
Wholesale and retail	17,40	20,06	13,95	11,10	11,20
Community	32,88	25,81	33,94	38,05	38,15
Other	10,81	11,89	5,14	11,54	11,57
Manager	5,74	4,51	1,03	0,98	1,08
Craft and trade	12,18	13,62	6,63	5,10	5,38
Agricultural labourer	9,50	81,33	30,88	27,50	27,03
Domestic worker	7,17	81,25	23,29	25,69	29,71
Union	29,02	6,71	7,79	5,25	5,14
Non-union	72,48	31,9	92,44	94,75	94,86

Individuals in rural areas constitute close a third of the total labour force and the employed. Yet, half of the poverty in the labour market and 73% of the poverty amongst the employed is rural. Thus rural areas are greatly overrepresented. Despite this, there are two aspects to Tables 3.7 and 3.8 that caution against an exclusive focus on the rural dimensions of labour market vulnerability. First, the rural share (by head-count) falls when the poverty line increases to R650 per month. Second, even at the lower poverty line, the rural shares fall significantly as the basis is changed from P_0 to P_1 and then to P_2. This indicates that there are significant pockets of urban unemployed and low-earners. These low-earners are the unregistered self-employed who were highlighted in the earlier CDF analysis.

The last three blocks of both tables offer further cross-sections on vulnerability within the employed. From the preceding discussion we know that these blocks are predominantly intra-group insights about the determinants of vulnerability amongst poorly educated Africans. We also know that this analysis still spans both males and females and rural and urban areas. The sectoral and occupational analyses complement each other. A full 85% of the low-earners work in the agricultural and community service sectors. The occupational distribution shows that this result is largely due to the shares of low earners that are agricultural labourers and domestic workers (35% and 38%, respectively).[18] As both of these occupations and sectors, as well as the third major vulnerable sector (wholesale and retail), are non-unionised it is hardly surprising to find that unions have a close to zero share of low-earners at the low poverty line. This rises to an 8% head-count share at the higher line, corresponding to the increasing share of manufacturing workers within the working poor.

Conclusion

This chapter has sought to show that important, useful and indeed graphically powerful information can be gleaned by using the tools of poverty analysis to describe individual earnings in the labour market. Rather than rely on median or, worse still, mean income levels, this analysis has sought to understand more rigorously the distribution of earnings and the extent and incidence of low earnings in the labour market. While a choice of poverty line could have dictated this analysis from the outset, the preferred option was to begin by using the tools of dominance testing to understand the poverty-sensitive segmentations in the labour market. Thereafter, we specified a poverty line in order to discuss the incidence of poverty in the labour market. We then used two poverty lines to calculate poverty shares across different groups within the labour market.

One of the key results here is that domestic workers and farm workers together are the two most vulnerable groups in the labour market. It is the importance of these groups that correlates with the total dominance of African and coloured race groups and the significance of women among the most vulnerable. The picture presented in this chapter has important implications for the modelling of earnings. It strongly suggests that there are a number of different labour markets in South Africa. It seems clear that, for Africans and coloureds, unregistered self-employment is qualitatively different from the formal sector. In addition, there are important differences between men and women in the labour market. We have flagged the fact that the processes determining labour force participation and selection into employment differ by gender. This is also true of the allocation into self-employment and into occupations. We have also flagged the potential importance of differences between urban and rural labour markets. The importance of education, in turn, was powerfully displayed through the distribution functions. It appears, though, that education is more important in determining earnings than whether an individual gets a job or not.

We have ensured that all labour market participants are extensively discussed in our analysis by exploiting a particular strength of the FGT poverty framework: namely, its ability to integrate the unemployed into the analysis of earnings vulnerability. This was fully reflected in our CDF analysis and in the share decompositions. However, in conclusion, it is important to recognise that this framework has not been broad enough to incorporate those who are not participating in the labour market. It is clear from the discussion in the first part of this chapter that the participation fault line is a key aspect of vulnerability that should not be forgotten. We showed that South Africa's labour participation rates are extremely low. Moreover, the key correlates of low participation are seen to be the same as those associated with earnings vulnerability. Thus, in almost every case, the analysis of earnings is an understatement of vulnerability, as it ignores the desperation of those on the fringes of the labour market.

Notes

1. A more detailed discussion of our selection procedure for the employed and unemployed in the OHS 95 will be provided by the authors upon request.

2. At best, we can impute the size of this group from the questionnaire.

3. The largest subcategory here were those individuals who, upon saying that they wanted a job, reported themselves as housewives who preferred not to seek work. These people numbered 113 729, approximately 2,7% of all those previously coded as unemployed.

4. Unfortunately, the OHS 95 does not break down the code for 'Other' in the questionnaire, which would have been useful, given its fairly high share for African females in particular.

5. Some have argued that codes 7 and 8 should not be included when defining the unemployed. Both codes, though, represent those individuals who, at the time of interview, still did not have a job. In addition, code 8 also includes those who may have previously undertaken training, a fact that would not exclude them from being part of the unemployed. Ultimately, though, the numbers of individuals involved in these two codes is small enough to make little difference to the overall unemployment rates derived.

6. Statistics South Africa has recently opted to publish the narrow definition as the official unemployment rate. The evidence makes it plain that such a choice should not lessen the appreciation of the very low rate of labour absorption in the economy, in an environment of very poor official unemployment insurance.

7. The 35-hour week is used as the cut-off period between full-time and part-time work in the questionnaire.

8. Given this, we use the terminology of 'low earners' and 'working poor' and 'low-earnings line' and 'poverty-earnings line' interchangeably.

9. The OHS 95 has a broad category for workers in elementary occupations, and the approach here has been to extract those labourer categories deemed to be of interest in earnings analysis.

10. 'Various informal occupations' refers to individuals coded as general managers in enterprises such as shebeens, taverns, spaza shops, butcheries, and so on.

11. The PG is therefore calculated as $P_1 = \int_0^z (1 - Y/z) f(Y) dY$

12. The choice of this low-earnings line is discussed later in this chapter. All the head-count results that are discussed in here are taken from Table 3.7 (page 101).

13. Given that three discrete distribution functions were generated, it was decided, *ex post*, to maintain the three locational definitions of Statistics South Africa, rather than opting for only a rural–urban split.

14. There are 50 subsectors within 9 major sector divisions and approximately 150 occupations within 9 major occupational groups.

15. The complete coverage of these sectors is mining and quarrying, manufacturing, agriculture, hunting, forestry and fishing and, finally, financial intermediation, insurance, real estate and business services.

16. The number for managers would be biased downwards, in that we would include employed persons who are unregistered self-employed and, therefore, would not conform to the classic conception of managers employed in the formal sector. Across all race groups, this class of managers number about 101 000 individuals.

17. In all these calculations, national frequency weights were assumed and missing values for monthly income were all omitted. The original intragroup measures are available from the authors, as are the actual weighted measures.

18. Note that the sample by occupation is incomplete in both tables, excluding individuals in other job grades. An 'other' category, however, in representing skill levels across the job ladder, would have had little meaning and was thus omitted.

4

Modelling Vulnerability and Low Earnings in the South African Labour Market

Haroon Bhorat
Murray Leibbrandt

Chapter 3 provided a detailed overview of the correlates of vulnerability in the South African labour market using the methodologies found primarily in household poverty studies. One of the key results of the chapter was to show that, in terms of the race and gender covariates, Africans and females were particularly disadvantaged in the labour market. In addition, Chapter 3 highlighted the importance of rural-versus-urban labour markets in explaining access to employment and the quality of employment. The importance of education was powerfully displayed through the use of cumulative distribution functions (CDFs). It appeared, though, that education was more important in determining earnings than whether an individual gets a job or not. Herein lies the limitation of this descriptive approach; it is incapable of comprehensively and simultaneously highlighting the different determinants and factors impinging on labour market selection and earnings processes. The next step in such an analysis, therefore, is to combine these differing covariates, which we identify as important, into an econometric model. Such a model would determine the relative importance of these covariates in explaining each stage of the labour market process, namely participation, employment and earnings.

The modelling work in this chapter therefore flows directly from the descriptive discussion of Chapter 3 in the sense that we use this analysis to formulate and specify our modelling work. Given the large number of previous studies that model earnings in South Africa, it is also useful to anchor our approach relative to this recent econometric work. Hence, the intention of this chapter is twofold. Firstly, we undertake a comparative analysis of all the South African earnings function literature, with a focus on the specification of the models and their differing treatments of sample selection issues. Secondly, we propose and estimate a model of our own which attempts to highlight the full dimensions of vulnerability in the South African labour market.

Previous earnings function models in South Africa

The 1990s have produced a wealth of work on earnings function (see Moll 1998; Mwabu & Schultz 1996a, 1996b & 1998; Fallon and Lucas 1998; Winter 1998; Hofmeyr 1999; Lucas & Hofmeyr 1998). This new literature has been spawned largely by the fact that a number of reliable national sample surveys were conducted during the 1990s. The availability of these data sets has for the first time encouraged the application of rigorous and econometrically sophisticated analysis of South African labour market issues.

We have selected four of these studies from this literature for further discussion, as we feel this is adequate to illustrate the type of choices that need to be made when modelling the South African labour market. The selection also allows us to illustrate how our approach compares to the existing literature. We summarise the methodology and the results of these studies in the box on page 109.

To the uninitiated, it is hard to read across this literature and make comparisons. The major reason for this is the bewildering array of differences in specification, conceptualisation, estimation techniques and data. These differences are rarely discussed or justified. The four studies presented in the box all use ordinary least-squares estimation techniques in estimating the earnings function, and all but one use the 1993 South African Living Standards Measurement Survey (LSMS) data. Thus, to a large measure we control for the differences due to data and techniques. This allows us to focus on issues relating to specification and conceptualisation.

In terms of specification issues, each study makes different choices about whether to deal with race, gender and location via dummy variables or via separate equations. Then there are differences in how education, age and experience effects are captured. Some studies use a set of dummy variables and interactive dummy variables for all of these explanatory variables. On the other hand, education effects are also assessed through the use of splines.

For us, the choices are largely defined by the descriptive analysis in Chapter 3. This picture revealed that the vulnerable are almost exclusively found within the African and coloured racial groups, with the African group accounting for close to 90% of all low-earners and no-earners. In our modelling we therefore confine our attention exclusively to African individuals. We also know that within the African group females carry a larger than proportionate burden of low participation, high unemployment and low earnings. In addition, low-earning African females tend to be found in different sections of the labour market to males. Given these factors, there is a strong likelihood that estimates based on aggregate African models are likely to throw up average parameters that are not useful representations of either male or female groups. In addition, we explicitly want to compare African female and male models. Thus, in all instances we run separate estimations for African males and females.

Recent econometric approaches to earnings in the South African labour market

Study and data	Specification of earnings function	Coverage of earnings function	Labour market sample selection	Results
Mwabu & Schultz (1996a) (LSMS 1993)	● Separate earnings equation by race gender and location (tests against combined model for all) ● Three education splines and also includes some tertiary training dummies ● Earnings normalised to wage rate per hour	● Formal sector earnings	● Potential labour market participants (the economically active population) ● Sample selection term has to cope with the participation decision and whether employed, unemployed or informally employed	● Wage rates of whites five times that of Africans. Half due to education differences ● African rates of return to education higher for secondary and tertiary
Fallon & Lucas (1998) (LSMS 1993)	● Separate earnings equations for African, white and Other ● Gender and regions specified as dummy variables ● Education measured as years. Includes an experience–education interaction effect ● Dummy variables for part-time and for public sector	● Formal sector, casual and self-employed earnings	● Actual labour market participants ● Sample selection term only has to cope with the unemployed	● Average African gender wage differential is 78% ● Average African union wage differential is 71% ● Average African public sector premium is 47%
Winter (1997) (OHS 1994)	● Separate earnings equations by race and gender ● Includes hours of work as an explanatory variable ● Education measured as years	● Formal sector workers	● No sample selection term despite the fullest analysis of participation	● South African participation rates are lower than international trends ● Sharp gender differences in participation ● Discrimination accounts for over 70% of the gender wage gap for all groups except coloureds
Hofmeyr (1998) (LSMS 1993)	● Separate earnings equations for all earnings categories ● Only male earners included ● Race and location specified as dummy variables ● Education measured as dummy variables ● Includes hours of work as an explanatory variable	● Paid employed, including informal self-employed, casual employed, formal non-unionised and formal unionised	● Potential labour market participants ● Sample selection term has to cope with unemployed and the unpaid and each of the four paid earnings categories using multinomial logit	● Substantial earnings differentials between the imposed segments of the labour market including formal unionised and non-unionised
This study (OHS 1995)	● *Only African individuals* ● *Separate models for male and female* ● *Tests against combined model for urban and rural* ● *Education splines*	● *All employees and self-employed*	● *Potential labour market participants* ● *selection into the labour market and then into employed*	

On the basis of this descriptive support, we are prepared to impose these restrictions. Such restrictions are also in line with the more careful econometric work represented in the box. We are confident, therefore, that they will improve the quality and usefulness of the resultant estimates.

Besides the racial and gender dimensions of vulnerability, the descriptive analysis in Chapter 3 also revealed strong rural and urban differences within both African male and female groups. It is important for our policy conclusions that we explore these differences. Initially, we do so by estimating models for all African women and all African men in which we include a rural and urban dummy variable. We then go on to estimate separate models for rural and urban areas so that we can compare the coefficients and statistically test for significance between these coefficients. Thus, in assessing rural and urban differences, we do not impose separate specifications from the outset. Rather we assess the specifications as part of the estimation process.

These are the major choices that we make regarding our earnings equations. As we explain later, we estimate labour participation and employment equations along with our earnings equation. Each of these three equations includes certain explanatory variables that clearly pertain to that equation and not to the others. However, our earlier descriptive analysis makes it clear that there are age, education and provincial aspects to labour market vulnerability at each of these three levels. All three equations will include a set of dummy variables capturing age and provincial effects and a set of three educational splines that capture the returns to schooling at primary, secondary and tertiary level.

On the conceptual level, hardly any of the South African work spells out even a rudimentary model of the South African labour market as the context for estimation. Earnings function work only makes sense against such a context, and part of the difference between the models must lie in the fact that the earnings functions are set up, often only implicitly, in differently defined labour market contexts. We tease out this point through a close examination of the sample selection equations that are used in each of the studies. Each researcher chooses a sample selection equation based on a demarcation of the relevant sample (labour market) of the study as well as the relationship between the subsample of earners and this broader sample. Thus, inspection of the interface between the earnings equation and the sample selection equation reveals much about the overall labour market context within which the earnings function work is located.

We illustrate with reference to the four studies presented in the box. The most important columns are the two reflecting the coverage of the earnings function and labour market sample selection.

The Mwabu and Schultz (1996) study is the most careful of all four studies in terms of testing for the adequacy of different specifications for the earnings function. However, the focus of the earnings function – formal sector earnings – is assumed from the outset and not derived. The selection equation begins with all potential labour market participants. It includes an extensive array of agricultural asset variables that are the hallmarks of a participation equation in a conventional developing country. However, the resultant selection term is insignificant in all but one of the earnings functions and it is therefore omitted for the final set of earnings function estimations. Indeed, as Mwabu and Schultz point out, these variables are jointly insignificant even in the participation equation, thus raising some problems for the identification of the two-equation model.

To us, this insignificance is hardly surprising for two reasons. First, one of the legacies of apartheid has been the decimation of any smallholder and subsistence farming classes (Lipton *et al.* 1996). Thus, it is hard to conceptualise any clear relationship between these agricultural assets and labour market participation. Second, the earnings equation is narrowly focused on formal sector earnings. This leaves participation in the labour market, selection into employment and participation in the informal sector to be dealt with by the participation equation. We would expect such a diversity of forms of participation and selections to be inadequately captured by a single participation equation. Even assuming that all unemployment in South Africa is voluntary, and therefore indistinguishable from the decision regarding whether or not to participate in the labour market, the participation equation also has to deal with the awkward issue of participation in the informal sector versus the formal sector.

The Fallon and Lucas (1997) study covers a far broader section of the labour market in the earnings function itself. Formal sector employees, the self-employed and part-time workers are all included as earners. The selection equation then selects from the chosen sample of all labour market participants into this reduced sample of earners. The selection equation therefore covers the selection from a pool of participants into earnings; that is, an employment–unemployment equation. Of course, this makes the selection equation coherent and interesting in its own right. However, this coherence is achieved at the cost of ignoring the issue of participation in the labour market and therefore using a narrower sample than the other studies. The employment probit includes a set of variables defining 'other household income'. These variables would usually be thought of as factors influencing participation rather than factors influencing employment. The exception would be if unemployment were viewed as voluntary. Fallon and Lucas clearly do not believe this to be the case. However, this then leaves the participation–unemployment nexus hanging in the air.

Winter (1998) offers a full analysis of participation in the South African labour market. Indeed, it was her clear documentation of the importance of South Africa's very low participation rates and the gender and racial biases in these participation rates that informed our insistence in this study that participation is one of the aspects of labour market vulnerability in South Africa. Having provided this exhaustive analysis of participation, Winter uses her earnings function work to document the importance of earnings discrimination by gender in the South African labour market. The focus of this earnings analysis is on formal sector workers. In estimating earnings functions by gender, she does not include a sample selection term. Indeed, she could not, as she has provided extensive coverage of participation but no coverage of unemployment. She has left the selection into employment unexplored and therefore has a missing subsample in her labour market.

Like Fallon and Lucas, Hofmeyr (1999) attempts to capture all earners within the ambit of the earnings function estimations. Hofmeyr uses the same earnings categories as Fallon and Lucas, but goes further by splitting formal sector workers into unionised and non-unionised sections. However, Hofmeyr differs from all previous studies in his approach to selection. He sets up a full sample of potential labour market participants and presumes that they are allocated into one of his four categories of earners or into unpaid household help (helping another household member who is self-employed) or into no employment. This selection is done simultaneously in a multinomial logit allocation equation in which 'no employment' is defined as the default category. It is interesting to see how the characteristics of those allocated into the earnings segments differ from those without employment. However, it needs to be stressed that 'no employment' covers non-participants and unemployed. Thus, the model cannot provide useful information on either participation or on unemployment.

The original rationale for such a multinomial logit model is an occupational choice model (Roy 1951). Hofmeyr is well aware of the fact that the South African labour market offers an uncomfortable context for such a choice-theoretic view of the allocation process. He wants the model to cover both supply and demand elements and therefore choice and constraints from the individual point of view. It is not clear that the model is up to such a task, as is evidenced by the fact that the model allocates many individuals to incorrect segments of the labour market.

Hopefully this review of four recent econometric studies will provide a relevant and useful context for the presentation of our approach to modelling. Our special focus is on the vulnerable in the labour market. Preceding empirical work in this book has made it quite clear that vulnerability needs to be defined in such a way that it encompasses labour market participation and selection into employment, as well as the determinants of earnings. The biggest conceptual issue that we face with regard to the formulation of our modelling is to give detailed attention to all three of these stages in the labour market.

The model set-up

Our model structure deals with these stages sequentially. First, we begin with a full sample of potential labour market participants and estimate a participation probability model. Then, for the reduced sample of labour market participants we estimate an employment probability model. Finally, we estimate an earnings function using the sample of employed Africans. Such a sequential model can be loosely justified by the assumption that labour market participation and employment are first-choice activities of all potential labour market participants and that we are therefore modelling a rationing process. The participation equation attempts to throw light on the key factors selecting participants. Once the participants are determined, the second stage models the employment allocation process. The final stage models earnings of those who succeed in obtaining employment.

This is certainly a plausible South African scenario, particularly for the employment–unemployment step between participation and earnings. We argued above that other econometric studies of the South African labour market have tended to blur the distinction between participation and unemployment in their selection equation. While this is not particularly important if the purpose of the exercise is to cleanse the earnings equation of sample selection problems, it is of no use if the purpose of the analysis is to examine the determinants of participation and employment.

Such analysis is particularly important in the South African context because of the debates that exist over usage of the narrow versus the expanded definition of unemployment (ILO 1996; Nattrass & Seekings 1998).[1] In discussions over the two unemployment definitions, insufficient attention has been given to the fact that a movement from a broad to a narrow definition of unemployment involves an assertion that discouraged workers are not participating in the labour force.[2] Thus, the subsample of unemployed shrinks to the narrow definition and the subsample of participants expands to take in the discouraged work-seekers. By distinguishing between participation and unemployment, we can assess the difference that the change in definition makes to *both* participation and unemployment.

Related to the narrow-versus-broad unemployment issue is the question of voluntary versus involuntary unemployment. All analysts recognise that unemployment is predominantly involuntary in South Africa. Even more important is the fact that the unemployment questions in all recent surveys are designed to select from the sample of potential labour market participants those who want jobs but do not have them. Thus, the surveys themselves are structured to capture the involuntarily unemployed. Yet, as pointed out earlier, the earnings function literature in South Africa has tended to present a messy interface between participation and unemployment in their selection equations. Indeed, given that most selection equations are starkly framed in terms of participation versus non-participation in the labour market, it is only by assuming that unemployment is voluntary that the specified selection equations can be made tenable. By including both participation and employment equations in our work, we are clearly defining unemployment as a state that occurs despite a decision to participate in the labour market. It is therefore clearly involuntary.

Our estimation starts out with a full sample of potential labour market participants. It then shrinks the sample to cover actual labour market participants, and then shrinks the sample further to cover earners. It is now well established in the labour economics literature that the estimates derived in the employment model and in the earnings model may be biased because of the fact that they are both based on non-random, reduced versions of the original sample of potentially employable Africans (Heckman 1979). Thus, in all versions of our modelling we control for the possibility of sample selection problems. We use a probit model to estimate our participation equation. Then we use another probit model to derive employment probability estimates conditional on the characteristics of all labour market participants and *conditional on the fact that these are the actual participants taken from a full sample of all potential participants*. Then we derive estimated earnings coefficients conditional on the individual characteristics of the earners and *conditional on the fact that these earners are a subsample of all labour market participants and an even smaller subsample of potential participants*.

In each instance, we use the Heckman two-step approach to cope with the sample selection issue (Greene 1993; Breen 1996). Having estimated the participation probit, we use these estimates to derive our estimate for the inverse Mills ratio (lambda) for inclusion in employment probit. It is the inclusion of this lambda that allows us to make the employment probit conditional on positive participation. We then use the estimates from the employment probit to derive a new estimated Mills ratio, reflecting selection into earnings. The inclusion of this second lambda in the earnings equation makes the earnings equation conditional on participation and selection into employment. It seems plausible to argue that the selection into employment and the determination of earnings for those employed are simultaneous processes rather than sequential ones. We also allow for this possibility by deriving another set of estimates for the employment probability model and the earnings function based on a single, integrated maximum-likelihood model.

One of the strengths of a clear delimitation of the participation, employment and earnings stages in the labour market is that it facilitates the selection of a coherent set of variables for each equation. For example, as mentioned earlier in the discussion of Fallon and Lucas (1997), it is fairly common to see household variables in an employment–unemployment probit. However, such variables would normally relate to a participation process rather than an employment process. Thus, our participation equation includes a full set of household composition variables by age as well as variable reflecting income from other household members (and the square of this variable to allow for non-linearities). In terms of the two-stage selection model, these household variables identify the lambda that is included in the employment probit.

The employment equation therefore only contains information about the personal characteristic of each job-seeker (age, education and location). As these variables are all also plausible explanatory factors in the earnings function, this raises a tricky identification issue in terms of the selection lambda that is derived from the employment probit for inclusion in the earnings equation. There are two factors that lead us to suspect that this is not a problem in our estimations. First, age would seem to be important in the employment–unemployment equation, whereas potential experience (and potential experience squared) would appear to be the more relevant age-related variable for the earnings function. Thus, age effects are specified differently in the two equations. Second, the lambda carried through into the earnings equation incorporates the first lambda from the participation equation as an identifying explanatory variable. This lambda is an additional variable in the employment equation.

Data issues

Thus, there seems to be a comforting degree of agreement between tidy econometric practice and the type of labour market that we estimate in order to capture the key aspects of labour market vulnerability in South Africa. However, it would be disingenuous of us not to conclude this section by clearly spelling out the constraints that the data have imposed on our modelling. One key limitation is the inability to use the survey data to demarcate clearly an informal and a formal sector. Models of segmentation in developing countries give explicit attention to these earnings segmentations (Glick & Sahn 1997, Heckman & Hotz 1986 and Andersson, undated). We cannot do this.[3]

Yet descriptive analysis highlights the fact that, for Africans, self-employment clearly offers inferior earnings. However, further analysis showed that it was African female domestic workers who dominated this self-employment category (Bhorat 1999). As we are estimating separate earnings equations by gender with full sets of sectoral and occupational dummy variables and an explanatory variable for hours worked, this self-employment effect will be adequately captured in the female earnings equations.

Our participation equation is also far from perfect. It is common to define potential labour market participants by age (16–65). This is the definition used in earlier descriptive analyses in this book. However, if we follow through with this definition here, then the non-participant subsample is dominated by young adults who are still in education. It might be the case that some young adults are staying in school because of poor employment prospects in the labour market. However, given South Africa's high repetition rates and educational backlogs, the routine school-leaving age is also well above sixteen years. Such people are not potential labour market participants. That said, it would be distortionary to deal with this issue by raising the age of labour market participants as not all young adults are in school. Indeed, this same age cohort represents a high youth unemployment problem that is a key facet of the modelling work. Thus, our solution is to remove all people who are in education from the sample.

This significantly reduces the subsample of non-participants. As Table 4.1 illustrates, the number of participants enrolled in education is just over four million, accounting for close to one-quarter of all potential African labour market participants. In our derivation of labour market participants, then, we firstly exclude those in the last three categories, being either retired, permanently disabled or unclassified.

For African females, there remain a large number of non-participants who are engaged in home production, but there are very few males in this category. The structure of the

TABLE 4.1

African participants, by type of activity

Activity	Male	Female	Total
Working full-time	3 597 992	2 009 485	5 607 477
	42,71%	22,29%	32,15%
Working part-time	245 596	294 602	540 198
	2,92%	3,27%	3,10%
With a job, but absent from work	39 512	30 360	69 872
	0,47%	0,34%	0,40%
Going to school/university/college	2 061 942	2 039 084	4 101 026
	24,48%	22,62%	23,51%
Unemployed (looking for work)	1 677 274	1 981 823	3 659 097
	19,91%	21,98%	20,98%
Not working, not looking for work	293 627	678 380	972 007
	3,49%	7,52%	5,57%
Housekeeping	21 096	1 337 700	1 358 796
	0,25%	14,84%	7,79%
Retired (pensioner)	253 188	431 601	684 789
	3,01%	4,79%	3,93%
Permanently unable to work	233 189	211 216	444 405
	2,77%	2,34%	2,55%
Other	1 060	2 224	3 284
	0,01%	0,02%	0,02%
Total	8 424 476	9 016 475	17 440 951
	100%	100%	100%

questionnaire is such as to classify all male non-labour market activity as self-employment, to impute earnings to these activities and to include such males as unregistered self-employed earners. With the removal of African individuals in education, the subsample of non-participants as a whole drops to 12 207 447, or 70% of the size of the original sample. Out of this narrower sample, then, 11% of the activities undertaken involve home production. Of this 11%, the overwhelming majority (98%) of participants are female.

The above decisions taken in dividing the sample of African participants have the following import for our modelling:

- When the broad definition of unemployment is adopted, we have a very small subsample of male non-participants, and the female subsample consists exclusively of those engaged in home production.

- When we adopt the narrow definition of unemployment, male non-participants are dominated by discouraged workers and female non-participants are a mix of discouraged workers and women engaged in home production.

There is one final data difficulty in the participation equation. It is not possible to attribute children to specific parents. We include a variable capturing the number of children in the household, but this is certainly only a loose proxy for the influence of own children on participation.

Model results

Tables 4.2 to 4.4 present the influence of the different covariates on the probability of participation and employment, as well as on the level of earnings of the employed. For the covariates which are dummies, the following are the referent variables:

- Location:Urban
- Age:16–24
- Province:Western Cape
- Sector:Agriculture
- Occupation:Farm worker
- Union status:Union member

As explained above, the equations are all run for African individuals only. In addition, separate male and female equations are estimated for both the expanded and strict definitions of unemployment. The key results for participation, employment and earnings, respectively, are presented in Tables 4.2, 4.3 and 4.4. Table A-9 through Table A-14 in the Appendix represent the output when all of these models are re-estimated separately for rural and urban areas.

Participation equation

Table 4.2 presents the results from the participation decision in the labour market. The urban dummy variable is significant for females, but not for males, across both the narrow and expanded definitions of unemployment. Hence, for females, living in an urban area increases the probability of participating in the labour market, while for males location has no bearing on their participation decision. Further evidence in this regard comes from the Table A-8 and Table A-9 in the Appendix. These tables present results for male and female participation equations in urban and rural areas. The coefficients in the male equations in both urban and rural areas are very similar to each other and to the coefficients in the aggregate model. It would seem that there are no noteworthy differences in male participation in urban and rural areas. However, this is not always the case with African females, and we will highlight these differences in our discussion below.

The education splines suggest that schooling is an important variable in determining whether or not individuals participate in the labour market. For African males, according to the expanded definition, both primary schooling and secondary schooling have a positive bearing on the participation decision. Surprisingly, having tertiary education docs not appear to influence the decision to participate or not. This insignificance could be due to the relatively small share of African males with tertiary education (6,5%), coupled with the fact that this level of education will not determine a decision of whether to enter the labour market or not. However, with a switch to the narrow definition of unemployment and the consequent reclassification of the discouraged workers as non-participants, all three splines become significant. The significant tertiary variable here implies that tertiary education greatly increases the probability of being employed or of being an active job seeker relative to being one of the discouraged work-seekers who now dominate the non-participants.

For females, the education splines are slightly different. Only secondary education is significant for the expanded definition, while for the narrow definition, secondary and tertiary schooling is significant. As with males, a small percentage of females have tertiary education. Remembering that the non-participants here include discouraged work-seekers, the data shows that of the female non-participants by the narrow definition, only 1% have tertiary education compared to 11% for participants. Again, the possession of secondary or tertiary education does distinguish females who are employed or actively searching for employment from those who do not participate.

The above suggests that education is important in determining whether an individual participates or not. However, its significance seems to increase when using the narrow definition of unemployment. This is manifested in much better educational qualifications amongst participants relative to non-participants when non-participants are dominated by discouraged work-seekers.

The age dummy variables are all significant, barring the case of females 46–55 under the expanded definition. In addition, all significant coefficients have the same positive sign, barring the case of females 56–65 under the expanded definition. In other words, the age dummies suggest that the probability of participation increases for all age cohorts relative to the youngest cohort, namely 16–25 years. This is not a surprising result, as those adults who are older are more likely to have a job or to be seeking a job, irrespective of the definition of unemployment used. However, the fact that this age effect strengthens with a move to the narrow definition of unemployment is alarming, as it suggests that a significant proportion of the youth cohort are discouraged work-seekers.

While not presented in Table 4.2, the equation also included a full set of provincial dummy variables. These dummies generally had similar results across the genders and definitions. Provinces with significant results were the Northern Cape, KwaZulu-Natal, North West,

TABLE 4.2

African male and female labour participation equations for expanded and narrow definitions of unemployment

	Male				Female			
	Expanded		Narrow		Expanded		Narrow	
	Marginal effects	x-bar	Marginal effects	x-bar	Marginal effects	x-bar	Marginal effects	x-bar
Urban	0,0099	0,504329	0,0072	0,504329	0,1418*	0,390973	0,1321*	0,390973
None–Grade 3	0,0029*	4,43131	0,004**	4,43131	0,0027	4,20941	0,0030	4,20941
Grade 4–8	0,0052*	1,44132	0,0159*	1,44132	0,0517*	1,27643	0,0568*	1,27643
Tertiary	0,00241	0,105839	0,0161*	0,105839	–0,0231	0,103659	0,0115**	0,103659
26–35	0,05796*	0,349291	0,13893*	0,349291	0,09665*	0,342574	0,1309*	0,342574
36–45	0,07255*	0,248674	0,18949*	0,248674	0,07898*	0,252344	0,1831*	0,252344
46–55	0,05132*	0,143162	0,1616*	0,143162	–0,0115	0,149113	0,1371*	0,149113
56–65	0,01766*	0,053417	0,1440*	0,053417	–0,12882*	0,050201	0,0781*	0,050201
No. of children under 7 years	0,00166	0,785774	0,0060	0,785774	–0,02125*	1,11372	00258*	1,11372
No. of children aged 8–15	–0,00156	0,878397	–0,0095*	0,878397	–0,00989*	1,14248	0,0168**	1,14248
No. of males aged 16–59	–0,009189*	1,96432	–0,0317*	1,96432	–0,00988*	1,33687	–0,0164*	1,33687
No. of females aged 16–59	–0,00937*	1,51446	–0,0259*	1,51446	0,02978*	2,15132	0,0116*	2,15132
No. of adults over 60 years	–0,03313*	0,319228	–0,0958*	0,319228	–0,00307	0,34587	–0,0381*	0,34587
Other household income	6,12e–07*	17 352	–9,90e–07*	17 352	–2,24e–06*	20 880,8	–9,73e–07*	20 880,8
Other household income squared	2,75e–12*	1,1e+09	7,16e–12*	1,1e+09	2,44e–12*	2,0e+09	4,83e–13*	2,0e+09
Observed probability	0,91173		0,7753		0,6584		0,4865	
Predicted probability (at x-bar)	0,9348		0,80972		0,6773		0,4878	
Number observed	15 658		15 658		19 548		19 548	
Chi^2	1 084*		2 450		2 190		2 144*	
Pseudo R^2	0,1120		0,1426		0,0870		0,0792	

* Significant at the 1% level.
** Significant at the 5% level.

Mpumalanga and the Northern Province. The referent province was the Western Cape. In each of these cases, being in the respective province decreased the probability of participating in the labour market relative to those in the Western Cape. All of these provinces have a higher percentage of rural economically active than the Western Cape. For the narrow definition, these results also pick up the much larger number of discouraged work-seekers in these provinces relative to the Western Cape.

The household block of variables includes two 'number of children' variables, three 'number of adults' variables and two 'household income' covariates. Here, the gender biases of child rearing become immediately evident. For males, the number of children of any age in a home is insignificant in determining their participation decision. For females, however, it is clearly established that the greater the number of children under the age of seven or between the ages of eight and fifteen, the less the probability of their participation in the labour market.

With the exception of adults older than 60 in the female expanded equation, the 'number of adults' variables are all significant. What is interesting, though, is that in most cases the coefficients are negative. This indicates that the presence of a greater number of adults in the household acts as a deterrent to participation in the labour market. For females, though, the signs are positive when considering the number of female adults aged 16–59 in the home. In other words, by both definitions of unemployment, females are more likely to participate in the labour market the larger the number of working-age women in the home. This fact may be picking up those women involved in home production, who, because they will not be participating, cause other females to participate in the labour market. The more working-age males in the home, though, the less likely are women to participate.

While the larger the number of aged in the home causes the probability of participation to fall for males by both definitions, this is not true for females. For females, the expanded definition estimate is insignificant, while the narrow definition is significant. These results in general suggest that for males and females, the presence of an aged person (in all likelihood, a pensioner) acts as a deterrent to participation in the labour market.

Finally, the household income variables are both significant across genders and definitions, with the same negative sign. It is evident that the greater the value of other household income available to an individual, male or female, in a household, the more likely it is to reduce the probability of their participation in the labour market. In other words, access to income within a household is an important determinant in an individual's decision to participate. However, the small but positive values for the household income squared coefficients suggest that effect is dampened as income increases.

Table A-9 and Table A-12 in the Appendix show that, in a few key areas, the aggregate female participation patterns that we have discussed above have blurred important rural–urban differences. We highlight two cases. First, the education results for urban females are stronger than for the whole sample of females. Thus, for urban women under the expanded definition, only primary schooling is significant in increasing the probability of participation. For the narrow definition, all three educational splines are significant. This would suggest that, for urban women, their educational qualifications are a more important determinant of their decision to participate, when compared with the sample of all females. Second, for urban women, the presence of children between the ages of eight and fifteen is not significant in determining participation, across either definitions of unemployment. This would suggest that in urban labour markets, women are less likely to give up a job or stop searching for a job due to older children being in the home. It may also reflect a work life-cycle phenomenon, in which women re-enter the labour market after rearing the children at home. Noticeably, this is a purely urban characteristic, as this variable is negative and significant for rural females.

Employment equation

Having considered the determinants of participation, we retain the sample of those individuals who decide to participate, and in turn estimate the probability that these participants will find a job. The results from the employment probit are presented in Table 4.3. Maintaining consistency with the participation models, we also estimated separate employment equations for urban and rural areas. These estimations are reported in Table A-10 and Table A-13, respectively, of the Appendix. Note that there were too few narrowly unemployed females in urban areas for the urban, female employment equation to generate a set of estimated coefficients.

Many of the variables in the employment equation are the same as those included in the participation equation. However, we do not include household structure or household income variables in the employment equation. As discussed earlier in this chapter, the employment equation is set up to capture the rationing process through which jobs are allocated to some of those who are seeking work. The household variables are seen to influence the decision to seek work but not the process of finding employment.

We begin with the last variable first. The coefficients for lambda are significant for males and females for the narrow definition, but under the expanded definition, only for males. Lambda represents the inverse Mills ratio, and is a measure of the selectivity bias in the sample. The significant results suggest that sampling bias did exist in the sample and needed to be corrected for through the inclusion of lambda. Labour market participants do not look like a random sample chosen from all of the economically active population. This difference is particularly acute when participants are defined based on the narrow definition of unemployment.

The location results show that, for African males across both definitions, living in an urban area reduces the probability of being employed. For females, the result also holds for the narrow definition of unemployment. Given that employment opportunities present themselves overwhelmingly in urban areas, the negative coefficients would seem to be surprising. Table A-10 and Table A-13 in the Appendix allow us to unpack this a little further. These tables contain figures for the actual and estimated probabilities of employment in urban and rural areas, respectively. It can be seen that both of these probabilities are very close for urban and rural areas. The predicted probabilities of employment are based on an average set of characteristics for urban or rural work-seekers, respectively. The mean values for all variables shown in Table A-10 and Table A-13 indicate that the average rural work-seeker is not as well-educated or as well-located as the average urban work-seeker. The marginal effect of the urban–rural dummy variable in Table 4.3 is based on an average set of characteristics for the *combined* urban and rural sample. Thus, it assesses the probability of employment for an average worker who has characteristics that lie in between those reflected in the separate urban and rural estimations. This worker has less favourable attributes than the average urban worker does and, *for such a person*, rural areas offer a higher probability of employment.

The case of female participants under the expanded definition appears to offer an important exception. Table A-10 and Table A-13 show that the actual and predicted probabilities of being employed are close to 10% higher in urban areas than in rural areas, and the urban–rural dummy variable in Table 4.3 is positive – reflecting a higher probability of employment in the urban areas. However, even here, the urban–rural dummy variable is not statistically significant. This reflects the fact that an African female with average aggregate characteristics would have better characteristics than the rural average and worse than the urban average. She would therefore have a higher than 50% chance of employment in rural areas and a lower than 60% chance of employment in urban areas.

TABLE 4.3

African male and female employment equations for expanded and narrow definitions of unemployment

| | Male | | | | Female | | | |
| | Expanded | | Narrow | | Expanded | | Narrow | |
	Marginal effects	x-bar	Marginal effects	x-bar	Marginal effects	x-bar	Marginal effects	x-bar
Urban	–0,08119*	0,518166	–0,06044*	0,536173	0,01502	0,470573	–0,11547*	0,512476
None–Grade 3	–0,01214*	4,46674	–0,00877*	4,49146	–0,00381**	4,4932	–0,00940*	4,58104
Grade 4–8	0,00911	1,46147	0,00007	1,49287	0,03556*	1,53057	–0,02063*	1,66111
Tertiary	0,04735*	0,108512	0,03623*	0,116307	0,14162*	0,126277	0,15301*	0,153247
26–35	0,00314	0,356938	–0,00214	0,357391	0,2068*	0,378007	0,08557*	0,370626
36–45	0,05499*	0,261804	0,01259	0,27969	0,35464*	0,259706	0,16435*	0,278516
46–55	0,11750*	0,146699	0,04410*	0,156069	0,38832*	0,129088	0,2040*	0,143411
56–65	0,25410*	0,049023	0,09665*	0,053912	0,41972*	0,033449	0,23622*	0,039938
Eastern Cape	–0,06235**	0,12238	0,04477**	0,108051	–0,12400*	0,162958	0,05221	0,15373
Northern Cape	0,00402	0,01065	–0,02210	0,01137	–0,0151	0,007157	0,02185	0,007811
Free State	–0,00515	0,087579	0,07063*	0,089931	0,03244	0,089192	0,0729**	0,091194
KwaZulu-Natal	0,03850	0,192919	0,02811	0,192312	–0,04242**	0,221515	0,05947	0,225838
North West	–0,01404	0,115938	0,04595**	0,115271	–0,04376	0,098021	0,09928*	0,093327
Gauteng	0,05342*	0,249739	0,04712*	0,268261	0,00861	0,193928	0,03198	0,219473
Mpumalanga	–0,0207	0,092567	0,06406*	0,090007	–0,08506*	0,0792	0,07478**	0,071484
Northern Province	0,08420*	0,08616	0,08594*	0,079052	–0,17369*	0,118059	0,06257*	0,10429
Lambda	–1,4131*	0,156201	–0,43850*	0,329335	0,0018	0,502512	–0,44005*	0,740367
Observed probability	0,7173043		0,8434		0,5460		0,73894	
Predicted probability (at x-bar)	0,7419969		0,8740		0,55423		0,76711	
No observation	14 203		11 931		12 810		9 426	
Chi^2	2 677*		1 585		1 902		1 245	
Pseudo R^2	0,1483		0,1548		0,1078		0,1156	

* Significant at the 1% level.
** Significant at the 5% level.

The education splines firstly show that, across both genders and definitions, the possession of primary schooling or less reduces the probability of finding employment. Indeed, for females by the narrow definition, this negative coefficient holds for secondary schooling as well. In contrast, the coefficient for tertiary education is positive across both genders and definitions. Collectively, the education splines indicate that individuals with lower levels of education have less of a chance of getting a job than those with high-level, and specifically tertiary, education. This analysis confirms time-series labour demand analysis done elsewhere on the South African labour market. Such studies indicate that labour demand patterns reflect a growing demand for higher-skilled labour, and stagnant or declining demand for less skilled workers (Bhorat & Hodge 1998).

The age variables, as with the previous equation, are not surprising, as they show an increased probability of employment in older age cohorts relative to those in the 16–25 group. This reflects the large number of youth who are unemployed. The insignificant results for all except one age cohort for males by the narrow definition may be picking up the large number of discouraged work-seekers who are fairly evenly distributed across these age groups. The provincial results are mixed. Some of the provinces, such as the Northern Cape and KwaZulu-Natal, yield mostly insignificant results. However, African males in Gauteng have a greater probability of finding employment than their counterparts in the Western Cape. The parallel coefficients for females, though, are insignificant. The Northern Province, one of the poorest provinces in the country, yields positive coefficients except for females by the expanded definition. One factor that may be influencing these results is the large coloured labour force in the Western Cape, which means a much lower share of African employment in the province relative to the rest of the country. Indeed, while the Western Cape accounts for 14% of total employment in the country, the province accounts for only 3% of African employment.

We have already referred to the separate urban and rural employment estimations that are presented in Table A-10 and Table A-13 in the Appendix. We conclude this section by noting further interesting results from these tables. For males, for example, secondary education is seen to be important in predicting employment in urban labour markets. The insignificance of secondary education in the aggregate male employment equations therefore reflects the lack of significance of secondary education in rural areas. Contrary to these mixed results for secondary schooling, across all four equations in both urban and rural areas, tertiary education is crucial in predicting employment. Noticeably, the effect of primary schooling or less is weaker in rural areas. The location cuts also show more consistent results for the provincial dummies. Along with Gauteng, the Western Cape is seen to be the most favourable location for rural work-seekers. However, this is not as clear-cut for urban work-seekers, especially when discouraged unemployed are not included as labour market participants.

The earnings function

Table 4.4 presents the earnings function for all those employed, by gender and again by the two definitions of unemployment. The move from narrow to expanded definition of unemployment does not affect the classification of earners but only the sample selection variable (lambda) in the earnings function. Thus, the results of the estimations do not and would not be expected to differ much by the choice of narrow versus expanded unemployment. However, as employment and earnings were estimated together in one maximum-likelihood process, we continue to report the two sets of earnings estimates. Once again, we report disaggregated urban–rural equations in Table A-11 and Table A-14 of the Appendix. In all estimations, earnings are measured by the log of the monthly total wage earned by individuals, which is the manner in which the survey reported total pay.

From the results, it is clear that being in an urban area increases the earnings of the employed. It is an effect that holds true for males and females and for both definitions of unemployment. The education splines are particularly interesting. They show that, for African males and females, each year of primary schooling and secondary schooling is important in increasing earnings, but that each year of tertiary education is not. Table A-11 and Table A-14 in the Appendix show that the insignificant impact of tertiary education holds true for the disaggregated urban and rural estimates as well. Hence, while tertiary education has been shown to be crucial in determining whether an African individual gains employment, it is not relevant in predicting the level of earnings. Notice that the rates of return to secondary schooling are in each case higher than the returns to primary schooling or less. Hence the return to earnings of one additional year of secondary schooling ranges from 8,1 to 10,9%, while in the primary schooling case, the figures are 3,5% and 5,1%. Furthermore, the returns to males on secondary education are higher than for females, but lower than females in the case of primary education. Males also get higher returns to education in urban areas than in rural areas, but the returns to females do not appear to differ in this way.

The provincial dummies show that African individuals in the Eastern Cape, Northern Cape and Free State, in all cases, are likely to earn less than their counterparts in the Western Cape. The differential ranges from about 11% for males in the Eastern Cape to 56% for females in the Free State. The coefficients for both males and females appear to be relatively insensitive to the two unemployment definitions. The Northern Province is the only other province where the results are all significant. However, in this case, the coefficients are all positive. This seems contrary to poverty estimates of the province which place it far below the Western Cape. However, what this may suggest is that for the African employed, the Northern Province offers better earnings potential than the Western Cape. Indeed the mean wage in the Western Cape is only about half that of employees in the Northern Province. The urban–rural estimates add needed detail to this picture. It is not the Northern Province as a whole that offers better earnings but

TABLE 4.4

African male and female earnings equations for expanded and narrow definitions of unemployment

	Male		Female	
	Expanded unemployment	Narrow unemployment	Expanded unemployment	Narrow unemployment
Urban	0,1192892*	0,1294798*	0,1780*	0,1912*
None–Grade 3	0,034631*	0,0357029*	0,0488*	0,0514*
Grade 4–8	0,1087725*	0,1078169*	0,0816*	0,0927*
Tertiary	0,0367241	0,0312919	0,0234	0,0318
Eastern Cape	–0,1070717*	–0,1116288*	–0,1117**	–0,1465*
Northern Cape	–0,155832*	–0,147461*	–0,2329*	–0,2267*
Free State	–0,3030291*	0,3149274*	–0,5577*	–0,5694*
KwaZulu-Natal	0,0350547	0,0377735	0,0538	0,0411
North West	–0,0153048	–0,0194882	–0,0891	–0,1180**
Gauteng	0,0536299	0,052913	0,1422**	0,1357**
Mpumalanga	–0,0353655	–0,0467185	0,1254**	0,0945
Northern Province	0,1192166*	0,1087125*	0,2051*	0,1613*
Mining	0,607814*	0,6068056*	0,2840**	0,2831**
Manufacturing	0,6394293*	0,643446*	0,2494*	0,2535*
Electricity	0,8829402*	0,8850715*	0,5171*	0,5237*
Construction	0,4777885*	0,4826215*	0,3753*	0,3761*
Wholesale trade	0,5040102*	0,5100534*	0,1957**	0,1995*
Transport	0,7384904*	0,7407738*	0,5106*	0,5179*
Finance	0,6486260*	0,6500433*	0,4674*	0,4708*
Community and social services	0,677428*	0,6803405*	0,3619*	0,3653*
Other	–0,2943609*	–0,291168*	0,2713*	0,2735*
Armed forces	0,5296329*	0,5256727*	0,7866	0,7881
Managers	0,7602302*	0,767167*	0,9501*	0,9552*
Professionals	0,7286019*	0,7230151*	1,029*	1,031*
Technicians	0,4671531*	0,4656222*	0,9203*	0,9212*
Clerks	0,2231234*	0,2237144*	0,5926*	0,5953*
Service and sales	0,1635076*	0,163773*	0,3514*	0,3532*
Skilled agricultural workers	0,1874371*	0,1916955*	0,0711	0,0797
Craft workers	0,1862878*	0,1865975*	0,2341*	0,2371*
Machine operators	0,1460807*	0,1461151*	0,3355*	0,3383*
Unspecified	–0,0151913	–0,0098603	0,1577	0,1641
Domestic helpers	–0,0466067*	–0,0482176	0,2067*	0,2073*
Mining labourers	–0,0668179**	–0,0656155	0,2000	0,2033
Manufacturing labourers	–0,0591869*	–0,0579945*	0,2727*	0,2732*
Transport labourers	–0,0401749	–0,0409864	–0,2676	–0,2347
Domestic workers	–0,8043337*	–0,7996188*	–0,3591*	–0,3596*
Union members	0,1997917*	0,1941152*	0,2131*	0,2145*
Experience	0,033548*	0,0322203*	0,0194*	0,0220*
Experience squared	–0,000409*	–0,0003958*	–0,0002*	–0,0002*
Log of hours per month	0,1089995*	0,1036497*	0,1246*	0,1250*
Constant	5,543329*	5,601965*	4,838*	4,672*
Lambda	–0,139954*	–0,25413766*	–0,2660*	–0,2271*
Number observed	14 124	11 886	12 723	9 393
Model Chi^2	2 775*	1 687,44*	1 939,9*	1 284,5*

* Significant at the 1% level.
** Significant at the 5% level.

urban employment in the Northern Province. Indeed, for rural Northern Province and all other provinces, average earnings are significantly lower than in the Western Cape.

The sectoral dummies show a strong and clear pattern: relative to agriculture, all the African employed earn more on average. This result holds true for both males and females and according to both definitions. For males, the ranking of the largest wage differentials does not alter by unemployment definition. The sector which pays the most relative to agriculture is electricity, where individuals earn about 88% more than those in farming. This is followed by transport, community and social services and finance. The relatively low ranking of finance, given that it is nationally the highest-paying sector, is due to the low representation of African workers here. For females, though, finance does rank higher, although the differential – at about 47% – is lower. The ranking change for females is due to the low ranking of community services, where females earn only about 36% more than women in agriculture. This can be explained by the large number of female basic service workers, particularly domestic workers, in this sector. Note that for the two large employers in the economy, mining and manufacturing, male workers will tend to earn 60% or more than those in farming, while for females the differential is much smaller, at about 25%.

The results by occupation show that for the skilled occupations (managers, professionals and technicians), these individuals are likely to earn between 47 and 76% more than agricultural labourers. As we move to the semi-skilled occupations (clerks, service and sales, skilled agriculture, craft workers and machine operators), the differentials are smaller. Hence, for these occupations, individuals of identical characteristics earn between 15 and 22% more than farm workers. In the unskilled category, though, the results are slightly different and, in some cases, surprising. For females, household domestic workers earn about 36% less than farm workers. The coefficient for male labourers in manufacturing, though, is surprising. Male labourers in manufacturing are seen to earn about 6% less than male farm labourers. For females, though, manufacturing labourers earn more. Hence, it would seem that the often perceived higher wage for unskilled workers in manufacturing industry is driven by the wage differential between women, and not men, in these two sectors. One can see these same forces and a similar logic operating in the case of domestic helpers. The negative mining labourer coefficient for males (expanded definition) may reflect the fact that the mining industry's average skill levels have been increasing in the last decade. Hence those at the bottom have found their wages lagging in preference to those higher up in the internal labour market. Indeed many of the workers in the mining industry would be in the semi-skilled categories.

The union-wage effect is shown here to be about 20% for males and marginally higher, at 21%, for females. This is substantially lower than the cross-section estimate of Fallon and Lucas (1998), where the differential was over 50%. However, their time-series analysis delivered an estimate in the range of 25 to 35%, which is more in agreement with the number here. It cannot be doubted, though, that union membership is associated with significantly higher earnings for African workers. Table A-11 and Table A-14 in the Appendix reveal that there is a particularly strong union effect in rural areas. The union premium is about 23% for males and 30% for females.

The experience variable indicates that an additional year of experience generates a return to earnings of about 3% for African males. For African females, the return is lower, at about 2%. The log of hours worked is significant for both genders and definitions. The coefficients suggest that an increase in the percentage of hours worked will increase earnings by between 10 and 12%. This is quite important as it indicates that an important determinant of earnings is the hours that the African employed are working. Table A-11 in the Appendix suggests that, in urban areas in particular, the returns could be quite high should males or females opt to work more. This finding is particularly noteworthy, as the previous chapter has shown that nearly all of the earners in the sample are working close to a 40-hour week. Thus, this finding is not contingent on the presence in the sample of a significant number of part-time and infrequent workers.

Finally, as with the employment equation, the Mills ratio is shown to be significant and negative for all cases. There was therefore a sample selection bias, which was corrected for The sample of earners is not a random selection of people drawn from the pool of participants. The significance of lambda once again vindicates the selection procedure utilised here.

Conclusion

This study has tried to be as meticulous and transparent as possible in modelling the labour market. The short review of other models highlighted their strengths and drawbacks, while also offering the reasoning for the methodological approach taken here. Perhaps the strongest point to emerge from the methodological section was the insistence on a very carefully managed, three-phase labour market selection procedure, from participation to employment and then to earnings.

The participation equation showed that discouraged workers are statistically closer to the non-participants than to the narrowly unemployed. This strongly suggests that those searching for employment are more likely to get a job than those no longer searching, and therefore hints at the importance of structural unemployment in understanding the participation decision. What makes this finding so bleak is the fact that many of the youth are already in this non-searching category. Our employment analysis showed that the rural and urban unemployed have different characteristics but similar probabilities of getting employment. What is important about this is that it highlights an asymmetry. Urban work-seekers could take rural jobs but, on average, rural work-seekers do not have the characteristics to compete in the urban job market. Rural work-seekers should thus be looking for work in rural areas. This suggests also that spatial rigidities are essential to understanding employment creation in the domestic economy. The significance of the sample selection terms in the earnings functions also make it clear that those who get employment are different from those who try and do not. The key differences seem to be age and education.

Across the equations, the age and education variables are important determinants. The age results for the participation and employment equation reflect in different ways the importance of youth unemployment. In the participation equation, the older age cohorts all have a higher probability of participating than do the youth. In turn, the stronger effect in the narrow definition case points to the significant proportion of the youth who are discouraged job-seekers – a fact which has important policy ramifications. The employment probit again suggested that the youth were the least likely to gain employment relative to those in the older age cohorts. The operation of the labour market appears to be stacked against new entrants, and the only way to counteract this is for new entrants to embody characteristics that are significantly better than the average worker already in employment.

The education results showed very interesting variation across the three equations. Hence, while the non-tertiary education splines tend to be significant and positive in the participation equation, the non-tertiary splines are negative in the employment estimation. This suggests that while non-tertiary education levels tend to increase the probability of participation, these levels are not sufficient to ensure employment. This is a result that matches well with the economy's current and, in all likelihood, future labour demand patterns, where firms' specifications are directed primarily toward highly skilled workers in the economy. However, it is clear that for those who already have a job, the returns to schooling operate as expected, with secondary schooling yielding a higher rate of return than primary schooling. The fact that we have concentrated so heavily on the vulnerable was shown by the insignificant tertiary coefficient, indicating very low levels of schooling amongst the African workforce. Essentially, though, the results across the equations show that education levels operate differentially at each phase of the labour market process.

Through our use of a three-phase model and concentration on the most vulnerable in the labour market, this chapter has added value to the burgeoning earnings function literature on the South African labour market. In addition, the results obtained, particularly in the case of covariates such as location and education, offer some important background information for policy-makers interested in the problems of and solutions to long-term sustainable employment for the domestic economy.

Notes

1. The formal distinction between these two categories is extensively discussed in Chapter 3.

2. The ILO (1996) argues that there are so many discouraged workers that they must be doing something. In other words, the 'discouraged worker' category is an artifact of inaccurate survey work. This is a plausible argument for some survey data sets. However, as argued in Chapter 3 and in Bhorat (1999), the OHS 95 gives serious attention to these issues and we would therefore argue that the patterns are robust enough to accept. It is interesting to restate the central conclusion of our earlier review of the unemployment issue. In OHS 95, the 'discouraged worker' category is notably smaller than previous estimates but the narrow unemployment category is larger. This suggests that part of the inaccuracy of earlier survey work may have involved an inaccurate capturing of search activity.

3. Our review of Fallon and Lucas (1997) and Hofmeyr (1998) showed that the LSMS data is similarly flawed when it comes to an analysis of the informal sector. It would appear therefore that there is no data set that can be used to explore formal sector/informal sector interactions in South Africa. The problem of uncovering the informal sector in the OHS 95 data set is taken up in Chapter 3 and Bhorat (1999).

5

Household Incomes, Poverty and Inequality in a Multivariate Framework

Murray Leibbrandt
Ingrid Woolard[1]

In previous chapters, we have provided detailed descriptions of South African poverty and inequality, and used established poverty and inequality decomposition techniques to further the analysis. Wherever possible, we have tied our analysis to the role of the labour market. What remains is to provide a sense of the importance of the key correlates of poverty and inequality relative to one another. Is the provincial impact more important than the rural–urban divide in terms of location factors? Is it possible to compare the impact of state welfare assistance relative to educational interventions? Which education interventions seem to provide the best return? How large is the burden of unemployment on households? What contribution will employment creation make to household poverty and inequality?

All of these questions are important policy issues in South Africa, and this chapter provides a framework to address them. Such an exercise requires an integrated household earnings generation model which includes all of the key correlates and indicates the relative importance of each one. This necessitates a multivariate approach based on a model of the determinants of household income.

Such an approach is common in the labour economics field, where an earnings function serves as the basis for much of the empirical work that is done on the relative importance of various factors influencing individual earnings and earnings inequality (Willis 1987). However, we apply this approach to household incomes rather than individual earnings. There are far fewer precedents for such work (Glewwe 1991 and Ravallion 1996). The best-developed literature in this spirit uses binary dependent variable models to look at the factors determining whether households lie above or below a poverty line. These poverty regressions have been a standard part of any World Bank country poverty profile for the last ten years. However, such regressions form only part of what we need to do here. We are interested in four interrelated areas:

- the determinants of household income;
- whether these relationships are stable across deciles;
- the determinants of household poverty status (the poverty regression issue); and
- the contribution of explanatory factors to household income inequality.

Econometric issues

Estimation issues

The sequencing of these questions ties in well with the methodological approaches raised in previous chapters. We derived poverty and inequality indices and decompositions from a framework that started by focusing on the full distribution of household income, either in the form of a cumulative distribution function (poverty) or a Lorenz curve (inequality). Here, we start with household income before looking more closely at poverty and inequality. The estimation of the first three models requires the use of techniques that are well established in the literature and can therefore be briefly dealt with here. The fourth technique is new and will be discussed in more detail.

We motivate for the use of per capita income as the appropriate dependent variable. Having decided on this, we estimate the percentage contribution to per capita household income of our explanatory factors by regressing the log of household per capita income on these factors.[2] This is a household analogue to the literature on individual earnings functions. The estimates are presented in Table 5.1. Household incomes are definitely not normally distributed in South Africa, but are closer to being log-normal. This provides one justification for the use of a logged form of the dependent variable (Willis 1996). However, the ordinary least squares procedure gives heavy weighting to the mean values of the dependent and explanatory variables in estimating coefficients. Again, the fact that the distribution of income is generally skewed and that our particular interest is in understanding factors operating in the bottom of the distribution make this weighting problematic.

Quantile regressions provide estimates that tell us whether relationships are stable across deciles. In doing so, they provide a check on the ordinary least squares estimates. Quantile regressions estimate a conditional quantile. That is, given a set of explanatory factors and a position in the error distribution, what is the predicted income? Thus, median regression, the most common quantile regression, gives the best estimate of the relation between x and y for households at the median of the conditional error distribution. The 10% quantile regression gives the best estimate of the relation between *x* and *y* for households at the tenth percentile of the conditional error distribution, and so on (Rousseeuw & Leroy 1987 and StataCorp 1997).[3]

The third area focuses more explicitly on the contribution of our explanatory factors to allocating households above and below the poverty line. This is the standard poverty regression issue. We estimate a series of probit models here.[4] The coefficients from these models are difficult to interpret, and we therefore always report a set of marginal effect estimates for each coefficient. These marginal effects are estimated holding all other variables at their mean value.

Technically speaking, the fourth area is the most challenging. There is some international work in this area that has made use of sets of surveys conducted over time.[5] These data have enabled researchers to throw light on factors driving household income inequality by focusing on the *changes* to static decomposition results over time. Unfortunately, we do not have a set of reliable surveys over time in South Africa, and so we will stick to the use of the 1995 October Household Survey and its accompanying Income and Expenditure Survey. Fortunately, there have been two major advances in recent years. At the moment, these are only reflected in unpublished work (Fields 1998 and Bourguignon *et al.* 1998). Both of these approaches are much more promising than any preceding methods. In this study, we will focus on the Fields approach.

Fields frames his work in terms of two questions: the levels question and the differences question. The levels question seeks a precise method of attributing shares of income inequality to the chosen set of explanatory factors. The differences question seeks to pin down the contribution of each explanatory factor to *changes* in inequality between groups.

In the present context, the levels question estimates the contribution of a range of explanatory factors to the inequality of household per capita income in models covering all South African households (Table 5.5), white households and African households (Table 5.6) and African urban and rural households (Table 5.7). A summary presentation of inequality shares in all households is given in Table 5.4. The differences question goes on to examine the role of these explanatory factors in explaining the differences in the income inequality patterns *between* white and African households (Table 5.6) and African urban and rural households (Table 5.7).

In addressing the levels question, we start with the standard ordinary least squares model of household income generation that we estimated in answering the first question. Fields shows that such a model can be used to carry out an exact decomposition of the contribution of all the variables in the model to the *variance* of log per capita income. In our model, Y_{it} is household per capita income. We use the same set of explanatory factors, $x_1 \ldots x_j$, as we have in addressing the first three areas. Using ordinary least squares regression, we estimate the coefficients, *aj*. The value of these coefficients reflects the percentage contribution that each factor makes to household per capita income. Clearly, this still focuses on the determinants of income and not income inequality. However, the heart of the Fields technique is to prove that an inequality share for each of the factors can be derived from the following formula:

$$s_j = \frac{\text{cov}[a_j Z_j, lnY]}{\sigma^2(lnY)}$$

$$= \frac{a_j \times \sigma(Z_j) \times \text{cor}[Z_j, lnY]}{\sigma(lnY)}$$

Strictly interpreted, this provides us with the share of factor Z_j in explaining inequality, as measured by the log variance. The elements of this formula are intuitive, showing that a factor may play a large role in explaining income inequality if:

- it has a large a_j; that is, it is an important factor in explaining earnings;
- it has a large standard deviation, $\sigma(Z_j)$; that is, it is a variable that is highly unequal itself; or
- it is highly correlated with the log of income, $\text{cor}[Z_j, lnY]$.

The presence of the standard deviation of lnY, $\sigma(lnY)$, in the denominator ensures that all of these effects are interpreted relative to the magnitude of the inequality in lnY.

Looking at Tables 5.4–5.7, we can see that, in some cases, the contribution of individual variables to inequality is represented, whereas in other cases the contribution of a block of variables to inequality is represented. Block contributions are simply derived by aggregating individual contributions.

The role of the residual requires some discussion. One strength of this regression-based methodology is the fact that the regression model generates a residual, which is treated as one of the factors contributing to inequality in lnY. In telling us what portion of the inequality in lnY is explained by the residual, we are implicitly being told what portion of inequality is left unexplained by our explanatory factors.

Finally, although log-variance is a recognised inequality measure, it is not one that enjoys routine usage. This is not a cause for concern, though, as Fields shows that the estimated shares that are derived using the log-variance are those that would be derived for a broad class of the most popular income distribution measures. Thus, the decomposition is very robust.

The differences question goes on to examine the role of these factors in explaining the differences in the income inequality patterns between two groups. Unfortunately, Fields shows that the differences question cannot be addressed in such a way that the answer is independent of the choice of inequality measure. For any chosen inequality measure $I(.)$, the contribution of the jth factor (including the residual) to the change in a particular inequality measure between country/group/time 1 and country/group/time 2 is expressed as follows:

$$\pi_j(I(.)) = [s_{j,2} \times I(.)_2 - s_{j,1} \times I(.)_1] / [I(.)_2 - I(.)_1]$$

It is an empirical question whether the choice of inequality measure makes a large difference or a small one in any particular context. Therefore, we use two inequality measures in our decomposition work: the Gini coefficient and the log-variance.

Choice of variables

The usefulness of the answers that we attain from any modelling is dependent on the formulation of a suitable household income generation equation. There are two aspects to suitability here. The first is that the right-hand-side variables provide the links that we need between households and the labour market. The second is econometric. It is difficult enough to formulate a suitable specification for individual earnings and near impossible to do so at the level of the household (Glewwe 1991). We make no pretence at deriving a structural model based on a careful analysis of household welfare and decision-making. Rather, we choose a variable set that is consistent with the South African inequality and poverty situation that we have sketched in the preceding chapters.[6] Then, we work hard to ensure econometric adequacy for our estimates (Ravallion 1996). Although our particular focus is on the role of the labour market, many variables make a contribution through the labour market or interact with the labour market variables. Therefore, the scope cannot be defined too narrowly. The estimations below all use the following variable set:

- *Household head*: South Africa has a history of migrant labour and divided families. This legacy is still very much with us, and female-headed households in rural areas are often regarded as the most vulnerable of all households. We therefore specify a dummy variable set that covers female and male, resident and absent possibilities. The household with a resident male head is the default.

- *Household composition*: In line with international findings, poorer households are generally larger than better-off households. In addition, poorer households usually have more children. As mentioned in the discussion of the household head, household composition was highly disrupted as households attempted to adjust to apartheid policies. Therefore, it is not adequate merely to flag household size (and household size squared) in the equations. We specify a set of variables capturing the numbers of children aged less than 7, children 8–15, females 16–59, males 16–59 and adults older than 60. These variables can be expressed as numbers or shares. We have tested and used both alternatives.

- *Locational and regional effects*: Earlier tables clearly showed that the incidence of poverty is far higher in South Africa's rural areas and particularly in the previously African areas. This is captured through a rural–urban dummy variable in which 'urban' takes on the value of 1. In addition, the best set of proxies for regional economies within South Africa are the nine provinces. We therefore include a full set of provincial dummy variables, with the Western Cape being the default.

- *Race*: Previous chapters have repeatedly flagged the importance of race as a dominant and lingering marker of both inequality and poverty. There are four race dummies, with African being the default.

- *Labour market factors*: The dominant theme of the earlier decomposition analyses in this book was the role of employment and unemployment in inequality and poverty. In this block, we therefore include variables capturing the extent of successful integration into wage or self-employment and the extent of the unemployment burden. To allow for the impact of migrant labour, we include a variable capturing the number of remitters providing remittance transfers into the household.

  These labour market variables are not dummy variables. Rather, two types of variables are constructed. First, the number of working, unemployed or absent migrant adults is used. Second, these numbers are converted into shares of the economically active adults in each household, and these shares are used. The shares of these three variables do not have to add up to 100%. As a rule, remitters are not counted as formal members of households. In addition, adult household members that are not participating in the labour market are neither employed or unemployed. Thus, only in the case of households with no migrants and full labour market participation by adults will the shares of employed and unemployed sum to 100%.

- *Education levels*: Education is key at both the individual and household levels. In 1995, and even today, the provision of education is overwhelmingly (especially for African and coloured groups) the responsibility of the state. We capture the influence of education through a set of variables covering adult household members with no education, primary, some secondary, completed secondary and any form of tertiary education. The completed secondary variable is important because secondary education ends with a standardised, national matriculation examination.

  As with the labour market variables, we reflect these educational variables either in terms of numbers of adults or in terms of shares of adults. In interpreting these education effects, the derivations are important. In the case of the number of adult household members with no education, all household members with some education are represented as a zero. For 75% of all households (99% of white households and 66% of African households) a zero (or a zero share) is recorded for this variable. The tertiary education variable has a similar pattern. In this case, 88% of African households have no adults with tertiary education, and therefore they record a zero share for this variable. The respective figure is 63% for white households.

- *Social welfare*: South Africa has an array of child maintenance grants, unemployment insurance schemes and universal state-funded old age pensions. As of 1995, and even today, the extent and coverage of child support schemes and unemployment insurance has been patchy. Pensions are by far the dominant form of social transfer in South Africa. We therefore include a variable capturing the number of old age pensioners in the household or the share of pensioners as a percentage of adults.

This variable list is not exhaustive. There are two major omissions. First, a potentially important labour market effect that is not explicitly captured in the models is the type of employment. International literature sometimes attributes sectoral and occupational varia-bles to households (Huppi & Ravallion 1991). This allocation of individual labour market characteristics to households is usually based on the labour market participation of the head of the household or the major earner in the household. Given that the survival strategies of South African households generally involve participation in a diverse array of activities, it is difficult to justify this practice here. Rather, one of our specifications estimates separate equations for rural and urban households. The major *a priori* reason why employment, unemployment and education coefficients would differ across these two estimations is because the labour markets differ by sector and occupation in urban and rural areas.

Second, aside from human capital, there is not a block of variables reflecting assets and wealth. The 1995 OHS and IES data do not contain very rich information on assets, and are particularly weak on the agricultural assets that are usually fully specified in developing coun-tries. One variable that is contained in the data is the valuation of the place of residence. When this variable is included in the models, it makes a very small contribution and has no impact on the values of the other coefficients. However, it needs to be acknowledged that the inclusion of this variable is only a limited exploration of possible interactions between assets and income generation.

Specification issues

In estimating our models, two specific econometric (and conceptual) issues arise. First, there are a range of possible interactions between household size and household composition and the other right-hand-side variables. Second, there are endogeneity issues that require attention.

We confront the first problem in a number of ways. First, we use per capita income as the left-hand-side variable in preference to total household income. We could have used income per adult equivalent instead of per capita income. However, we do not want to include the influence of household composition on the left-hand-side variable because we have included a full set of household composition factors on the right-hand side of all models. Finally, as observed when we defined our variables, we specify all models using numbers of household members as well as shares of the household.

Estimates are very sensitive to these choices between various household size and composi-tion blocks and between the use of numbers versus shares in defining education, labour market and welfare variables. The specification that is most successful in untangling the relationships between household composition, education, pensions and the labour market is one that retains a full household composition block as numbers and then uses shares for education and labour market and pensions blocks. We report these results in the discussion below.[7]

The second major econometric issue involves endogeneity on the right-hand side of the equation. Aside from race, none of the explanatory variables are truly independent. South Africa's history is such that race is certainly partly responsible for the movement in nearly all of the other right-hand-side variables. For example, in simple regressions of race on the education and labour market variables, the race dummies are always significant.

We acknowledge this problem by estimating our models for all households and then separately for African and white households. The estimations by race are interesting in their own right, as they provide useful information on the within-race determinants of income, poverty and inequality. Inspection of Table 5.1 reveals that the estimated coefficients for the 'all households' regression lie close to the African estimates and within the range implied by appropriate weighting of the separate African and white estimates. While this is not a rigorous control for the influence of race, dramatic changes that took the estimated coefficients outside of this range would certainly have implied a major endogeneity problem with race that is not adequately dealt with by the inclusion of race dummies.

Besides the racial factor, there are other endogeneity issues that require attention. An important labour market possibility is the fact that the labour market and education blocks may operate differently in urban and rural areas if urban and rural labour markets are very different. It is true that the estimated coefficients for all households and for African households change appreciably if the models are estimated without the urban–rural dummy variable. Thus, we always include this dummy variable or estimate separate equations for urban and rural areas. In order to ensure that this spatial effect is not wrapped up with the racial effects, we limit these rural–urban estimations to African households. Thus, in all models, the flow is from national households to African households and then to urban or rural African households.

The final endogeneity issue that we address concerns the influence of education on the labour market variables. It is not easy to think of an explicit control at the household level. The usual labour market procedure would be to handle the indirect impact of education on occupational attainment (for example) through a multinomial logit estimation of education on occupations. However, the labour market variables are not categorical, as the relevant variables are shares of adult household members that are employed or unemployed or remitters. A roughly analogous procedure to the multinomial logit is to regress all of the educational variables on each of the three labour market variables. This was done, and while some of the educational coefficients were significant, the R-squared coefficients for these models were very low indeed. An additional piece of evidence in support of this is derived by inspection of the last two columns of Table 5.1. These show that the impact of education on African household per capita income is very sensitive to separate rural–urban divisions, but that the labour market variables retain their consistency despite this.

In sum then, this section has laid out the case for a fairly simple, linear specification of our chosen variables as the basis for all of our modelling. We now proceed to address the four issues that we tabled at the beginning of this chapter with the help of four models that all use this specification.

Estimation, results and discussion: the important determinants of household income, poverty and inequality

Before we move on to a variable-by-variable discussion, there are a few general points to be made about the four models. When looking over Tables 5.1 and 5.2, it is noticeable that the median-based quantile estimates – based on the median of the error distribution – are generally quite close to the mean-dominated estimates derived by OLS. However, this is not true of the bottom-decile quantile case. The coefficients for this regression are usually lower than at the median or at the top decile. In African households, it is only the share of remitters and old age pensioners that offers an exception. Lower 'returns' to factors at the bottom of the error distribution hint at the fact that factors play a larger role where income is more widely dispersed. The factors therefore appear to be positively correlated with household income inequality. We will have more to say later on about such contributions to inequality.

The first thing to note about the poverty results of Table 5.3 is that the white model does not work well at all. This is a reflection of the fact that there are not enough poor white households in many of the categories to estimate the coefficients. On the other hand, the African model shows that, generally, the factors that are a positive influence on incomes are also positive influences on the probability of not being poor. Some factors show themselves to be more important in the poverty regression than in the full income models. Old age pensions in African households are an example of this.

For both African and white inequality models, there are substantial amounts of residual (unexplained) inequality (44% and 63%, respectively). As in the case of the poverty regressions, for white households in particular, we are left with the strong impression that we have not come to grips with the key factors driving inequality. It might well be that a focus on wealth and asset variables would be necessary to explain white inequality. While this is speculative, there is no denying the fact that that the within-race equations leave far more residual inequality than the 'all households' model (30% residual inequality) that explicitly deals with race through the racial dummy variables. This is also true of the African urban and African rural equations in which a large amount of the inequality (42,1% and 55,7%, respectively) is left unexplained. Thus, we seem to have a better model of all household income inequality in South Africa than within-race group inequality or African urban–rural inequality.

TABLE 5.1

The determinants of household income[a]

	Percentage contributions to household income (Ordinary least squares estimates on log per capita income)				
	All households	White	African	African urban	African rural
Head:					
Femres	−0,2701286	−0,305298	−0,2556111	−0,2040247	−0,293596
Femabs	−0,1709232	−0,1741878	−0,161133	−0,0551329	−0,2313877
Maleabs	0,1396368	0,0767289	0,1643966	0,1768707	0,1557935
Composition:					
Kid7	−0,1655144	−0,2724278	−0,1500638	−0,1692102	−0,1431333
Kid15	−0,1589389	−0,22314	−0,1479725	−0,1844129	−0,1336192
F16_59	−0,064871	−0,0924504	−0,0685099	−0,0706807	−0,0616601
M16_59	−0,048516	−0,0432652	−0,0493758	−0,0388929	−0,0519207
Ad60	0,0070972	−0,1528326	0,012329	−0,0311293	0,0341542
Province:					
Eastern Cape	−0,1615817	−0,0732565	−0,1120541	−0,0519413	−0,1851876
Northern Cape	−0,2101004	0,1728977	−0,2477614	−0,1297678	−0,6558229
Free State	−0,3017424	−0,1825402	−0,2846519	−0,1610042	−0,6839104
KwaZulu–Natal	0,091771	−0,0249695	0,1710477	0,1880675	−0,1776282
North West	−0,0413994	−0,0243796	0,0075066	0,0422307	−0,3501167
Gauteng	0,167128	0,1195842	0,2092098	0,2341174	−0,2290835
Mpumalanga	−0,0654942	−0,1153256	−0,0090146	−0,1568967	−0,2903379
Northern Province	0,0921316	0,0586052	0,1553172	0,2308377	−0,2055513
Urban	0,2386275	−0,2051718	0,2764435		
Race:					
Coloured	0,1652885				
Asian	0,4500624				
White	0,8450188				
Education:					
Shno_ed	0,0177529	0,6961734	0,0072023	0,1054994	−0,0387509
Shprim	0,0764243	0,2909542	0,0791113	0,1252036	0,0621953
Shsec	0,3641685	0,4393242	0,3187812	0,3098628	0,305834
Shmatric	0,5072614	0,4111087	0,5068706	0,5086073	0,4591706
Shtert	0,4202615	0,3251523	0,5269322	0,4554513	0,6646113
Labour market:					
Shwork	0,6812947	0,4659047	0,7659807	0,8308757	0,735619
Shunemp	−0,3260304	−0,3031824	−0,2934526	−0,3835213	−0,2292114
Shmig	0,1736706	0,3392358	0,1644313	0,1753879	0,1205743
Welfare:					
Shoap	0,0747939	−0,5387748	0,3447923	0,2879481	0,3781855
Cons	8,067799	9,433772	7,938406	8,10466	8,333174
	N = 28 578	N = 5 224	N = 18 476	N = 7 744	N = 10 732
	Prob > F = 0,000	Prob > F = 0,000	Prob > F = 0,000	Prob > F = 0,000	Prob > F = 0,000
	AdjR^2 = 0,70	AdjR^2 = 0,37	AdjR^2 = 0,56	AdjR^2 = 0,44	AdjR^2 = 0,37

[a] Bold coefficients are significant at the 1% level using unweighted sample data.

TABLE 5.2

The determinants of household earnings at different quantiles of the error distribution (shares)[a]

| | Quantile regression | | | | | | | | |
| | All households | | | African | | | White | | |
	Median	(0,1)	(0,9)	Median	(0,1)	(0,9)	Median	(0,1)	(0,9)
Head:									
Femres	**−0,26**	**−0,26**	**−0,32**	**−0,24**	**−0,24**	**−0,30**	**−0,29**	**−0,21**	**−0,39**
Femabs	**−0,17**	**−0,13**	**−0,24**	**−0,16**	**−0,12**	**−0,24**	**−0,14**	0,01	**−0,23**
Maleabs	**0,15**	**0,24**	0,09	**0,15**	**0,20**	0,12	0,10	0,20	0,03
Composition:									
Kid7	**−0,18**	**−0,17**	**−0,16**	**−0,16**	**−0,16**	**−0,14**	**−0,31**	**−0,29**	**−0,29**
Kid15	**−0,17**	**−0,17**	**−0,16**	**−0,16**	**−0,17**	**−0,15**	**−0,22**	**−0,23**	**−0,20**
F16_59	**−0,07**	**−0,08**	**−0,06**	**−0,07**	**−0,10**	**−0,06**	**−0,09**	−0,06	−0,11
M16_59	**−0,05**	**−0,06**	**−0,05**	**−0,06**	**−0,08**	**−0,04**	−0,04	−0,06	−0,05
Ad60	0,02	0,02	−0,02	0,02	**0,04**	−0,02	**−0,15**	**−0,18**	−0,12
Province:									
Eastern Cape	**−0,14**	**−0,16**	**−0,06**	**−0,11**	**−0,17**	−0,12	−0,07	−0,07	−0,17
Northern Cape	**−0,19**	**−0,28**	−0,11	**−0,16**	**−0,35**	−0,26	**−0,19**	**−0,22**	−0,16
Free State	**−0,34**	**−0,35**	**−0,20**	**−0,32**	**−0,37**	**−0,25**	**−0,23**	−0,10	−0,17
KwaZulu-Natal	**0,10**	**0,06**	0,16	**0,17**	0,10	0,14	−0,04	**−0,14**	−0,04
North West	−0,03	−0,07	**0,08**	0,00	−0,04	−0,02	−0,11	−0,10	0,09
Gauteng	**0,17**	**0,16**	**0,18**	**0,19**	**0,18**	0,09	**0,09**	**0,14**	0,02
Mpumalanga	−0,04	**−0,18**	0,07	0,02	**−0,18**	0,07	**−0,11**	0,03	**−0,27**
Northern Province	**0,09**	**−0,12**	**0,38**	**0,12**	**−0,13**	**0,37**	−0,06	0,03	0,013
Urban	**0,25**	**0,24**	**0,19**	**0,27**	**0,24**	**0,26**	**−0,14**	0,00	−0,77
Race:									
Coloured	**0,17**	**0,16**	**0,15**						
Asian	**0,43**	**0,50**	**0,55**						
White	**0,79**	**0,88**	**0,94**						
Education:									
Shno_ed	0,03	0,06	**0,00**	0,03	0,03	−0,02	0,86	**1,84**	0,04
Shprim	**0,07**	**0,12**	**0,08**	0,07	0,11	0,07	0,45	0,51	0,08
Shsec	**0,37**	**0,30**	**0,41**	**0,29**	**0,28**	**0,34**	0,17	**0,50**	0,22
Shmatric	**0,43**	**0,29**	**0,54**	**0,53**	**0,38**	**0,61**	**0,29**	**0,20**	**0,40**
Shtert	**0,54**	**0,50**	**0,57**	**0,62**	**0,41**	**0,59**	**0,35**	**0,42**	**0,46**
Labour market:									
Shwork	**0,68**	**0,71**	**0,62**	**0,79**	**0,68**	**0,74**	**0,51**	**0,68**	**0,27**
Shunemp	**−0,35**	**−0,38**	**−0,20**	**−0,28**	**−0,35**	**−0,15**	**−0,34**	**−0,51**	−0,07
Shmig	**0,19**	**0,17**	**0,14**	**0,18**	**0,22**	**0,11**	0,19	0,18	−0,09
Welfare:									
Shoap	**0,15**	0,00	0,05	**0,40**	**0,45**	0,18	**−0,52**	**−0,28**	**−0,54**
Cons	**8,05**	**7,35**	**8,80**	**7,93**	**7,38**	**8,74**	**9,45**	**7,99**	**11,31**
N =	28 583	28 583	28 583	18 481	18 481	18 481	5 224	5 224	5 224
R^2 =	0,41	0,44	0,36	0,00	0,27	0,33	0,22	0,25	0,17

[a] Bold coefficients are significant at the 1% level using unweighted sample data.

TABLE 5.3

The determinants of household poverty[a]

	Contributions to the probability of being poor (Probit marginal effects estimates at mean values)				
	All households	White	African	African urban	African rural
Head:					
Femres	**0,0781478**	**0,0219131**	**0,1136566**	**0,0373425**	**0,157935**
Femabs	**0,0497033**	0,0009678	**0,0745141**	−0,018173	**0,1414804**
Maleabs	**−0,0442584**	No poor households	**−0,0731561**	−0,0255452	**−0,0992155**
Composition:					
Kid7	**0,0313683**	−0,0000713	**0,0487308**	**0,0270438**	**0,0541386**
Kid15	**0,0271427**	0,0000927	**0,041356**	**0,0325001**	**0,0407004**
F16_59	**0,0300596**	0,0004054	**0,0482446**	**0,0333742**	**0,0471798**
M16_59	**0,0209923**	0,0000933	**0,0333056**	**0,017946**	**0,0366794**
Ad60	−0,0040401	0,0000364	0,0025527	**0,0123253**	−0,0050099
Province:					
Eastern Cape	**0,1273211**	0,0000488	**0,1081468**	**0,0489737**	**0,386569**
Northern Cape	**0,1421202**	0,0002972	**0,1319067**	**0,0425478**	**0,3694423**
Free State	**0,2431827**	−0,0001416	**0,2410857**	**0,0827216**	**0,4602548**
KwaZulu-Natal	−0,030258	0,0006555	**−0,1136445**	**0,0783361**	**0,1881312**
North West	**0,065554**	−0,0004	0,026282	**0,0221716**	**0,2995115**
Gauteng	**−0,0529552**	−0,0000628	**−0,1514906**	**−0,1175519**	**0,2343683**
Mpumalanga	**0,0409939**	No poor households	−0,0023541	**0,0693216**	**0,2528469**
Northern Province	−0,0090761	No poor households	**−0,0744267**	−0,0402356	**0,2264175**
Urban	**−0,1129563**	**−0,0021825**	**−0,1653923**		
Race:					
Coloured	**−0,060042**				
Asian	**−0,1206235**				
White	**−0,204393**				
Education:					
Shno_ed	−0,0195861	No poor households	−0,0370429	**−0,1045847**	0,0118241
Shprim	**−0,0487069**	No poor households	**−0,0716319**	**−0,0946805**	−0,0431914
Shsec	**−0,1347915**	−0,0007906	**−0,2072631**	**−0,1246659**	**−0,2074922**
Shmatric	**−0,1780758**	−0,0003662	**−0,2896607**	**−0,1680733**	**−0,3226574**
Shtert	**−0,1150711**	−0,0003629	**−0,1861881**	**−0,1513875**	**−0,1750088**
Labour market:					
Shwork	**−0,2817501**	−0,0012705	**−0,4445696**	**−0,3294419**	**−0,4563091**
Shunemp	**0,1094686**	0,0008389	**0,1611013**	**0,1513047**	**0,114812**
Shmig	**−0,0614882**	No poor households	**−0,1003269**	**−0,0736301**	**−0,0914207**
Welfare:					
Shoap	**−0,1600474**	0,0009599	**−0,3029865**	**−0,2021589**	**−0,304651**
Cons					
	N = 28 578	N = 4 485	N = 18 476	N = 7 744	N = 10 732
Prob > Chi^2 =	0,000	0,000	0,000	0,000	0,000
PseudoR^2 =	0,39	0,31	0,29	0,32	0,21

[a] Bold coefficients are significant at the 1% level using unweighted sample data.

In the 'all households' estimations of the *head of household* block, the female coefficients have the anticipated signs and values. Relative to having a male head that resides at home, average household income (per capita) is 27% lower if there is a female head at home and 17% lower there is a female head working away from home. Households with an absent male head earn 14% more on average. The poverty probabilities are consistent with this, in that households with resident female heads increase the probability of being poor by 7,8% relative to households with resident male heads.

The above picture remains consistent across races and deciles although the respective coefficient magnitudes vary. It is noteworthy that the disadvantage associated with a resident female head relative to a resident male head is particularly acute in African rural households and in white households. The former finding is expected, given the conventional picture of disrupted African rural households. The latter is more surprising. The quantile results are even more surprising in that, for both race groups, they show higher female disadvantage when the top decile of the error distribution is given explicit attention.

The head of household block of variables makes a very small contribution to overall inequality (1,6%). It is more important in explaining African inequality (2,6%) and especially African rural inequality (3,1%).

It is dismal to note the negative sign of the *household composition* estimates in Table 5.1 and the positive signs in Table 5.2. These imply that each household member is a net burden on per capita household income, and increases the probability of being poor. This is robust across deciles and across racial and urban–rural estimations. Surprisingly, adults who are 60 or older provide the single exception to this trend. In particular, it can be seen that this positive coefficient is significant in the bottom-decile quantile equation and in the African rural OLS equation. However, in most models the coefficient is negative but not significant. Finally, this coefficient is negative and significant in white households.

As a whole, household composition factors account for an important share of inequality in the 'all household' model as well as in all of the African models. Tables 5.5–5.7 show that the major contributors responsible for this are the two factors covering children (Kid7, Kid15). The decompositions show that these high inequality contributions arise from the high negative income coefficient associated with these two factors and from the strong negative correlation between these factors and per capita income.

These findings are not that startling because, in static estimations, it is almost by definition that children make negative contributions to per capita income. More worrying is the fact that economically active females and males (F16_59 and M16_59) also make negative income contributions on average. These negative coefficients are even larger in the bottom-decile quantile regression. The female economically active variable also makes a sizable contribution to inequality in African and African urban models.

TABLE 5.4

Contributions of different factors to household income inequality, for all households and by race

	Shares of total inequality				
	All households	White	African	African urban	African rural
	(Gini = 0,638)	*(Gini = 0,466)*	*(Gini = 0,552)*	*(Gini = 0,519)*	*(Gini = 0,526)*
Head:					
Femrcc Femabs Maleabs	0,016	0,017	0,026	0,023	0,031
Composition:					
Kid7	0,050	0,023	0,055	0,047	0,06
Kid15	0,053	0,032	0,060	0,062	0,059
F16_59	0,017	0,000	0,021	0,026	0,018
M16_59	0,005	−0,004	0,003	0,004	0,003
Ad60	0,000	0,029	−0,001	0,004	−0,002
Province:					
Eastern Cape Northern Cape Free State KwaZulu-Natal North West Gauteng Mpumalanga Northern Province	0,030	0,019	0,033	0,046	0,023
Urban	0,045	0,006	0,047		
Race:					
Coloured Asian White	0,170				
Education:					
Shno_ed	−0,001	−0,001	0,000	−0,004	0,002
Shprim	0,006	0,001	0,006	0,006	0,004
Shsec	0,061	0,006	0,041	0,035	0,028
Shmatric	0,093	0,081	0,060	0,074	0,036
Shtert	0,038	0,049	0,035	0,038	0,032
Labour market:					
Shwork	0,100	0,082	0,147	0,174	0,128
Shunemp	0,022	0,005	0,021	0,037	0,016
Shmig	0,001	0,001	0,007	0,010	0,004
Welfare:					
Shoap	−0,001	0,021	−0,001	−0,003	0,002
Residual	0,296	0,633	0,443	0,421	0,557

TABLE 5.5

The contribution of explanatory factors to household income inequality for South African households of all races[a]

	All households – (Gini 0,52) (log-variance 1,455) $\sigma(lnY) = 1,206$			
	Logper capita income(OLS)	Standard deviation of factor	Correlation of factor with LnY	Contribution to inequality
	(a_j)	$\sigma(Z_j)$	$Cor[Z_j, lnY]$	(By 2,a)
Head:				
Femres	**−0,2701**			
Femabs	**−0,1709**			0,016
Maleabs	**0,1396**			
Composition:				
Kid7	**−0,1655**	1,008	−0,360	0,050
Kid15	**−0,1589**	1,071	−0,377	0,053
F16_59	**−0,0649**	1,053	−0,297	0,017
M16_59	**−0,0485**	0,980	−0,114	0,005
Ad60	0,0071	0,635	−0,105	0,000
Province:				
Eastern Cape	**−0,1616**			
Northern Cape	**−0,2101**			
Free State	**−0,3017**			
KwaZulu-Natal	**0,0918**			0,030
North West	−0,0414			
Gauteng	**0,1671**			
Mpumalanga	**−0,0655**			
Northern Province	**0,0921**			
Urban	**0,2386**	0,498	0,457	0,045
Race:				
Coloured	**0,1653**			
Asian	**0,4501**			0,170
White	**0,8450**			
Education:				
Shno_ed	0,0178	0,263	−0,304	−0,001
Shprim	0,0764	0,294	0,345	0,006
Shsec	**0,3642**	0,400	0,503	0,061
Smartic	**0,5073**	0,376	0,587	0,093
Shtert	**0,4203**	0,257	1,206	0,038
Labour market:				
Shwork	**0,6813**	0,374	0,472	0,100
Shunemp	**−0,3260**	0,244	−0,331	0,022
Shmig	**0,1737**	0,198	0,039	0,001
Welfare:				
Shoap	0,0748	0,142	−0,057	−0,001
Cons	**8,0678**			
Residual	1,000	0,656	0,544	0,296

[a] Bold coefficients are significant at the 1% level using the unweighted sample data.

TABLE 5.6

The contribution of explanatory factors to household income inequality for African and white households and the contribution of explanatory factors to differences in African and white income inequality[a]

	African households (Gini 0,55) (log-variance 0,98) σ(lnY) = 0,990				White households (Gini 0,47) (log-variance 0,65) σ(lnY) = 0,81				Contrib. to differences between African/white inequality	
	Log per capita income (OLS) (a_j)	Std. deviation of factor $\sigma(Z_j)$	Correlation of factor with LnY $Cor[Z_j,lnY]$	Contribution to inequality (By 2.a.)	Log per capita income (OLS) (a_j)	Std. deviation of factor $\sigma(Z_j)$	Correlation of factor with LnY $Cor[Z_j,lnY]$	Contribution to inequality (By 2.a.)	Gini (By 3)	Log-variance (By 3)
Head:										
Femres	**−0,2556**				**−0,3053**					
Femabs	**−0,1611**			0,026	**−0,1742**			0,017	8	4
Maleabs	**0,1644**				**0,0767**					
Composition:										
Kid7	**−0,1501**	1,072	−0,336	0,055	**−0,2724**	0,645	−0,105	0,023	23	12
Kid15	**−0,1480**	1,125	−0,359	0,060	**−0,2232**	0,760	−0,152	0,032	21	12
F16_59	**−0,0686**	1,124	−0,268	0,021	**−0,0925**	0,668	0,003	0,000	13	6
M16_59	**−0,0494**	1,036	−0,050	0,003	**−0,0433**	0,690	0,099	−0,004	4	1
Ad60	**0,0123**	0,618	−0,161	−0,001	**−0,1528**	0,707	−0,215	0,029	−16	−6
Province:										
E. Cape	**−0,1121**				**−0,0733**					
N. Cape	**−0,2478**				**−0,1729**					
F. State	**−0,2847**				**−0,1825**					
KZ-Natal	**0,1710**			0,033	**−0,0250**			0,019	10	6
N. West	0,0075				**−0,0244**					
Gauteng	**0,2092**				**0,1196**					
Mplnga	−0,0090				**−0,1153**					
N. Province	**0,1553**				**0,0586**					
Urban:	**0,2764**	0,490	0,343	0,047	**−0,2052**	0,277	−0,083	0,006	27	13
Education:										
Shno_ed	0,0072	0,290	−0,207	0,000	**0,6962**	0,031	−0,039	−0,001	0	0
Shprim	0,0791	0,319	0,235	0,006	**0,2910**	0,039	0,053	0,001	3	2
Shsec	**0,3188**	0,395	0,321	0,041	**0,4393**	0,087	0,119	0,006	23	11
Smartic	**0,5069**	0,296	0,396	0,060	**0,4111**	0,406	0,392	0,081	−5	2
Shtert	**0,5269**	0,196	0,331	0,035	**0,3252**	0,384	0,316	0,049	−4	1
Labour market:										
Shwork	**0,7660**	0,366	0,518	0,147	**0,4659**	0,393	0,362	0,082	49	27
Shunemp	**−0,2935**	0,264	−0,265	0,021	**−0,3032**	0,126	−0,113	0,005	10	5
Shmig	**0,1644**	0,228	0,179	0,007	0,3392	0,067	0,032	0,001	4	2
Welfare:										
Shoap	**0,345**	0,133	−0,025	−0,001	**−0,5388**	0,165	−0,190	0,021	−12	−4
Cons	7,9384				9,4338					
Residual:	1,00	0,659	0,666	0,443	1,00	0,641	0,796	0,633	−58	7

[a] Bold coefficients are significant at the 1% level using the unweighted sample data.

TABLE 5.7

The contribution of explanatory factors to household income inequality for African urban and rural households and the contribution of explanatory factors to differences in African urban and rural income inequality[a]

	African urban households (Gini 0,52) (log-variance 0,96) σ(lnY) = 0,978				African rural households (Gini 0,53) (log-variance 0,80) σ(lnY) = 0,897				Contrib. to differences between African urban/ rural inequality	
	Log per capita income (OLS) (a_j)	Std. deviation of factor σ(Zj)	Correlation of factor with LnY Cor[Zj,lnY]	Contribution to inequality (By 2.a.)	Log per capita income (OLS) (a_j)	Std. deviation of factor σ(Zj)	Correlation of factor with LnY Cor[Zj,lnY]	Contribution to inequality (By 2.a.)	Gini (By 3)	Log-variance (By 3)
Head:										
Femres	**−0,204**				**−0,294**					
Femabs	**−0,055**			0,023	**−0,231**			0,031	77	−2
Maleabs	**0,177**				**−0,156**					
Composition:										
Kid7	**−0,169**	0,928	−0,285	0,047	**−0,143**	1,144	−0,328	0,06	114	−2
Kid15	**−0,184**	0,983	−0,334	0,062	**−0,134**	1,191	−0,334	0,059	−17	8
F16_59	**−0,071**	1,116	−0,324	0,026	**−0,062**	1,129	−0,238	0,018	−63	7
M16_59	**−0,039**	1,024	−0,090	0,004	**−0,052**	1,043	−0,048	0,003	−6	1
Ad60	−0,031	0,557	−0,213	0,004	**0,034**	0,650	−0,088	−0,002	−51	3
Province:										
E. Cape	**−0,0519**				**−0,4852**					
N. Cape	**−0,1298**				**−0,6558**					
Free State	**−0,1610**				**−0,6839**					
KZ-Natal	**0,1881**				**−0,1776**					
North West	**0,0422**			0,046	**−0,3501**			0,023	−196	17
Gauteng	**0,2341**				**−0,2290**					
Mplnga	**−0,1569**				**−0,2903**					
N. Province	**0,2308**				**−0,2056**					
Education:										
Shno_ed	0,105	0,226	−0,165	−0,004	−0,039	0,315	−0,137	0,002	50	−3
Shprim	0,125	0,255	0,198	0,006	0,062	0,341	0,154	0,004	−24	2
Shsec	**0,310**	0,378	0,978	0,035	**0,306**	0,380	0,217	0,028	−56	7
Smartic	**0,509**	0,350	0,405	0,074	**0,459**	0,238	0,294	0,036	−318	27
Shtert	**0,455**	0,242	0,341	0,038	**0,665**	0,154	0,277	0,032	−54	7
Labour market:										
Shwork	**0,831**	0,356	0,576	0,174	**0,736**	0,361	0,432	0,128	−381	42
Shunemp	**−0,384**	0,266	−0,356	0,037	**−0,229**	0,263	−0,243	0,016	−175	15
Shmig	**0,175**	0,266	0,204	0,010	0,121	0,199	0,138	0,004	−51	4
Welfare:										
Shoap	**0,288**	0,125	−0,079	−0,003	**0,378**	0,138	0,035	0,002	42	−3
Cons										
Residual:	1,000	0,635	0,649	0,421	1,000	0,669	0,746	0,897	1209	−29

[a] Bold coefficients are significant at the 1% level using the unweighted sample data.

Conventional wisdom in South Africa has it that Gauteng and Western Cape are the two most well-off provinces in South Africa. The Western Cape is the omitted dummy in the *provincial* dummy variable block, and our models therefore allow for an assessment of this claim in the multivariate context. For example, it is interesting to note that the Free State is revealed to be the least well-off province across all models, and that the Northern Province appears to be one of the better-off provinces. Both of these results are strongly contra the conventional provincial poverty rankings.

More generally, the results reveal a fairly complex situation that differs strongly along rural and urban dimensions. For 'all households' and for African households, the results suggest that Gauteng and also KwaZulu-Natal and the Northern Province have higher mean and median incomes than the Western Cape after controlling for all other factors. They also have relatively lower average probabilities of being poor. The African urban–rural results show that this aggregate outcome is the result of two contrasting processes. In urban areas, the general trend tabled above is strongly observed. However, in rural areas all provinces are strongly disadvantaged relative to the Western Cape both in terms of mean income and in terms of the probability of being poor. This rural result is due to the fact that the Western Cape did not absorb any of the predominantly rural and very poor homeland areas in 1994, whereas many other provinces did.

Table 5.4 shows that the aggregate provincial contribution to 'all household' inequality is 3%. This is lower than expected. However, the provincial block is competing with the urban–rural dummy variable in this model as both are components of the contribution of spatial factors. The inequality contribution rises to a high of close to 5% for urban African inequality. In this case, the provincial contribution is picking up the fact that, for some provinces, 'urban' implies large metropolitan cities whereas in other provinces it implies very much smaller secondary cities.

The estimation of *urban–rural* differences in household per capita incomes reveals smaller than expected coefficients in all the OLS and quantile models. The models even suggest that, holding all other variables constant, mean and median household incomes are higher in rural white households than urban white households with similar characteristics. Moreover, the contribution to inequality in 'all households' and in African households is just short of 5% in both cases. This is certainly a lesser share than expected. However, the estimated poverty marginal effects indicate large and significant increases in the probability of being poor associated with rural households – particularly for African households. In any event, our provincial discussion above has flagged the fact that the separate urban and rural equations for African households allow for a much fuller assessment of the influence of urban–rural dimension on all explanatory factors. This is clearly a more important dimension than is indicated by estimating an urban–rural dummy variable in Tables 5.1–5.6.

The analysis of the contribution of the explanatory factors to differences in urban and rural inequality provides a useful tool for direct comparison of the urban and rural equations. The final two columns of Table 5.7 present the results of the differences decomposition using two inequality measures: the Gini coefficient and the log-variance. The urban and rural Gini coefficients are almost exactly the same (0,52 and 0,53, respectively). Therefore, there is very little difference to explain by a large number of factors. This is what lies behind the unstable results for the Gini coefficient decomposition in Table 5.7. In the log-variance case, African urban inequality (0,96) is about 20% higher than African rural inequality (0,80). This is a substantial difference, and it is hardly surprising that the log-variance is far more successful in decomposing the full extent of this difference (100%) in a stable way. Table 5.7 reveals that 42% of the wider urban distribution can be attributed to Shwork, 27% to the share of adults with matric, 17% to the provincial block and 15% to the share of unemployed. Education and labour market factors are therefore seen to play the largest role in driving the differences between the African urban and rural equations and, more specifically, in explaining the greater urban inequality.

As with the urban–rural situation, the influence of *race* is captured both as a dummy variable set and in equations that are separately specified by race. However, unlike the urban–rural case, the racial dummies are strikingly large in their own right. Relative to African incomes, there are large premiums associated with coloured, Asian and especially white incomes. The quantile regressions suggest that the 84% mean difference between African and white households with the same characteristics may underestimate the difference, as both the bottom-decile and top-decile estimates are higher. Table 5.3 reveals that racial differences in the probabilities of being poor are also very large.

In addition, it can be seen from Table 5.4 that the most important of the block contributions to inequality is the one due to race. In the 'all households' models, race accounts for 17,3% of total inequality. Even if the inequality contributions of individual factors are aggregated into group shares, the contribution of race remains the largest of any of the variable groups. In the multivariate context, these findings are particularly startling as this racial contribution does not include racial biases in education or the labour market. As such, it is a lower-bound inequality estimate that starkly confirms the continuing importance of race in South Africa. When race is included as a single explanatory factor in this model, it accounts for 39% of the total inequality. This upper-bound estimate is very much in line with the between-race contributions that we derived in Chapter 1 using the Theil and Atkinson measures.

The final two columns of Table 5.6 present the results for the decomposition of the difference between African and white inequality using two inequality measures: the Gini coefficient and the log-variance. Both measures suggest that the inequality within white households is lower than the inequality within African households. The difference that needs to be explained is 4% in terms of the Gini coefficient and 39% in terms of the log-variance. Thus, as with the urban–rural case earlier, the two measures seek to explain markedly varying inequality differences.

Given this situation, it is hardly surprising that the log-variance is more successful in decomposing the full extent of the difference (100%) in a stable way. Both measures suggest that the old age pension and residual factor go against the trend and contribute to a situation in which white households are more uneven than African – when everything else is held constant. All the other factors work in the direction of the measured total difference, in that they explain a move to a wider African distribution. For both the Gini coefficient and the log-variance, Shwork, Urban, Kid7 and Kid15 and Shsec are seen to be the major factors responsible for the greater African inequality.

Shwork is by far the largest contributor. In this case, as the standard deviations of the African and white Shwork variables are very similar, this difference is largely attributable to differences in the income coefficients and in the correlations between Shwork and log per capita income. Indeed, the Shwork income coefficient (76,6%) and correlation coefficient (0,518) are both the largest of any variables in the African model.

The second largest contributor to the difference is the urban–rural factor. This is due to the fact that both the income coefficient and the correlation coefficient are positive in the African model and negative in the white model. The shift from urban to rural widens the distribution of income in both models, but it corresponds to a shift down the distribution in the African case and a slight shift up the distribution in the white case. Thus, the difference is quite marked.

The impacts of the two children variables (Kid7 and Kid15) and the Shmatric education factor are very similar in size and in underlying explanation. In all cases, the standard deviations and the income correlations of the factors are much larger in African households. white households of all income levels rarely have large numbers of children and almost all adults have some secondary education. Thus, these three factors are not major drivers of white inequality. In African households, there is a far bigger range of numbers of children in the household and shares of adults with secondary education. In addition, households with large numbers of children tend to be found in the lower half of the African distribution and households with higher shares of adults with secondary schooling tend to be found in the upper half of the African distribution. These three factors are therefore much more important contributors to African household inequality than to white inequality.

The education block follows the race block in Tables 5.1–5.7. However, in order to make sense of the education results it is necessary to talk about the labour market. Thus, we discuss the labour market results before we discuss the education results.

Indeed, the contribution of an increased *share of working adults* in the household is the highest of any single continuous variable in all income, poverty and inequality models. In the 'all households' model, each additional worker makes a large contribution to household per capita income (68%), to the probability of avoiding poverty (28%) and to inequality (10%). The contributions are even higher for African households – at 77%, 44% and 14,7%, respectively. In addition, the high income benefits are robust across quantiles. While income and poverty contributions stay high when urban and rural African households are examined separately, there is an interesting reversal in the estimated coefficients. For household per capita income, urban benefits are greater than rural – at 83% and 74%, respectively. For the probability of poverty avoidance, urban benefits are less than rural – at 33% and 46%, respectively. A plausible explanation of this reversal would be the fact that better-remunerated employment is available in urban areas compared to rural areas, thus raising the income benefits of increases in the share of employed adults to urban households above those to rural households. However, given the scarcity of employment in rural areas relative to urban areas and the absence of viable alternative activities for rural households, increased access to any employment makes a larger contribution to lifting a household out of poverty in rural areas than in urban.

We have already extensively discussed the dominant role of the share of working adults in explaining the differences in inequality between African and white households and between African urban and rural households. To some extent, this has pre-empted a discussion of the direct contribution of Shwork to inequality. Across all inequality models, this contribution is attributable to:

- The size of the income coefficient. A unit increase in the share of working adults raises per capita household income by 76%.
- The large standard deviations for this variable. There are large differences across households in the shares of economically active adults that are employed.
- The high correlation of this variable with lnY.

Unemployment makes a large negative contribution to income and poverty. However, the magnitude of this influence is never more than half that of the comparable employment coefficient in all models. Thus, there is not an opposite-but-equal symmetry between the impacts of unemployment and employment. In a trivial sense, this is to be expected because the income contribution made by working members to their households depends on the quality of employment, whereas the direct income contribution of the unemployed is always zero. There is another plausible explanation for this result. If unemployed household members have weaker labour market characteristics than those members of the household that are already employed, then the lost potential earnings of the unemployed would be lower than the actual earnings of the employed.

It is important to note that this analysis of the relative contributions of the employed and the unemployed does not imply that the costs to households of unemployment are lower than expected. In an absolute sense, a rising share of unemployed members takes a heavy income toll on households. Moreover, the quantile regression results in Table 5.2 show that this toll is higher when the estimate is anchored around the bottom decile than when it is anchored around the median or the top decile. This is particularly true for African households. Thus, the absolute cost of unemployment is higher for those at the bottom of the distribution.

From Table 5.4, it can be seen that the contribution of unemployment to inequality is low in all models. Particularly unexpected is the fact that the contribution to African rural inequality (1,6%) is less than the contribution to African urban inequality (3,7%). This is a reflection of the fact that the negative income coefficient is less in rural areas (−0,23 compared to −0,38) and that the negative income correlation is also weaker in rural areas (−0,243 compared to −0,356). Both of these findings require careful interpretation. The lower income coefficient for unemployment is most likely a reflection of the poorer earnings possibilities in rural areas. The lower (negative) correlation coefficient reveals that a household with a high share of unemployed adults is likely to be closer to the bottom of the urban distribution than the rural. Thus, rather than signalling the unimportance of the unemployment problem in rural areas, this is a reflection of the endemic nature of the unemployment problem in rural areas. The unemployed are found in all rural households including those in the middle of the income distribution. Therefore, unemployment is not strongly correlated with those households at the bottom end of the distribution.

The impact of *migrant remittances* on income, poverty and inequality is small. Rather surprisingly, this is the case even for African rural households. Thus, this is the one labour market factor that does not throw up any interesting results in the multivariate context.

The *education* variables show very strong 'returns' (in terms of income and poverty avoidance) to households in which a large share of adult members have secondary education and higher. The significance of completed secondary education (matric), as distinct from some secondary education, is also clear. There are so few adults in white households with no education or only primary education that these coefficients are always statistically insignificant when estimated with unweighted sample data. We will therefore ignore these coefficients. Focusing only on the secondary, matric and tertiary levels, it can still be seen that there are important differences across races in terms of the household returns to education. African returns are higher at all levels and across all quantiles. This is even more marked in the poverty regressions. Table 5.3 shows that household education levels are not an important factor in avoiding poverty for white households. In contrast to this, African households get very large poverty avoidance returns from increasing the shares of adults with higher levels of education.

The income contribution of secondary-schooled adult household members is about 32% for African households in both urban and rural areas. However, there are interesting urban–rural differences at the matric and tertiary levels. For urban areas, matric generates the highest return (51% compared to 45%). In rural areas, this is reversed (46% and 66%). All of these returns are high. However, it would seem that adults with completed secondary education have good opportunities for income-generation in urban areas, whereas the best rural opportunities require tertiary education. This is plausible. In the 1980s and early 1990s, the best rural income-earning opportunities for Africans have generally involved skilled employment in the public sector (Leib-brandt & Woolard 1995).

When the focus shifts to the poverty regressions, rural returns are markedly higher than urban for secondary schooling (a 21 versus a 12% decrease in the poverty probability) and matric (a 32 versus a 17% decrease in the poverty probability) and marginally higher for tertiary education (15 and 18%, respectively).

In the 'all households' and white households inequality models, the education variables make the largest block contribution to inequality of all variable sets. In all other models, this block is the second-largest next to the labour market block. Within this education block, Table 5.3 shows that Shmatric makes the largest contribution to inequality of any education factor in all of the models. Next to Shwork, it is the second largest contributor to inequality of all of the individual factors. In the 'all households' and white households models, the Shmatric contribution is only marginally smaller than Shwork. All of these findings clearly establish the importance of educational factors in inequality. Earlier, we flagged the importance of Shmatric in differences between rural and urban inequality and the importance of Shsec in explaining differences between African and white inequality.

Judging by the 'all households' equations, *pensioners* appear to have a small impact on average household earnings. However, this is an instance of the 'all households' situation representing a bad average of two disparate African and white trends. In the case of white households, a rising share of pensioners in the household makes a negative contribution to income and a positive contribution to inequality. In all African models, a rising share of pensioners makes a positive contribution to income. This is especially notable in rural areas. In addition, the impact on poverty is very strong. Earlier, we addressed the role of pensions in poverty alleviation. The multivariate work now affirms our earlier contention that pensions are well targeted in terms of their welfare objectives.

Old-age pensions also yield some interesting inequality results. For African households, they make a *negative* but very small contribution to inequality. This is a consequence of the fact that pensions make a positive contribution to income but households with pensioners in them are in the lower-income groups. This variable is therefore negatively correlated with lnY. This is somewhat surprising, as it is well known that pensions play an important role in the social safety net for African rural households. However, the correlation coefficient is very close to zero, implying that households with pension incomes are not the poorest of the African poor. Indeed, in African rural households the correlation is slightly positive, giving this factor a small positive role in inequality.

Conclusion

There is a large body of work, including our own in earlier chapters of this book, that teases out and describes the key dimensions of poverty and inequality in South Africa. From the policy point of view, there is a pressing need to provide a sense of the relative importance of these key dimensions. There is virtually no precedent for such work in South Africa. In this chapter, we have taken a first step in this direction. We have estimated and discussed four multivariate models of household income determination, household poverty and household inequality. Econometric adequacy is elusive in such household-level models, but we have endeavoured to be as careful as possible in our estimations.

For this study, the major issue at stake is to understand the role of the labour market in driving income determination, poverty and inequality. Our interpretation of results has been slanted towards this angle. For example, urban and rural differences have been seen to reflect different types of employment and levels of unemployment in rural and urban labour markets. This labour market angle is justified by the results themselves. Employment of adult labour market participants is shown to be the biggest single contributor to household per capita income, household poverty avoidance and household inequality. Unemployment of such adults imposes a high cost on households. The aggregate impact of new job creation is especially significant, as it involves the removal of the negative unemployment effect and the addition of the positive employment effect. On average, the net impact of this would be very close to a 100% improvement in average per capita household income and a 40% reduction in the probability of the household being poor. In addition, the aggregate contribution of these labour market variables to 'all household' inequality is 12,3%.

While education is not only a labour market issue, education and the labour market are intimately related at the policy level. This chapter has repeatedly shown the important, positive contributions made by household members who are educated to at least the secondary-school level. Households get particularly high returns from adult members with completed secondary schooling and tertiary education. Moreover, the block of education variables is always amongst the top two contributors to household inequality.

All in all, then, our models certainly justify the fact that we give detailed attention to the labour market and to the role that education plays in determining labour market outcomes. The discussion in this chapter has not been particularly precise about urban-versus-rural labour markets or the factors determining unemployment and earnings. The reason for this is that we exclude the way in which the labour market operates in South Africa. Within the labour market, it is individuals that are employed or unemployed, and it is individual characteristics that determine this, as well as consequent earnings for the employed. Thus, the labour market analysis needs to move away from households and focus on individuals.

There are two additional findings from our modelling that warrant emphasis. First, the provincial analysis reveals some interesting dimensions. The analysis of provincial poverty shares that we undertook in an earlier chapter concluded that provincial shares are very sensitive to the choice of poverty measure. In the multivariate context, the relative income and poverty rankings appear to be quite different from the conventional views and quite unstable across different equations. Thus, the multivariate models certainly provide additional support for our earlier cautionary note. This is important, because provinces are institutional intermediaries in the social service delivery process in South Africa and, to some extent, provincial budget allocations are based on measurement of need *across provinces*. The policy question that arises is: what are the currently used needs rankings and how are they derived? The multivariate models have also shown that there are important urban–rural differences in mean income and poverty *within* provinces. Appropriate intraprovincial service delivery rules are therefore going to be vital in ensuring successful anti-poverty policy – no matter how provincial shares are derived.

Finally, the multivariate models confirm the ongoing importance of race as a fundamental factor structuring South African poverty and inequality. This is in line with our earlier racial decomposition work and greatly strengthens this work by showing that race retains its direct importance even after controlling for its indirect influence on access to education, location and employment opportunities. This is a daunting indicator of the magnitude of the project South Africa faces to redress our racial legacy.

Notes

1. We thank Servaas van der Berg, Gary Fields and Haroon Bhorat for their extensive comments on earlier drafts of this chapter.

2. In order to be consistent with earlier work here, the estimates that we report in the main text are based on sample data weighted up to the national population by using the appropriate frequency weights. However, the reported levels of statistical significance are based on the unweighted sample data.

3. The quantile regression coefficients are actually fitted by iterative programming. The statistical package Stata does not allow quantile regressions to use frequency weights to boost the sample observations to population levels, as there will be too many observations to converge to a solution. The estimates in Table 5.2 are therefore unweighted.

4. Ravallion (1996) provides a thorough and jaundiced review of such probit-based poverty regressions. We will use the probit approach as a complement to the ordinary least squares and quantile approaches.

5. See the articles in Fiszbein and Psacharopoulos (1995) for a good example.

6. The variable set is identical to that used in the poverty profile presented in Chapter 2.

7. All other estimations are available from the authors.

Public Expenditure and Poverty Alleviation – Simulations for South Africa

Haroon Bhorat

There can be no doubt that one of the key dilemmas facing the South African government is that of eradicating, or at least reducing, the incidence of poverty in the society. The Growth, Employment and Redistribution (GEAR) strategy, while dedicating itself to this broad goal of poverty alleviation, is also heavily directed by a programme of fiscal austerity. Stringent fiscal deficit targets have been laid down which have thus far been met, and will continue to be fulfilled. It is in this policy milieu that the issue arises of the cost-effectiveness of current poverty alleviation schemes funded through the national budget. It has often been noted that the most cost-efficient and indeed simplest poverty alleviation intervention is that of targeted income transfers. Indeed, South Africa's very own old age pension scheme has long been held up as a model of an effective and efficient welfare transfer scheme. The purpose of this chapter is to note the government's current poverty alleviation and social security strategies, but then to abstract from them to allow for the expenditure simulations to be undertaken.

The specific intention of undertaking these policy simulations is to determine, in a hypothetical world, the cost to the state of alleviating poverty through an extensive income transfer scheme. What follows is deliberately general and somewhat grandiose, as the focus is to deliver baseline estimates of what the potential one-off costs of different income transfer schemes could be. Different permutations of such a hypothetical income transfer scheme are considered, using an established methodology drawn from the literature on household poverty analysis. These involve the public expenditure commitment necessary to generate zero poverty in the society – with consideration given to the different household and individual categories in the economy. In addition, an attempt is made to provide some sensitivity analysis, where intermediate expenditure outlays are correlated with reduced (but non-zero) poverty levels. This analysis will in turn provide a comparison and assessment of two alternative types of income grant schemes, namely the additive versus the multiplicative grant.

The theoretical approach

The most useful measure for simulating the effects on poverty of various policy interventions is the poverty gap measure. The poverty gap measure is derived from the general class of poverty measures developed by Foster, Greer and Thorbecke (1984). The FGT index of poverty measures can be represented in general form as:

$$P_\alpha = \frac{1}{n} \sum_{i=1}^{n} \left(\frac{z-y_i}{z}\right)^\alpha \bigg| (y_i \leq z) \tag{1}$$

where n is the total sample size, z is the chosen poverty line, and y_i is the standard of living indicator of agent i. The parameter α measures the sensitivity of the index to transfers between the poor units. Note that the index is conditional on the agent's income, y_i, being below the designated poverty line, z. The poverty gap measure (PG) is generated when $\alpha = 1$, and therefore for a given poverty line z is presented as follows:

$$P_1 = \frac{1}{n} \sum_{i=1}^{n} \left(\frac{z-y_i}{z}\right) \bigg| (y_i \leq z) \tag{2}$$

Clearly, the PG represents a direct measure of agents' incomes relative to the poverty line. It is a money metric of poverty in the group under scrutiny. A first advantage of the FGT index is its additive decomposability, which allows for subgroup poverty measures to be summed to form a society-wide measure without any loss of generality. More importantly here, the PG measure, in being linked to money values, can be utilised to run simulations on the poverty impacts of income transfers to the poor — for any given reference group in the society. Remembering that P_1 is a measure not simply of how many poor agents there are, but also of how poor the poor are, we do arrive at a fairly nuanced analysis of the welfare outcomes of poverty alleviation strategies.

By using the poverty gap measure, then, it is possible to calculate the minimum financial cost of poverty alleviation. This is done by assuming that the poverty outcome in each subgroup is for P_1 to be zero. Expressed differently, this means that the income to each agent in the subgroup or society (y_i), would at least be equal to the value of the poverty line (z). This value can be determined from the equation (2) by calculating

$$\sum_{i=1}^{n} (z-y_i) \big| (y_i \leq z) \tag{3}$$

In other words, we sum the value of the resources required to place each agent in the society just above the poverty line.

A reformulation of this, and one that is easier for calculation purposes, is nzP_1, which is derived directly from equation (2). Using the latter as a basis, we can therefore present the minimum financial cost of alleviating poverty, as measured by P_1, to the subgroup or society by the value associated with nzP_1 (Kanbur 1987:71). This figure represents the minimum commitment required of the state, in that it assumes perfect targeting, with zero administrative and other costs generally associated with welfare transfer schemes. It is also assumed that the scheme would elicit no behavioural responses from any potential recipients. These responses are particularly important when individuals' returns to labour supply fall within the range of the transfer value. While these assumptions are of course extreme, and are discussed in greater detail later on, the value of nzP_1 does provide a very useful first step in trying to gauge the importance and magnitude of the problem facing society.

The value of nzP_1 can be extended to include subdivisions of the total sample. Hence, what can be determined is a matrix of the minimum financial commitment required to eradicate poverty amongst different groups at the household and individual level in the society. It is also useful to determine the poverty impact when committing to expenditure less than the value of nzP_1. In this way, we engage in sensitivity analysis that provides results which correlate intermediate expenditure changes to intermediate alterations in the poverty gap. It has to be remembered that these results would also not explicitly take account of the administrative and other set-up costs associated with an income grant programme. Following from Kanbur (1987), it is possible to deal with this sensitivity analysis through a methodology that allocates specific income grants to agents. There are two alternative ways of operationalising such a fiscal intervention. One would be an additive income grant and the other a multiplicative grant. An additive income transfer would be an absolute transfer independent of the income earned by the recipient. For example, one could think of a R50 increase to old age pensioners or single unemployed mothers as an additive income transfer with imperfect targeting. A multiplicative transfer would be set as a fraction or percentage of the recipient's given income, and hence the absolute amount received would differ across agents. An example here would be to lower average tax rates for individuals whose earnings fall within a certain income range. Simulation of each of these two types of transfers – additive or multiplicative – will impart relevant information concerning the effect on poverty in the society or subgroup.

Examining the additive case first, and assuming that we account for the entire income distribution, an increase in everybody's income in the society by an absolute amount, Δ_I, will mean that equation (1) takes the following form:

$$P_\alpha = \int_0^{z-\Delta} \left(\frac{z-y-\Delta}{z} \right)^\alpha f(y)d(y) \tag{4}$$

Hence each agent gets a transfer in each scheme of Δ_i while the total cost of the scheme would be Δ. The calculations performed below will involve the provision of transfers only to poor agents. Given that our measure of poverty utilised here is the poverty gap, or P_1, it is possible to calculate the value of the marginal impact by:

$$\frac{dP_1}{d\Delta} = -\frac{P_0}{z} = -\frac{H}{z} \qquad (5)$$

where P_0 is the measure of the head-count index (H) – simply, the number or share of agents living below the poverty line. Equation (4) presents the unit change in poverty as measured by P_1, given a unit change in the transfer value, Δ_i, to each agent in the society. Hence, an increase of Δ_i to each agent in the society or subgroup would cause poverty to fall by a specified and calculable value. It is possible to see that the amount by which poverty will decline is in fact proportional to the head-count index, P_0. An increase of Δ_i would thus cause a parallel downward shift in the poverty deficit curve associated with the measure, P_1. In other words, the change in poverty can be measured here in relation to the poverty line, z, and the head-count index P_0. The head-count index is therefore an important indicator of the impact of public spending on poverty, despite not serving as the direct measure of poverty in the methodology.

The second simulation case is to assume that the expenditure is multiplicative in nature. Following from the above, the corresponding equations that present the distribution function associated with the multiplicative expenditure, Δ, and its impact on measured poverty, respectively, are as follows:

$$P_\alpha = \int_0^{z/(1+\Delta)} \left[\frac{z - y(1+\Delta)}{z} \right]^\alpha f(y)d(y) \qquad (6)$$

$$\frac{dP_1}{d\Delta} = -\frac{1}{1+\Delta}[P_0 - P_1] < 0 \qquad (7)$$

Note that the value of the transfer is expressed as a share of the income of each agent. Again, the head-count index (P_0) is a relevant variable in understanding how measured poverty is affected by budgetary allocations. Here, it is the weighted difference between P_0 and P_1 that calculates the degree to which poverty falls after an expenditure that is multiplicative in nature.

Simulations for South Africa

By making use of the preceding methodology, it is possible to estimate the one-off costs of eradicating poverty amongst different groups in society. An important conceptual issue is to deal adequately with the unit of analysis in the different simulations. This relates to the problem of individuals and households in poverty analysis. In the language of the labour market, individuals earn or receive income, but from a strict poverty perspective it is households that should be examined when trying to understand income in relation to poverty. The analysis here will be diligent in trying to ensure that both individual- and household-level impacts of poverty-alleviating expenditure are adequately dealt with. This is particularly important, as each approach offers separate conceptual advantages.

Expenditure for zero poverty

We have noted that the minimum expenditure required to yield zero poverty in the society is represented by nzP_1. The tables below provide these estimates for different subgroups in the society. A few things need to be noted about the tables. Firstly, the analysis is based on the October Household Survey of 1995 (OHS 95), which sampled about 30 000 households, drawn from 10 selected households in each of 3 000 clusters. For the household-specific data, the accompanying Income and Expenditure Survey (IES) was also utilised, and income rather than expenditure data manipulated to estimate household earnings. Secondly, for all the calculations that follow, the household poverty line chosen was R903 per month, a scale based on May *et al.* (1995). The resultant individual poverty line drawn directly from this measure was R293 per month, based on the assumption, albeit simplistic, of an average of three individuals in a household. Given that the expenditure figures below will be presented as annual commitments, the equivalent household poverty line is R10 836 and the individual annual poverty line, R3 516. Finally, given the date of the survey, the money values presented are in 1995 prices.

Table 6.1 provides baseline estimates of the minimum financial commitment required to eradicate poverty at the household level. The different subgroups of households are those characterised by the race of the household head and the location of the household. The total number of dwellings in the society is about 9,5 million, of which about 3 million are poor households. The national poverty gap measure for this group is about 0,13. As a consequence, the minimum financial commitment necessary to eradicate poverty at the household level in the economy, using the 1995 data, is approximately R12,9 billion per annum. The state's total expenditure in 1995, at current prices, was about R154,9 billion. Thus the cost of eradicating household poverty in the society constitutes 8,29% of this expenditure.

In terms of the race–household distribution of public expenditure, a disproportionate share is allocated to African households. While African households form about 70% of the total household population, they constitute 95% of poor homes in the society. As a result, R12,1 billion of the total expenditure will be allocated to households where the head is African. Coloured households are marginally underrepresented amongst poor households relative to their share in the total household population. Coloured dwellings thus form 8,3% of the population, and 4,8% of the poverty eradication expenditure. The commitment from government for these households is less than 1% of total expenditure outlays. No significant financial commitment is required from the fiscus to eradicate poverty amongst Asian and white households. For white households, despite the fact that they form close to 20% of all homes in the society, the commitment from the state constitutes under 1% of the poverty-eradication expenditure. The location results

TABLE 6.1

Minimum poverty alleviation expenditure for households[a]

Subgroup	Number of households (n)	Number of poor households	Poverty measure (P₁)	Expenditure per annum	% of total expenditure
Total	9 475 165	3 010 855	0,1251	12 844 378 281	8,29
African	6 625 570	2 749 295	0,1180	12 115 400 777	7,82
Coloured	783 595	187 707	0,0060	616 037 328	0,40
Asian	249 906	11 356	0,0001	10 267 289	0,01
White	1 816 094	62 497	0,0010	102 672 888	0,07
Urban	5 122 047	831 863	0,0360	3 696 223 966	2,39
Semi-urban	177 302	52 081	0,0020	205 345 776	0,13
Rural	4 175 816	2 126 911	0,0871	8 942 808 540	5,77

[a] The decomposability properties of the FGT measure are particularly useful here, and the P_1 measures are calculated according to the formula

$$P = \frac{\sum_{j=1}^{m} P_j n_j}{n}.$$

where the j individuals are summed by the m subgroups in the sample and then weighted by the total sample, n, to derive the composite P_1 value. It should be noted that by using this formula, the value for the minimum financial commitment by m subgroups will be equal to

$$nz \sum_{j=1}^{m} \frac{n_j P_j}{n}$$

In this table and all that follow, the poverty measure P_1 represents weighted shares of total poverty.

reveal the importance of rural household poverty in South Africa. To eradicate poverty amongst rural households, the state would need to commit to at least an additional R8,9 billion per annum, constituting 5,8% of the state's total expenditure in 1995. Notwithstanding the expected predominance of rural household poverty, 30% of fiscal expenditure on poverty allevi-ation would still need to be allocated to urban households.

The household poverty alleviation figures may be complemented by a description of the mag-nitude of commitment required from the state by the different labour market cohorts in the society. In a more general vein, this is an analysis of poverty and public expenditure at the individ-ual rather than the household level. Table 6.2 attempts to achieve this division of individual poverty alleviation expenditure by calculating the value of nzP_1 for individuals identified by their labour market status, where z is now R293 per month, and the unemployed are of course zero-earners.

The data illustrates, for example, that the state would need to spend approximately R15 billion more per annum to keep all individuals in the labour force out of poverty. This static figure constitutes 9,7% of total government spending in 1995. Note that the individual expenditure value is greater than the household figure above, indicating that the cost of keeping a household out of poverty involves economies of scale not realised when dissecting the sample by individuals only. The racial division for the labour force again shows the dominance of African individuals. While the state would need to spend about R485 million per year on white workers in order to keep them out of poverty, the corresponding figure for Africans is exactly 27 times greater. The racial disparities are also evident in that Africans form 69% of the labour force but 88% of all poor individuals in the labour force, while the corresponding figures for whites are 17% and 2,2%.

The second set of figures for the labour market concentrates on employed individuals, by race, gender, location, sector and occupation. It is immediately apparent that the resources required from the fiscus decline sharply when only employed individuals are included. The expenditure required falls by over R14 billion, suggesting that the large numbers of unemployed would capture a substantial portion (93%) of the state's poverty eradication expenditure. Hence, a labour market-focused poverty eradication programme would be overwhelmingly targeted at the unemployed. It is tempting, then, to describe the fault line of poverty in the labour market as running between the employed and the unemployed. However, as the following discussion will illuminate, pockets of poverty exist amongst specific categories of the employed as well, which may require modification of this strict division.

Expenditure on the employed by race, once again, yields over-expenditure on Africans relative to their share in the population. The financial resources required for the employed according to gender show that greater spending is required for women than men. Despite the fact that women form only 38% of the workforce, the state needs to spend twice as much on poor employed females, compared to males, in order to end poverty in this cohort. Female expenditure constituted 0,45% of total government expenditure in 1995.

It is the sector and occupation cohorts, though, that provide for an interesting analysis of labour market poverty. At the sectoral level, the two poorest sets of individuals are those in agriculture and community and social services. These two sectors account for 85% of all the poverty amongst employed individuals in the labour market. Community and social services has marginally more poor individuals than agriculture. These two sectors account for close to 90% of all the required expenditure on the employed poor. More specifically, the state would need to spend about R349,7 million in agriculture and R575,1 million in community and social services every year to eradicate poverty in these sectors. This sectoral picture of poverty is mirrored in the poverty results by occupation. The two poorest occupations are domestic workers and agricultural labourers. These two occupations account for 72% of all the employed poor in the labour market. Note that there are more poor individuals who are domestic workers than are farm labourers. As a result, the state would need to spend R454,7 million per annum on domestic services versus about R280 million on farm workers, in order to eliminate poverty in these

TABLE 6.2

Minimum poverty alleviation expenditure for labour market individuals[a]

Subgroup	Number of individuals (n)	Number of poor individuals (q)	Poverty measure (P_1)	Expenditure per annum	% of total expenditure
Labour force					
Total	13 817 522	4 499 617	0,3100	15 060 546 279	9,72
African	9 550 773	3 971 141	0,2700	13 117 249 985	8,47
Coloured	1 509 564	379 631	0,0300	1 457 472 221	0,94
Asian	414 511	49 675	0,0000	0	0,00
White	2 342 674	99 170	0,0100	485 824 074	0,31
Urban	8 528 908	2 100 535	0,1600	7 773 185 176	5,02
Semi-urban	263 791	81 463	0,0200	971 648 147	0,63
Rural	5 004 374	2 301 880	0,1300	6 315 712 956	4,08
Employed					
Total	9 947 208	721 625	0,03	1 049 231 500	0,68
African	6 146 540	622 992	0,03	1 049 231 500	0,68
Coloured	1 191 020	84 206	0,00	0	0,00
Asian	364 780	1 932	0,00	0	0,00
White	2 244 868	12 495	0,00	0	0,00
Male	6 127 107	269 078	0,01	349 743 833	0,23
Female	3 820 101	452 547	0,02	699 487 667	0,45
Urban	6 546 947	182 856	0,01	349 743 833	0,23
Semi-urban	189 015	10 036	0,00	0	0,00
Rural	3 207 066	528 733	0,02	699 487 667	0,45
Agriculture	1 266 183	288 918	0,01	349 743 833	0,23
Mining	463 743	2 085	0,00	0	0,00
Manufacturing	1 497 292	21 833	0,00	0	0,00
Construction	92 470	10 386	0,00	0	0,00
Utilities	472 457	370	0,00	0	0,00
Wholesale trade	1 730 487	68 001	0,00	0	0,00
Transport	510 099	4 081	0,00	0	0,00
Finance	643 354	2 526	0,00	0	0,00
Community services	3 271 123	323 425	0,02	575 063 423	0,37
Manager	570 923	7 201	0,001	34 974 383	0,02
Professional	351 518	347	0,000	0	0,00
Technicians	1 137 083	3 698	0,000	0	0,00
Clerks	1 205 348	10 194	0,001	34 974 383	0,02
Service	1 124 283	30 872	0,001	34 974 383	0,02
Skilled agric. workers	129 267	9 143	0,000	0	0,00
Craft workers	1 211 344	25 556	0,002	69 948 767	0,05
Machine operators	1 152 070	26 551	0,002	69 948 767	0,05
Domestic helpers	379 684	22 973	0,001	34 974 383	0,02
Agric. labourers	944 531	250 972	0,008	279 795 067	0,18
Mining labourers	256 891	8 925	0,001	34 974 383	0,02
Manufacturing labourers	352 742	12 770	0,000	0	0,00
Transport labourers	38 307	934	0,000	0	0,00
Domestic workers	713 035	267 439	0,013	454 666 983	0,29

[a] The full sample of employed individuals is not included here as 0,04% of the survey is coded as 'missing' in terms of their reported location.

cohorts. These two occupations would have accounted for 0,47% of the government's total expenditure in 1995.

From Table 6.2, then, it can be argued that the majority of public expenditure would be committed to the unemployed. However, a strict separation in poverty terms between the employed and the unemployed does not exist. This is particularly true in the case of farm workers and domestic workers, who represent the core of the working poor in the labour market. These two groups of workers would require a substantial public expenditure commitment aimed at poverty reduction. This suggests that should public expenditure take the form of a labour market intervention, due consideration should be given to the fact that poverty exists not only amongst the unemployed but also amongst sections of the employed. There would remain, though, the real danger of disincentive effects on the labour supply decision of these two cohorts of workers from this type of government support.

A perhaps stronger mechanism for displaying this shared poverty amongst the unemployed and a segment of the employed is found in Table 6.3. The table presents household level data, but these are households categorised according to their labour market status. Hence, each labour force individual – in this case, domestic workers, farm workers and the unemployed – is linked back to their respective households. The subgroups, therefore, are of households characterised by a labour market status variable. The sample in each category is mutually exclusive. Thus, the households that domestic workers are found in refer specifically to those dwellings where domestic workers, *and no unemployed individuals or farm workers*, reside. This is to avoid double-counting in our poverty measures, which would bias our poverty gap estimates. In addition, the households wherein combinations of these three labour force types are found are included under the subgroup 'combined'. Note that this category represents a minor share of these selected indigent household types. The data illustrates that while these four household types account for 54% of the total population, they represent 73% of all poor homes in the society. In terms of trying to gain a labour market view of household poverty, then, it is evident that these four subgroups of households are a fairly strong representation of how labour market earnings generate the observed household poverty levels in the society.

TABLE 6.3

Minimum poverty alleviation expenditure for selected households

Subgroup	Number of households (n)	Number of poor households	Poverty measure (P_1)	Expenditure per annum	% of total expenditure
Total	9 475 165	3 010 855	0,1251	12 844 378 281	8,29
Domestic workers	407 247	185 841	0,008	807 045 012	0,52
Agricultural workers	662 888	424 002	0,018	1 803 417 208	1,16
Unemployed	3 386 180	1 371 302	0,058	5 917 762 505	3,82
'Combined'	698 632	230 745	0,014	1 430 818 542	0,92

In terms of public expenditure, the state would need to spend about 77% of its total poverty eradication budget on these households. Hence, well over two-thirds of fiscal support for the poor would need to be targeted at only four types of dwellings in the society, accounting for 6,4% of the government's total expenditure. The largest share of the additional annual expenditure would accrue to households with unemployed individuals (R5,9 billion), followed by farm workers (R1,8 billion), combined worker households (R1,4 billion) and domestic worker dwellings (R807 million). Ultimately, if we were to use a general targeting rule of capturing the most disadvantaged labour market participants, together with ensuring that their households were the recipients of public support, this subgroup meets the requirement in a powerfully optimal manner. Clearly, public support that takes cognisance of both the individual and household dimensions of poverty can ensure that the effectiveness of the expenditure is maximised.

With regard to farm workers and domestic workers, an interesting switch occurs when moving from the individual level data to household data. In Table 6.2, domestic workers were poorer than farm workers, and hence required greater expenditure than the latter to place them out of poverty. However, the data on which Table 6.3 is based make it clear that farm workers come from poorer households than domestic workers. Not only is the number of farm worker homes in poverty larger than those of domestic workers, but the intragroup poverty measure (not shown in the table) is also higher for farm workers. The household head-count measure for domestics is 45,63, while for farm workers it is 63,96. The respective P_1 measures are 0,18 for domestics and 0,25 for farm workers. A possible reason for this outcome is that farm worker households are by their very nature found in rural or semi-urban areas. This location effect is a strong predictor for greater household poverty, given the nature of rural labour markets and the returns provided to labour in these areas. Hence, the data shows that close to 92% of all farm worker homes are in rural areas, while the corresponding figure for domestic workers is 49%. A second reason for this outcome was tested: namely that the probability of multiple earners is greater in domestic worker homes, so increasing the total household income earned. The data illustrates, however, that this is an unlikely source of the poverty differential, as the number of earners per household type is fairly equal. Hence farm worker households have on average 1,8 earners, while domestic worker homes have about 2 earners each.

Another interesting facet of the individual and household differences comes from comparing the unemployed as individuals to the households they live in. Hence, as individuals, they are the poorest in the labour force because the unemployed by definition earn no income. However, at the household level, the dynamic changes. While this sample of dwellings clearly outnumbers that of any other poor subgroup, the poverty measures tell a slightly different story. The poverty gap measure for households with unemployed is lower than that of domestics and farm workers. The household intragroup P_1 measure (again, not shown in Table 6.3) amongst the unemployed households is 0,16, while the head-count index is 40,50 – compared to 0,18 and 45,63 amongst domestics, and 0,25 and 63,96 amongst farm workers. Putting this differently, while there are more unemployed households living in poverty – so generating the largest share of overall household poverty – the extent of poverty within this sample is lower than amongst domestic or farm worker dwellings. It would appear, then, that farm workers come from the poorest homes in the society, while the unemployed in fact live in homes that are generally better-off than the other two categories.

There are a few lessons for policy prescriptions in the above empirical experiments. Firstly, the data suggests that, despite the very strict assumptions of zero running and fixed costs in the income transfer, the value of the financial commitment asked of the state for both individuals and households is fairly modest. This is supported by comparisons with the relatively large expenditure outlays in other functions of government. Secondly, the markers of household and individual poverty, such as race, location and occupation, are important determinants of this expenditure. An extension here is that labour market poverty should not simply be expressed as a distinction between the employed and the unemployed, given that pockets of deep poverty do prevail amongst the employed. Thirdly, the choice of generic subgroups in the form of individuals or households significantly alters the description of poverty, and therefore the magnitude of expenditure allocations. Finally, it is evident that should the state opt to target those households with domestic workers, farm workers or the unemployed residing in them, a large proportion of poverty in the society will be captured. As such, this kind of targeted expenditure is a creative and effective way to give credence to both the individual and household dimensions of poverty.

Additive and multiplicative income grants

It may be informative here to examine the possibility of non-zero poverty outcomes from public intervention. Thus, a hypothetical public transfer programme set at an intermediate absolute value per individual or household, independent of their income or as a share of their income, can be generated with the sample. In so doing, the sensitivity analysis will yield results that measure the responsiveness of the poverty gap measure to the stipulated state support. As with the previous section, this does not take into account all the added costs associated with such a welfare transfer scheme.

Table 6.4 presents the first case of an additive transfer to households. It is assumed here that each poor household in the society is allocated a lump-sum transfer from the state valued at R2 400 per annum, or R200 per month per household. As with Table 6.1, the household categories are listed by race and location. The total figures indicate that an annual subsidy of R2 400 to each poor home would cost the state an additional R7,2 billion. Expenditure of this value would in turn cause the poverty gap to fall from 0,125 to 0,063, a 49,5% decline in society-wide poverty. The value for (−H/z), as explained in equation (5), reflects the marginal decline in poverty associated with a marginal increase in the value of the subsidy, Δ. Hence, the results show that a R1,00 increase in the subsidy to each agent will cause P_1 to fall by 0,000022 units. An approximate halving of national household poverty requires the state to commit 4,66% of its total annual expenditure.

The racial dimensions of household poverty reappear very strongly here, as do the location effects. Note that given the fact that Asian and white households are likely to be less poor than coloured and African dwellings, the reduction in the poverty gap is larger for the former groups. Hence a transfer to all the poor will have the greatest impact on those closest to the designated poverty line. The stronger impact for urban, as opposed to rural, households reflects the same trend, although the effect is smaller than for the race-based data.

The above simulation was also carried out on individuals, using a subsidy value of R50,00 per month, or R600 per annum. While the results are not tabled here, they show that poverty amongst the labour force falls by 19%, while for the employed it declines by 41%. The large difference here is due to the zero-earners picked up in the labour force. The added cost to the fiscus of reducing poverty to this new level for the labour force would be approximately R2,7 billion, while for the employed the figure would be R433 million. Once again, for the employed the largest expenditure would be for domestic workers and farm workers. The sectoral data reveals that individuals in manufacturing and mining live closest to the poverty line, as a R50 monthly transfer would cause the poverty gap here to fall by over 90%. Clearly, then, even though a lump-sum transfer means the same cash-in-hand for all the poor, it is those who are relatively less poor – or closer to the poverty line – who will benefit the most from the expenditure.

Table 6.5 presents the results of the R2 400 per annum transfer to households containing domestics, farm workers and the unemployed. Once again, it is evident that a large share of the total poverty expenditure would be captured by this subset of households. In addition, the value of the transfer would appear to have the greatest poverty impact for the combined worker homes, as their poverty gap measure would fall by over half. The corresponding figure for the other categories is only marginally lower, though.

Given the uneven distribution of earnings within each of these household categories, the poverty impacts of the transfer do not accord entirely with the initial poverty gap measures. It still remains true, though, that equal transfers to households that differ in poverty status will have a differential outcome on each agent, depending on their position in the overall earnings distribution. It is interesting to note that to decrease poverty by half amongst domestic worker households, the state would need to spend a mere R446 million per annum – amounting to 0,29% of its total annual expenditure in 1995. The commitment for unemployed dwellings is greater given their sheer weight of numbers, thus accounting for 45% of all poverty-eradication expenditure.

The case of a multiplicative income grant programme is presented with the same set of assumptions about perfect targeting and zero running and other costs. However, the very nature

TABLE 6.4

Poverty impact on households of additive transfer of R2 400 per annum

Subgroup	No. of poor households	Total expenditure	Old poverty level	New poverty level	% change	Marginal decline in poverty (–H/z)	% of total expenditure
Total	3 010 855	7 226 052 000	0,125	0,063	–49,50	–0,00002182	4,66
African	2 749 295	6 598 308 000	0,119	0,061	–48,82	–0,00001926	4,26
Coloured	187 707	450 496 800	0,008	0,004	–53,91	–0,00000213	0,29
Asian	11 356	27 254 400	0,000	0,000	–58,01	–0,00000007	0,02
White	62 497	149 992 800	0,002	0,001	–57,90	–0,00000036	0,10
Urban	831 863	1 996 471 200	0,037	0,018	–50,83	–0,00000654	1,29
Semi-urban	52 081	124 994 400	0,002	0,001	–47,96	–0,00000041	0,08
Rural	2 126 911	5 104 586 400	0,088	0,045	–48,94	–0,00001487	3,30

TABLE 6.5

Poverty impact on selected very poor households of additive transfer of R2 400 per annum

Subgroup	No. of poor households	Total expenditure	Old poverty level	New poverty level	% change	Marginal decline in poverty (–H/z)	% of total expenditure
Total	3 010 855	7 226 052 000	0,125	0,063	–49,50	0,00002182	4,66
Domestic workers	185 841	446 018 400	0,008	0,004	–49,92	0,00000095	0,29
Agricultural workers	424 002	1 017 604 800	0,018	0,009	–50,69	0,00000231	0,66
Unemployed	1 371 302	3 291 124 800	0,058	0,030	–48,33	0,00000679	2,12
'Combined'	230 745	553 788 000	0,014	0,007	–52,46	0,00000160	0,36

of the programme means that its poverty outcomes will be different to those of an additive income grant. Only one table will be presented here, and it considers the sample of the three household types that capture most of the deep poverty in the society.

Table 6.6 therefore weighs the relative effectiveness of the additive versus the multiplicative transfer scheme. This is done by assuming a multiplicative case that in total would cost the same as the additive programme. Based on the data, and using the full sample of households, it was found that an income transfer of 35,7% of each agent's income was equivalent to the total cost of the additive grant programme.

What Table 6.6 suggests is that a multiplicative programme will have a smaller impact on poverty when compared with its additive equivalent. Across all the household types, the change in the value of the poverty gap was smaller in comparison with the results of Table 6.5. For example, while an additive transfer to unemployed households caused poverty to fall by 48%, it fell by only 40% in the equivalent multiplicative case. The reason, which is partially but not entirely illustrated in Table 6.6, is that a multiplicative system offers the poor less cash-in-hand

TABLE 6.6

Poverty impact on selected poor households with multiplicative transfer of 0,357

Subgroup	Old poverty level	New poverty level	% change	Marginal dexline in poverty (–H/z)	% of total expenditure
Total	0,125	0,073	–41,75	–0,104	4,66
Domestic workers	0,008	0,005	–42,21	–0,006	0,29
Agricultural workers	0,018	0,010	–44,01	–0,018	0,66
Unemployed	0,058	0,035	–39,95	–0,047	2,12
'Combined'	0,014	0,008	–46,09	–0,006	0,36

compared to those higher up in the income distribution. The lesson for policy-makers, then, is that in order to maximise the impact on poverty alleviation, additive grant schemes are a better option than the multiplicative programme, which disadvantages those at the lower end of the income profile.

Drawbacks of income transfer schemes

It needs to be stressed that despite the apparent care taken in deriving these calculations, they contain some stringent assumptions. Relaxing these assumptions in certain cases renders the results questionable, and also provides some of the reasoning for reluctance amongst policy-makers to institute such schemes. What, then, are some of these assumptions and the problems they raise?

Firstly, it is clearly not realistic to assume that such a hypothetical fiscal transfer scheme would have no administrative or set-up costs. Conceivably, these costs could considerably inflate the estimated expenditures derived above. Indeed, the fact that such a fiscal transfer scheme does not exist at present would entail a massive initial set-up cost, combined with concurrent expenditure in maintaining the scheme. Herein lies the second problem with the analysis: it does not build in the continued cost of the scheme from one year to the next, and how its value may fluctuate. Hence higher poverty levels in the society, brought on, for example, by rising unemployment levels, might see a rapid expansion in the scheme that could make it unaffordable very quickly.

A third, very serious drawback of such a scheme is that does not take labour supply incentives into account. Simply put, the offer of an income grant to employed or unemployed individuals may induce many to stop working or looking for work and live solely on the grant. Studies of labour demand patterns in the economy, though, have argued that in many cases individuals at the low end of the labour market are not going to be in great demand, and indeed large sections of the unemployed are unlikely to be employed anyway (Bhorat & Hodge 1999). In this environment, an income grant could offer much needed respite from indigence in an economy with very low job prospects. A final drawback of the analysis is that it assumes perfect targeting. In other words, it is assumed that every rand spent on the grant will go to the correct recipient. There would be no individuals or households getting the grant who are not eligible, and vice versa. Clearly this is an unlikely outcome in reality. Hence the spill-out effects of such a scheme are serious, and could conceivably mean that the scheme does not effectively reduce poverty to the levels initially aimed at.

For policy-makers, these are serious considerations which require intensive investigation before any agreement can be reached on implementing such a scheme. Hence it is vital that the potential capital and operational expenditure estimates of the grant scheme be first calculated and incorporated into the above estimates. The old-age pension scheme may be used as a guide to these associated costs. In addition, though, the potential for expenditure in the scheme to grow as more recipients gain access to the grant is particularly worrying. Indeed, the incentive effects already alluded to could be a significant factor in expanding the commitment of the scheme to levels well beyond what the state can afford. Even if the state were to consider redistribution within the budget to make finance available for such a scheme, the potential for it to expand as a result of a spurt in qualified recipients is a risk the fiscally constrained state cannot be expected to take. Furthermore, taking into consideration that a more generalised scheme such as the above simulations may not be perfectly targeted, government's reluctance to consider such a grant scheme is wholly understandable.

In this regard, we need to remember that the current social safety net, primarily in the form of the old age pensions scheme and maintenance grants, is already a significant anti-poverty fiscal intervention. It is these grants that have cumulatively contributed to indigent cohorts at least having access to some household income. In other words, the notion of a national income grant scheme must take account of the longstanding schemes that are still being delivered to households.

However, the evidence in other countries and in other studies points unequivocally to the fact that transfer schemes are an effective and efficient manner in which to alleviate poverty in a society. Given this fact, is there any way in which to conceive of a grant scheme that would prove more amenable to the concerns of policy-makers? There would seem to be two immediate alternatives in this regard. Firstly, it may be useful to think of a grant scheme in narrower terms rather than the general, far-reaching schemes suggested above. In this regard, the union movement's Basic Income Grant (BIG) to the unemployed forms a useful point of departure. It is focused, and may have more appeal to policy-makers, given the economy's almost complete inability to absorb these individuals into long-term formal employment. The scheme could be further narrowed down to include, for example, only those unemployed individuals who lost their jobs through structural decline in the economy – which would, in essence, mean targeting those who lost their jobs in the primary sectors. Such a scheme would dovetail well with the current Social Plan in the mining industry.

Secondly, it is possible to think of the poverty effects of an already existing income grant, such as the old-age pension scheme, which is up and running, is well targeted and does not have to concern itself with incentive effects. A key issue that could be explored here is the impact on poverty at the household level of increasing the value of the pension. Indeed, in most poor households, the old age pension is the only regular form of income there is. A more detailed analysis of the possible poverty effects of raising its value would be an ideal avenue for initiating policy discussion with the relevant fiscal authorities. While the budgetary constraints are recognised, it may be illustrated, through the use of the above methodology for example, that household poverty alleviation goals are best met through the old age pension system. In this way, redistribution within the budget towards this grant scheme could be achieved, particularly in the context of alleviating poverty in a cost-effective and efficient manner.

Conclusion

This chapter offers a number of important lessons about poverty and public policy, in addition to some notable pointers for future research. Hence, as a first approximation, the study has yielded detailed baseline estimates of what, free of all additional costs, is required of the state to reduce poverty in the society. While these estimates do abstract from the real obstacles facing such schemes, it is a first step in outlining the expenditure parameters of the poverty problem. In addition, the results show that a creative combination of individual- and household-level data can be very informative in the formulation of appropriate policy interventions. Relatedly, the centrality of the labour market and individual earnings in understanding poverty is displayed. In combining these two units of analysis, we see that poverty in South Africa is readily condensed into three, labour market-defined, household types. The additive and multiplicative grant programmes show firstly that a low financial commitment would go a long way towards reducing poverty. Secondly, the comparison of the two programmes offers the prescription that the additive scheme is friendlier to those who are relatively worse-off amongst the poor.

In terms of extending this work further, it is evident that estimates would need to account for the additional costs associated with the schemes. Secondly, it may be useful to derive a matrix of the required financial commitment from the state, over a short-run period of, say, five years. This would present a more realistic picture of potential expenditure by the state. But perhaps the most optimal way in which to enhance the analysis here is to apply the above methodology to more defined transfer schemes, such as a grant to the unemployed, or to already existing welfare interventions such as the old-age pension scheme.

7

Social Policy to Address Poverty

Servaas van der Berg

Social stability and racial harmony are indeed important components of the social infrastructure that any society has to offer, and this breaks down once the interracial differences – the average differences between groups – go beyond a critical level. What this threshold is varies from society to society – but the fact that it exists cannot be denied. (Kanbur, 1998:26)

The analysis contained in previous chapters indicates that poverty is still endemic in South Africa, that it has a strong racial dimension and that it has its origins largely in the labour market. Despite the continuing relevance of race for identifying the poor, the analysis has also shown that labour market discrimination has declined as a factor in the generation of poverty and inequality. What appears to contribute more are other factors also correlated with race, such as differentials in education, location (urban–rural) and family size and composition. Moreover, as will be argued below, if we take into account the large differentials in educational quality not considered in earnings functions, the residual role for labour market race discrimination in explaining earnings differentials may well be small. Thus, there is an urgent need to identify those factors that are amenable to policy intervention, in order to reduce poverty and inequality.

Unlike countries with low poverty rates, where transient poverty is relatively large – that is, movement in and out of poverty is relatively large compared to the stock of poverty at any moment in time (Van den Bosch *et al.* 1997:107) – it is likely that endemic poverty is more the norm in a country such as South Africa, which is marked by high levels of poverty and structural unemployment. There is no panel data available to support this conclusion, however. Endemic poverty combined with high expectations and high levels of inequality, particularly racial inequality, are likely to be bad for stability and therefore undermine prospects of growth. As Kanbur (1998:26) remarks, 'The core literature on income distribution and development is strangely silent on interracial or interethnic dimensions of distribution as development process, while the daily political discourse in many countries, particularly in Africa, has this as a constant topic of discussion and tension.' This racial dimension to poverty and inequality enhances the urgent need to develop policies to reduce poverty.

The similarities with Latin America are striking when we look at the pattern of inequality and many other aspects of South African economic life. The nations of Latin America share with

South Africa the status of middle-income developing countries, as well as high levels of inequality. For this reason, it is useful to draw on a recent analysis of inequality in Latin America by the Inter-American Development Bank (hereafter IADB) (1999):

- Latin American (as indeed also South African) inequality is associated with large wage differentials. 'In other words, it results not only from differences between owners of capital and workers, but from a divergence of incomes among workers' (IADB 1999:1).

- '(M)uch of Latin America's inequality relates to the difference between the top 10% of the population and the rest' (IADB 1999:1). This is also the case for South Africa. Thus, while the richest decile have a per capita income 60% higher than that of the second richest decile in the US, and 160% higher in Latin America, it is 208% higher in South Africa.[1]

- As in Latin America, it will be shown below that in South Africa 'much of this gap between the top 10% and the rest reflects the 'slow and unequal progress in improving the level and quality of schooling' (IADB 1999:2), and in particular high returns to and unequal access to higher education (IADB 1999:5). As in Latin America, primary education is virtually universal in South Africa, while the challenge at this stage remains 'to improve the quality of primary education and to universalise secondary education' (IADB 1999:5).

- In Latin America, '(f)amilies play many roles in the complex relationships that sustain income inequality. They mitigate the effects of high inequality by sharing resources, often across generations. They also play a role in determining how many of their members should try to find work, how many children to have, and how much education to give them' (IADB 1999:2). This is also true in South Africa where, in addition, migration and urban–rural remittances play a particularly important role in mitigating inequality (although the separation of migrants and their families of origin into separate households may accentuate measured inter-household inequality). Furthermore, family formation is strongly influenced by the pervasiveness of unemployment, leading to many young males attaching themselves to older households until a fairly high age (Simkins 1998). The presence of old-age pensions as an important source of income in rural areas also influences family structures through retaining older members within the household (Case & Deaton 1998).[2]

- The demographic transition presently offers both Latin America and South Africa some respite: fertility decline and aging are having opposite effects on dependency ratios, but the effect of fertility decline still dominates, thus reducing child dependency burdens and labour force growth rates. In South Africa, fertility decline started somewhat later and fertility is still higher than in Latin America, so the benefits of this effect on child dependency burdens are somewhat less strong and the rate of labour force growth higher than in Latin America.

- As in Latin America, the capital market largely bypasses the poor and even large segments of the middle-income group in South Africa. This not only excludes them from the economic mainstream, but reduces overall growth opportunities by wasting potential entrepreneurial resources.

- As in Latin America, the scope for more progressive taxation is severely limited, and a widening of the tax base plus progressive spending offer better possibilities for improving equity. But as the IADB report (1999:4) points out, economic instability is strongly related to inequality, and such inequality makes fiscal prudence politically much more difficult.
- Whereas Latin America has improved its macroeconomic performance in recent years, there is still considerable uncertainty whether South Africa's growth rates will be adequate to out-pace population growth.

Thus South Africa has much to learn from the experiences of and analysis of Latin American countries. In Latin America, there are some grounds for optimism:

> Although it may be little solace for those riding in the last cars of the development train, most of Latin America appears to be turning the corner; as these trends continue, they should provide a basis to reduce income inequality in the future, as long as adequate economic and social policies are in place (IADB 1999:3).

This conclusion as to prospects for reduced inequality in Latin America may equally apply to South Africa, but for the fact that economic growth is as yet far less entrenched in the latter. Adequate and sustained growth is required to ensure that the distributional conflict in South Africa does not remain a zero-sum game tearing at the fabric of social stability. Broadly speaking, two routes for reduced poverty suggest themselves. The one is to reduce inequity through various interventions, including those targeted mainly at the poor. The alternative route is concerned with an acceleration of economic growth. It is widely agreed in the development literature today that such growth contributes most to the reduction of poverty if it is strongly associated with utilising the major assets of the poor, particularly their labour (De Haan et al. 1997). Growth can strongly impact directly on poverty, even without improved distribution, but may also allow distribution to take place without engendering increased conflict. The macroeconomic conditions for growth fall outside the ambit of this book, but we shall return to growth as a factor in poverty reduction when we consider the growth effects of human capital provision.

Based on the work presented in this book, as well as the international literature, there are a number of more promising avenues for improving equity and targeting the poor. In the South African circumstances, the most promising routes appear to be:

- Social transfers to the poor, which already contribute in a major way to reducing poverty in South Africa (Ardington & Lund 1995; Van der Berg 1997; Case & Deaton 1998).
- Expanding and improving the educational system to reduce earnings differentials, improve access of the poor to available job opportunities and accelerate growth. Training, both on and off the job, would naturally also contribute in this regard.

- Improving access for the poor to other social services (health, housing and social infrastructure). Though this would not necessarily improve their incomes, it might improve other aspects of their life – for example, through improved sanitation, access to water, health services, nutrition and housing. However, as this book has focused almost exclusively on money-metric aspects of poverty (income poverty), we shall not discuss policy options in this field.

- Improving access for the poor to financial services, particularly credit facilities. This is a highly technical issue about which present household surveys can tell very little, and consequently it will not be discussed any further. This does not, however, detract from its importance for the poor and for broad-based economic growth.

The following two sections will focus on the two areas of social policy directly relevant to improving the incomes of the poor, namely education and social transfers (safety nets).

Education

The role of education in reducing poverty is of paramount importance, because of its contribution to improving the earnings potential of the poor, both in competition for jobs and earnings in a static labour market, and as a source of growth and employment in itself. As Kanbur (1998:20) puts it, 'The distribution of physical and human capital emerges from the theoretical and empirical literature as the key to distributional consequences of growth, and as the determinant of growth itself.' For this reason, we shall investigate the possible impact of education in terms of both its distributional consequences and its potential impact on economic growth. Then we will briefly discuss possible educational policy consequences of the economic debates on the role of education.

Education, inequality and poverty

Previous chapters in this book have shown that education is crucial in determining labour force participation, employment and earnings. This is similar to the results found in comparable societies. Ferreira & Litchfield (1998:32), for instance, report that between one-quarter and one-third of income differentials between households in Chile can be ascribed to differences in the educational attainment of the household head – a far greater proportion than captured by any other characteristic of the household.

Inequality of education has long been a determining factor in earnings distribution in South Africa. In recent decades, there has been a substantial reduction in schooling inequality, as reflected in the years of educational output (unadjusted for the quality of education). For instance, working from the same data set as most of the studies in this book, Lam (1999) shows the decline in inequality in years of education completed between two birth cohorts separated by thirty years (shown in Table 7.1). Note that not only mean-invariant measures such as the coefficient of variation have declined, but also the variance. This is important, for if earnings were log-linearly related to years of education, an increased variance could well be associated with increased earnings inequality even if the coefficient of variation declined, as Lam (1999) argues indeed occurred in Brazil.[3] In South Africa, schooling variance declined even amongst Africans. Between the different races, schooling inequality greatly declined, as shown in Figure 7.1, which shows the mean years of schooling by birth cohort. Africans in the cohort born in 1920 had a mean backlog of 8,0 years of education compared to whites; those born in 1950 still had a 6,0-year backlog, the 1960 cohort a 4,6-year backlog and the 1970s cohort a backlog that had been reduced to only 3,2 years.

Interestingly, Lam's comparisons of educational inequality in Brazil and South Africa are supported by the work of Filmer and Pritchett (1998), who find that Latin American educational inequality is still large, even more so than in many countries of Southern and Eastern Africa (though they did not include South Africa in their sample). Londoño (1996) confirms that Latin American educational performance – in terms of years of education completed – lags far behind most other countries at this level of economic development.

Moll (1998) convincingly shows that South African earnings inequality between race groups decreased between 1981 and 1993, whilst inequality in earnings within race groups was increasing. Thus, the net result was to leave overall earnings inequality largely unchanged, as shown in Table 7.2. It is likely that changes in education played only a minor role in the shifts in earnings. Moll argues that the growing earnings inequality within race groups was rather caused by the removal of labour market discrimination over the preceding decades, which allowed more wage mobility within race groups, with some Africans better positioned than others to benefit from the new opportunities for upward mobility. At the same time, poorly educated whites in particular lost the protection they had historically enjoyed in the form of barriers to African job advancement. But even in this case, education is important, in that it determines who can and who cannot benefit from the new opportunities for Africans in the labour market.

TABLE 7.1

Educational inequality for two South African cohorts (1995)[a]

	Cohorts 55–59	Cohorts 25–29
Mean	5,77	9,05
Standard deviation	4,51	3,60
Coefficient of variation	0,78	0,40
Gini	0,44	0,21

[a] Lam 1999:Table 2.

FIGURE 7.1

Mean years of education by race and birth cohort (1995) (3-year moving averages)[a]

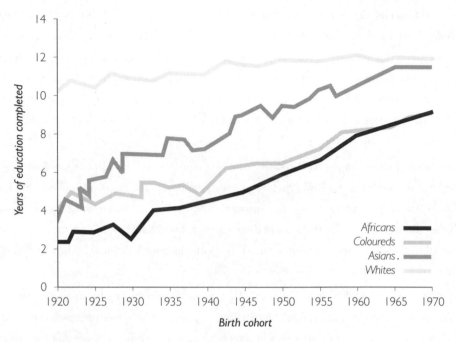

[a] *Source*: OHS 1995.

TABLE 7.2

Inequality of monthly earnings by race (1980 and 1993)[a]

	1980	1993
Gini coefficient	0,52	0,51
Coefficient of variation	1,19	1,12
L-statistic[b]	0,49	0,50
L-statistic: Africans	0,14	0,28
L-statistic: Asians	0,21	0,28
L-statistic: coloureds	0,25	0,35
L-statistic: whites	0,21	0,28
Within-group inequality	0,17	0,29
Between-group inequality	0,32	0,21

[a] Moll 1998: Tables 1 and 2.

[b] The L-statistic (mean logarithmic deviation) is an additively decomposable measure of inequality that ranges from 0 (complete equality) to infinity. If utility has a logarithmic form, L measures the difference between maximum social welfare with a given income (the ideal state of distribution) and the actual social welfare (Moll 1998:4). It is calculated as the mean of the natural logarithms of earnings, minus the natural logarithm of mean earnings.

When working with South African educational data, however, it is important to consider that the quality of education still varies considerably. In this respect, too, the similarities with Latin America are great, for there too 'the poor receive an inferior quality of schooling' (IADB 1998:53). To some extent, the old dividing lines of race have blurred in South Africa: large numbers of African pupils are now attending schools that formerly served whites only, while there is also growing diversity in the quality of schools serving mainly African pupils. Nevertheless, there are still considerable differentials in the ability of schools to have their pupils pass matriculation, with most formerly African schools performing much more poorly than white schools. Very high matriculation failure rates (more than half of matriculants failed in 1998, and only 13% received university exemption [Edusource 1999:5]), despite high repetition rates, also indicate that pass rates at lower standards are still perhaps artificially high. Thus educational attainment figures below the matriculation level, for Africans in particular, may be inflated relative to the cognitive education levels they have mastered.

But the quality differentials go beyond only the ability to get pupils to pass matriculation. These also lie in the quality of the matriculation itself, in terms of the standard at which matric is passed, as well as the subject choice. It is a source of much concern in South Africa, for instance, that few schools serving mainly Africans perform adequately in terms of providing good background in mathematics or science. So, for instance, only 45% of all matriculation candidates wrote mathematics in 1997 (with a marked male bias); only 21% passed it. For science, these percentages were even lower, at 25% and 16%, respectively. Moreover, a large proportion of those who wrote mathematics did so at the standard grade, a standard far below what is conventional in developed countries. Only 50% and 42% of teachers teaching mathematics and science have studied these subjects beyond secondary school level. In the Western Cape, the province with the best matriculation results, only 24% of matriculation candidates attempted mathematics at the higher grade, and only 20% passed it.

Another indication of the inequality in educational output can be gleaned from some data for the Western Cape. As pass rates are almost uniformly high, differentials between schools (inequality) in terms of pass rates are relatively low, as shown in Table 7.3. However, as soon as more advanced levels of school performance are evaluated (percentage A-candidates, or percentage exemptions), inequality increases considerably, with Gini coefficients of 0,56 and 0,80, respectively.

The differentials in the quality of education provided are also well illustrated by Figure 7.2, which shows, for African and whites aged 13 to 18, literacy and numeracy test scores for 1993 on an eight-point scale, where questions have been set at approximately Grade 7 (age 12) level. Even the performance of whites is not very encouraging, but what is particularly alarming is that Africans do far worse than whites on both these tests. This has to be seen against the fact that educational levels attained by Africans and whites at age 13 differ relatively little. The poorer

African attainment at higher age levels can thus perhaps be seen as the delayed effect of lower cognitive achievement levels on progression through high school and on matriculation pass rates. Figure 7.3 shows that though Africans aged 13 to 18 in 1995 had attained between 78% and 86% of white levels of years of education, their 1993 performance in terms of literacy scores ranged only between 50% and 63% of white levels, and their numeracy scores lagged even further behind, at 36% to 47% of white levels. Indeed, at the cross-country level, '. . . school children from higher income countries tend to achieve higher test scores, holding fixed other factors that influence student achievement.' (Lee & Barro 1997:23). Whether this is the effect of non-school factors (home environment or education of parents) or of qualitative differences in school productivity between rich and poor countries is not clear, but in South Africa test-score differentials by race are so large that it is likely that school and teacher quality play a determining role.

TABLE 7.3

Inequality of educational outcomes between schools in the Western Cape (1997)[a]

	% A-aggregate	% Exemption	% Pass
Mean	2,6%	23,0%	80,6%
Standard deviation	5,0%	22,0%	22,5%
Coefficient of variation	1,94	0,96	0,28
Gini coefficient	0,80	0,56	0,15

[a] Own calculations from Western Cape Education Department data.

FIGURE 7.2

Literacy and numeracy test scores by age and race (1993) (test level: age 12)[a]

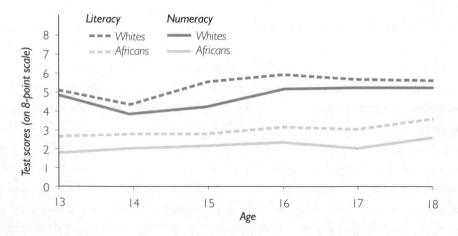

[a] *Source*: Case & Deaton 1999: Table 5.

FIGURE 7.3

African literacy and numeracy test scores and years of education relative to white levels by age (1993–95)[a]

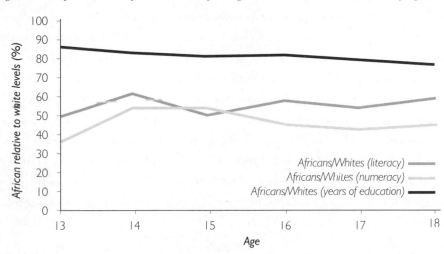

[a] *Sources:* OHS 1995; Case & Deaton 1999: Table 5.

Case and Deaton (1999) show that factors associated with higher test scores for Africans on both literacy and numeracy include the age of respondents, years of education completed (standardising for age) and education of the head of the household. Keeping all other factors constant, their regression coefficients suggest that almost ten years of additional education would be required to bring African cognitive levels in terms of both literacy and numeracy up to the same standards as those of whites ('four additional years generate one additional correct answer on the tests' [Case & Deaton, 1999:26]). This may be an exaggeration, but it does show that the former African school system is completely inadequate to integrate large numbers of people into the modern economy. From an economic viewpoint, this must be the yardstick by which the efficacy of the educational system should be measured.

Considering these quality differentials, some of the racial differentials in wages for persons with the same education and experience may in fact result not from labour market discrimination, but from pre-labour market discrimination in the quality of schooling. In some Latin American countries, where private education is important to improve educational quality, the Inter-American Development Bank (IADB 1998:54–5) found significant differentials in the labour market earnings for individuals from different income groups with similar education and experience, which the authors ascribe to differential quality of education. 'Estimates show that individuals from the lower deciles receive a primary education whose quality (measured in terms of income generation capacity) is 35% lower than that of the next decile above' (IADB 1998:54).

Not surprisingly, there is also increasing inequality developing within the African population as far as educational attainment is concerned. This largely follows the lines of income: more affluent families are better able to support their children through school, so that there is increasing stratification taking place within African society. Figure 7.4 shows that children from the top two deciles among Africans do considerably better than their poorer counterparts and only start falling behind whites at age fifteen. Case & Deaton (1999:21) conclude that private resources (expenditures) were indeed a major factor in determining South African educational outcomes under apartheid. 'Pupils in better-off African households do better in their education, and we find no parallel for whites. That the education of Africans but not whites is constrained by financial resources is further supported by the fact that many Africans who are not in school (but not whites) report lack of resources as the reason' (Case & Deaton, 1999:28). Furthermore, newly acquired access to better-quality schools for the more affluent is likely to have accentuated qualitative educational differentials amongst Africans.

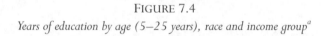

FIGURE 7.4

Years of education by age (5–25 years), race and income group[a]

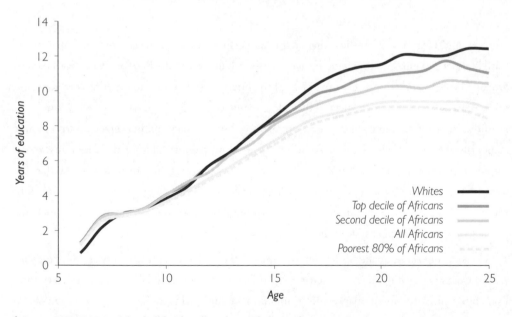

[a] *Source*: OHS 1995 ('at school' defined as all students/scholars without matric).

In the labour market, returns to education are determined by educational differentials in association with the demand for labour. Thus far, little is known about past patterns of returns to education and their evolution over time in South Africa, to say nothing about what these would have been in the absence of apartheid-based labour market interventions. It is therefore extremely difficult to predict with any confidence what would happen to labour market inequality given future educational outcomes and patterns of economic growth and development. However, international patterns of development point to growing demand for skills, and without a large spurt in the availability of such skills, educational premia are likely to remain high. Hence the reduction of labour market inequality requires a substantial improvement in the supply of skills through an improvement in both the quantity and quality of education. Studies on the returns to education for the United States for the whole of the 20th century (Goldin & Katz 1999) found that only an enormous expansion in secondary schooling after 1910 made possible a reduction in the returns to education until the 1950s, since which time returns to education again rose as skills demand outstripped supply. 'Skill-biased technological change' (Goldin & Katz 1999:25) was a major factor in the US (as has also been shown for recent decades by Murphy & Welch 1994), as has also been shown in South Africa (Bhorat & Hodge 1999).

Education and growth
The new growth literature has again brought to the fore the importance of human capital and technology for economic growth. The neoclassical growth model of Solow pointed to unconditional convergence of per capita incomes, for two major reasons:

- Firstly, capital accumulation would shift to less developed countries once diminishing returns to capital make further investment in developed countries unattractive.

- Secondly, if technology is a public good freely available to all, developing countries should enjoy the 'benefit of coming late', which would allow them to grow more rapidly than more developed countries by utilising existing technologies, without having to bear the cost of developing them (Fagerberg 1994).

Given these assumptions, catch-up and convergence should in principle have taken place. That this has not occurred, and that an increasing gap has instead arisen between the 'convergence club' – countries able to share in international capital movements and technology and indeed converging on the world leader – and the majority of the developing world (Baumol et al. 1989), calls for an alternative view of the growth process. The theoretical underpinnings for this have come to the fore with the new growth literature and the concept of endogenous growth.

One common feature of many endogenous growth models is in their modelling of technology as something whose benefits are to some extent appropriable. This allows for a different view of the role and the development of technology, for only if they can appropriate (some of) the benefits will firms find it attractive to invest in technological research and development.

A second common feature of the new growth literature is a new role for human capital as separate from labour or physical capital in the production process.

The new growth literature has spawned a further array of empirical studies attempting to isolate the crucial variables in international growth. Such attempts, whether based on a theoretical model or only on empirical observations, have been relatively unsuccessful, *inter alia* because the quality of the data used has been highly suspect, and the human capital and technology variables very difficult to specify or to measure. Thus it is not surprising that Levine & Renelt's (1992) finding still largely applies, that international growth regressions have been unable to identify convincingly any other contributor to long-term growth than capital accumulation.

Despite the failure to prove the role of human capital in long-term economic growth, most economists agree that the reason for this lies mainly in data deficiencies and variable specification rather than in the absence of such a relationship flowing from human capital to growth. (There is also no doubting the flow of reverse causality as well, which complicates empirical analysis.) Three forms of education–growth relationships have been variously tested, being consistent with *a priori* views of informed observers in this field:

- Improvements in education and in economic performance (growth) go together (which accentuates the difficulty of determining the direction of causality).
- Educational improvement is a condition for higher growth, so that high initial levels of education lead to high rates of economic growth, all other things being constant.
- The distribution of education is crucial, in a similar way as others have pointed to the initial distribution of other productive assets (land or capital) as a contributor to accelerated growth.

A more general explanation is also possible, namely that human capital is part of what has been termed 'social capability', a crucial ingredient that determines whether countries are able to attract international investment or utilise available technology so as to reduce the gap between themselves and developed countries (Abromovitz 1989). Social capability obviously incorporates more than only human capital (e.g. institutions, governance, etc.), but clearly human capital is a component.

Irrespective of the way we view the relationship between education and growth, the problem in taking further the work in this field appears to remain the paucity of dependable data in which the human capital variable can be specified in a form that accords with the theoretical point of departure. Much of the work has taken school enrolment (usually gross enrolment) as proxy for human capital, which it is not; almost all have had to ignore possible differentials in the quality of education; and studies differ in whether they use data on primary, secondary or tertiary education, or combinations thereof.

So, for instance, Barro (1999:15 & Table 1) finds that economic '(g)rowth is positively related to the stock of human capital at the start of each period, as measured by the average years of attainment at the secondary and higher levels of adult males. (Growth turns out to be insignificantly related to secondary and higher attainment of females and to primary attainment of males and females.)' However, though schooling appears to affect growth rates, it does not impact significantly on investment (Barro, 1999:16 & Table 2). If these results are robust, the implication must be that the effect of education comes through productivity improvement rather than through attracting more investment in physical capital. This is a finding that is crucial for South Africa, with its history of poor (but improving) multifactor productivity – but the data deficiencies warn against giving too strong weight to these results. Only lately have some researchers (e.g. Lee & Barro 1998) started the painstaking work of collecting the data that will be necessary to move beyond the present empirical impasse that research in this field has reached.

Education policy

Four broad issues of economic policy arise in the educational area, namely the question of the fiscal costs of education in aggregate, allocation of resources within education, the productivity of educational resource use and the economic requirements in terms of education. This last issue has been dealt with to some extent in the preceding section. National resources for education and the allocation of resources within education have been treated in detail in an excellent recent government report (South Africa 1998a), so they will only receive perfunctory treatment here. That leaves the question of educational productivity as the major policy issue to be discussed.

By international standards, South Africa allocates a large share of its national resources to public education; its public education spending ratio, at about 7% of GDP, is close to the highest in the world. Moreover, education spending has increased relatively rapidly. Shifting further fiscal resources to education does not appear to be a viable proposition. Moreover, larger financial flows to education in the past five years did not, in fact, increase real resources for education: the impact of the fiscal resource shift was overshadowed by wage increases for teachers, with the result that the total equivalent number of full-time teachers employed may even have marginally declined, while pupil numbers continued to rise. In some of the richer provinces, cutbacks in educational personnel could therefore not be matched by increases in personnel in the educationally worse endowed provinces. Internationally, the development process appears to give rise to the relative burden of teacher salaries falling (i.e. relative to per capita GDP):

> . . . from 1960 to 1990, the real average salary per primary school teacher increased from $10 428 to $26 820 in the OECD and from $4 869 to $7 179 in developing countries. The rising trend applies to all developing countries . . . In contrast, the figures for the CPEs have fallen markedly from $14 462 in 1965 to $4 771 in 1990. The ratios of estimated real salaries of primary school teachers to per capita GDP have typically declined over time; from 1965 to 1990, the value dropped from 2,5 to 2,2 in the OECD, from 4,9 to 3,6 in the overall group of developing countries, and from 7,4 to 1,7 in the CPEs. These ratios tend to be higher in developing countries, especially in Sub-Saharan Africa (5,1 in 1990) than in the OECD.' (Lee & Barro 1997:17–18) (All figures in 1985 PPP-dollars)

In South Africa, in contrast, teacher salaries outpaced the growth of national resources. One reason for this was the strong bargaining power of the teacher unions, which has allowed them to raise their salaries far higher than the rate of inflation. Furthermore, African teachers felt themselves left behind when African advancement in the public sector accelerated after democratisation, as there were few opportunities for promotion within the teaching sector that they could benefit from.[4] Thus their frustrations were vented in the wage bargaining process. After democratisation, then, when the need for resource shifts across the formerly racially-based departments was crucial, resources increasingly had to be directed to personnel spending, leaving a growing dearth of non-personnel spending. Thus, from 1995/6 to 1997/8 personnel expenditure in real terms increased by 20%, while non-personnel expenditure declined by 17% (South Africa 1998a:27).

As the growth in pupil numbers still exceeds the growth rate of the economy, the government team investigating the medium-term expenditure framework (South Africa 1998a) came to the conclusion that there is likely to be a major funding problem in education in coming years, unless:

- more funds are allocated to education, an option they regard as fiscally infeasible, and which internationally has been shown not always to improve educational outcomes (Gupta *et al.* 1999:4);
- pupil–teacher ratios rise even further, which is unacceptable to government, teacher unions and parents;
- teacher salaries decline in real terms, which is strongly opposed by the teacher unions;
- some combination of the above occurs.

From an economic efficiency point of view, it can be argued that the malaise affecting the South African educational system lies less in terms of allocative inefficiency than in *x*-inefficiency. Reallocating resources from one level of education to another, as many suggest for developing countries (Gupta *et al.* 1999), would bring little gain in South Africa, and it is not even clear which level of education most requires additional resources, as will presently be discussed. There is perhaps a stronger case for shifting more financial resources to non-personnel teaching resources; personnel spending is so dominant that even a small shift of this nature would have a major impact on the availability of classroom resources.

However, the clearest problem is one of utilising existing resources better, even in their present application. The major inefficiency in qualitative terms lies in what used to be the African school system – by far the largest part of the system – where the quality of learning in schools is often abysmal. Strong words from the President and the Minister of Education in recent years show that they blame this in part on a lack of discipline within schools, and in particular amongst teachers.

This is the result of a typical principal–agent problem. Outputs of the educational system are extremely difficult to monitor, as is teacher effort (input). Thus low teacher productivity is difficult to overcome. The educational authorities have responded to this problem by attempting to shift the monitoring to the parent community as the final 'principal'. Unfortunately, however, this policy has had limited success in those schools where the parents themselves have had little education and therefore do not feel confident about their ability to assess the contribution of teachers. Moreover, lines of authority are also not always clear and school principals often find it difficult to act against undisciplined teachers or pupils.

Thus there is still a large effort required to restore the 'culture of learning' to South African schools. The expenditure review team notes that the COLTS (Culture of Learning, Teaching and Service) campaign launched in 1996 'was the first more or less official recognition of the fact that efficiency and work effort problems, rather than funding by itself, were at the heart of the problems in the education sector' (South Africa, 1998a:35). The effect of the culture of learning on educational performance manifests itself completely differently in the case of East Asia, which appears to be outperforming other educational systems: ' . . . a major component of East Asia's academic performance is left unexplained by the family and school inputs that were included in the regressions.' . . . 'The significance of the East Asian dummy may reflect the existence of an "Asian value", which is broadly defined by the cultural and religious features unique to the East Asian countries' (Lee & Barro 1997:25). Thus culture and history play a strong role in education, and South Africa is presently poorly placed to benefit from this.

One avenue to improve the situation, as always where there is a principal–agent problem, is the provision of more information. At present, there is a paucity of information for the education authorities to analyse the educational situation and their policy options. They have only one measure of educational output available to them, and that is matriculation results, but these still do not identify the roots of the problem. In the first part of this chapter, we noted that literacy and numeracy levels amongst Africans are already far below par as early as age thirteen. Allocating resources based on matriculation results cannot adequately address a problem which requires far earlier intervention. Thus the question of whether resources should go to secondary or to primary level, even if matriculation pass rates were the criterion, cannot be properly answered without more data on the qualitative performance of different parts of the school system. This requires a large-scale and continued effort at measuring cognitive achievement at different levels within the educational system in order to better understand the relationship between the home background of pupils, educational inputs and enhancement of cognitive achievement. Moreover, identifying the poor-performing schools in order to take remedial action requires a better understanding of how schools perform, and the reasons for this.

Thus the returns-to-education literature, useful as it is, cannot assist South Africa very much in resource allocation across different levels of the educational system. In sum:

- It is not clear that more resources are the solution to problems of expansion of outputs. In fact, access to education is no longer a major problem, as is clear from Figure 7.5, which shows that more than 90% of children of all race groups remain at school until attaining matric or reaching at least the age of 16, and that among Africans it is common to remain in the school system much longer, due to poor progression rates, amongst other factors.

FIGURE 7.5

At school as percentage of each age group, by race (1995)[a]

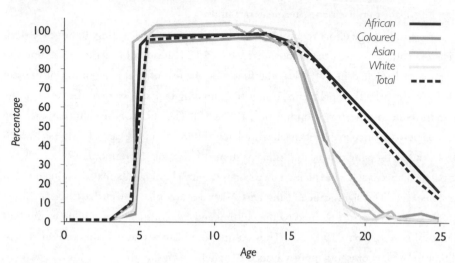

[a] *Source:* OHS 1995.

- The quality of the output varies considerably amongst schools and over time, so that the educational returns literature is always suspect.
- The needs of the economy in terms of the type rather than the level of educational output should also be considered, and may affect the returns to education (e.g. the importance of the choice of mathematics as school subject for further training).
- Returns to education are the result of the interaction between the supply and demand for human capital, and the latter is related to the growth path of the economy, which is itself changing. Moreover, insofar as growth itself may be determined by the availability of appropriate levels of education, there is an endogeneity problem that cannot be solved.

Social security[5]

Background to South African social security

The South African social security system is surprisingly developed for a middle-income developing country. This is evident from both coverage against contingencies and social security spending ratios (Van der Merwe 1996:296 & 318). This fact can perhaps be ascribed to the way that the system developed under apartheid – as a welfare state for whites – and expanded under social and political pressure to incorporate other groups (Van der Berg 1997). If one allows for the fact that South African occupational insurance is really a form of social insurance that does not flow through the budget, social security expenditure ratios have reached levels only attained by Western European welfare states in the post-World War II period (see Alber 1982:64, Table 4). In a country known for its racial inequalities and discriminatory social policies that were poorly targeted at the poor, it appears puzzling that social security is so advanced.

Access to modern employment has become a major dividing line within the population, with all insiders increasingly sharing in the privileged situation previously reserved for whites, and unemployed outsiders becoming further impoverished through lack of skills, geographic location and marginalisation in wider society. An intermediate group of people, though formally employed (often in agriculture, domestic service or mining, and including many women in the first two categories), is only tenuously linked to employment and to the modern consumer society because of their low wages, uncertain jobs or status as migrant workers. As in other developing countries, the large part of the labour force lacking formal employment cannot be reached by social insurance, and as will be shown, not all the employed are covered by social insurance. Yet there is a well-developed social assistance system that, although fiscally expensive – it costs more than 2% of GDP – reaches many of the poor.

In apartheid South Africa, an embryonic welfare state was erected to protect whites against various contingencies. Ironically, the extension of this system to other groups puts South Africa in the rather unique situation for a semi-industrial country of having the trappings of a modern welfare state. Today, South African social security has two main components:

- *Occupational (social) insurance*, which includes retirement benefits for a substantial proportion of the formally employed labour force; a somewhat inadequate system of worker's compensation against injuries sustained at work; a system of unemployment insurance which cannot address the major unemployment risks associated with structural rather than cyclical unemployment; and health insurance for the better skilled.[6]

- *Social assistance*, the three main pillars of which are social old-age pensions, disability grants and child and family grants – all means-tested to ensure targeting at the poorest.

An interesting dimension to the development of South African social security was the tension that existed between the liberal Anglo-Saxon *laissez-faire* position, which was sceptical of social security, and continental European influences, which were more supportive of it (Kruger 1992:117; Van der Merwe 1996:381). The latter influences were dominant in the old Boer republics and in the pre-British Cape Colony, and later came to the fore under Afrikaner Nationalist rule – only now with a racial bias. *Laissez-faire* enjoyed stronger support under direct British rule, and later from the predominantly English business class.

Although there was little poor relief and barely any other social services in the early period of European settlement, racial distinctions soon crept into the provision of services (Kruger 1992:113). British occupation in the early 19th century brought pre-Victorian views on the distinction between the 'deserving' and 'undeserving' poor, and strengthened the racial bias in the provision of social services, a pattern that remained dominant for almost two centuries.

The first pension fund, introduced in the old Transvaal (South African) Republic in 1882, was prescribed neither by legislation nor by convention, and could thus in no way have been regarded as social insurance. However, in the 1920s, occupational retirement insurance expanded rapidly to include many skilled (mainly white) employees. The norm of excluding the lower skilled (and therefore, in the context of apartheid, almost all Africans) from such coverage remained, though. It was only in the 1960s and the early 1970s, when rapid industrialisation increasingly drew African workers into industry, that occupational retirement insurance widened to also include less-skilled workers. The (mainly) white trade unions were instrumental both in this and in having coverage extended to more industries. Membership of both occupational and private retirement funds increased from 923 000 in 1958 to 9 309 000 in 1993 (Smith Committee 1995:D2.4a), a growth rate of almost 7% per annum over three and a half decades (though these figures include extensive duplication, in which many people belonged to more than one fund). The membership growth rate of 8% in the 1960s and 10% in the 1970s slowed to 3,7% in the 1980s, partly as a result of saturation of the market.

After the African trade union movement became a political force in the 1970s, social security only really came to the fore as an issue in 1981 when the government attempted to enforce preservation of pension rights when people changed jobs – ironically, an issue that the trade unions effectively mobilised against, and their victory became another milestone in the empowerment of African workers. African workers saw the Louw Committee's recommendation for compulsory preservation of pension rights upon withdrawal from a fund as an attempt to deny them access to their own money (Mouton Committee 1992:153; Rumney 1988:35). Moreover, according to Adler (1989:20), 'most African people see the State as the legitimate source of old-age pensions'. Thus, this measure met with such fierce resistance that the government was forced to withdraw the proposed bill. After this victory, trade unions took a far more active interest in retirement benefits. As low-income workers who retire often prefer a lump sum benefit so that they can buy land, cattle or a house (Basson, 1987:34) – partly because the means test favours holding certain assets rather than receiving income (Mouton Committee 1992:54; Sephton *et al.* 1990:45, 101) – many provident rather than pension funds were subsequently established. (Retiring pension fund members can receive at most one-third of their benefits as a lump sum payout and must take the rest as a monthly pension. Provident fund members, however, may take their full benefit as a lump sum.)

Thus social retirement insurance was initially instituted for whites (who dominated the skilled positions in formal employment), but eventually extended to Africans. However, the majority of the African labour force, who are either unemployed or in jobs not covered by social retirement insurance, remain outside this safety net.

The second pillar of the social security system consists of social assistance, that is, categorical transfers funded from general government revenues[7] to certain individuals in the form of social old-age pensions, disability grants or child support grants – conditional upon the recipient qualifying in accordance with a means test. Social assistance benefits presently still reach far more people than social insurance. The central feature is means-testing, which by its very nature encourages a 'poverty trap' and can also in certain circumstances lead to perverse incentives.

Modern social assistance in South Africa mainly dates from the period 1910 to 1933, when many new schemes were introduced, although Africans and Asians were initially often excluded from benefits (Kruger 1992:159) The exclusion of Africans was predicated on the 'civilised labour' view that people accustomed to modern lifestyles and consumption patterns had greater need of social protection than those in rural subsistence agriculture, who were not proletarianised and were thus presumed to be better placed to meet traditional subsistence needs:

> Rural natives were excluded from old-age pensions mainly on the assumption that Native custom makes provision for maintaining dependent persons. Urban Natives were excluded in consequence, regardless of their needs, owing 'to the difficulty of applying any statutory distinction between them and other Natives' (South Africa, Social Security Committee 1944:19, as quoted by Kruger 1992:165).

Military pensions date from 1919, and in 1928 social pensions were instituted for those whites and coloureds not covered by occupational retirement insurance, subject to age criteria and a means test to ensure that only the needy were targeted The white population dependent on social pensions remained relatively small despite an increasingly liberal means test, as occupational retirement insurance covered the more affluent. In 1943, take-up rates amongst the elderly were 40% for whites and 56% for coloureds (South Africa, Social Security Committee 1944:43–4, 58). By that year, only 4% of all social assistance spending was on Africans (mainly targeted relief and pensions for the blind), 1% for Asians and 16% for coloureds (South Africa, Social Security Committee 1944:15). But in 1944 the Smuts government extended social old-age pensions to Africans (Van der Merwe 1996:378), though benefit levels were less than a tenth of those for whites and the means test far more stringent. By 1958, Africans comprised 60% of 347 000 social old-age pensioners, although they received only 19% of old-age pension spending. By 1978, after their numbers had grown by 5% a year for two decades, Africans made up 70% of the 770 000 pensioners and received 43% of pensions. By 1990, this latter proportion had increased to 67%.

Around the time of World War II, other forms of social assistance also expanded. In 1936 and 1937, grants for the blind and the disabled were instituted, respectively, but these were initially confined to whites and coloureds and only extended to other groups in 1946. War veterans' pensions were instituted in 1941, and family allowances for large low-income families in 1947, but these excluded African people (Kruger 1992:167–70).

From the mid-1970s, attempts to confer political legitimacy on the homeland system and later the tricameral parliament led to a rapid increase in the funds for social assistance, especially for the elderly. Both the coverage of the African elderly population and the real value of the benefits paid increased markedly, and in 1993 there were almost twice as many African pensioners inside the homelands as outside. The flow of funds to the coloured and Asian communities also increased remarkably, but the fiscal costs of incorporating these relatively small groups into the mainstream social security system were manageable. The far greater fiscal challenge only came later, in the late 1970s, once the principle of moving to parity in social spending levels was reluctantly accepted. From that time onwards, fiscal expenditures on social assistance rose rapidly to incorporate Africans into the system and to eliminate the racial barriers which had allowed the white welfare state to prosper in the first place. This led to the rise in social old-age pension spending from 0,59% of GDP in 1970 (a decline from the 0,80% in 1960) to 1,82% by 1993 (Smith Committee 1995:D2.15) and a budgeted 2,51% in 1998/9 (calculated from South Africa 1998b:25, Table 1).

The levels and types of social grants were a product of the peculiar nature of political patronage in apartheid society and later attempts to deracialise benefit structures. Fiscal constraints precluded increasing African benefits to white levels; thus pension equalisation occurred through a combination of enhancing African pension benefits (by 7% per year in real terms from 1970 to 1993) and rapidly eroding real white pensions (white resistance was limited due to the marginal political position of those small numbers of elderly or disabled poor whites who qualified under the means test). In 1980, white pensions displaced more than 30% of the average wage, compared to only 8,6% for African pensions; by 1993, when pension parity was achieved and discrimination in the application of the means tests eliminated, the pension displaced 15,5% of the average wage (Van der Berg 1994).

Under apartheid, white employment was secure (given preferential access to human capital development and to some jobs) and most social security needs could be met through social insurance. The major additional social security measures required were social grants for the elderly and for the disabled, and child and parent allowances. Social assistance was thus set up as a safety net for the white (relatively) poor who, in the wider South African context, were not the poorest. In contrast, the safety net for other groups was initially rudimentary or nonexistent. But as apartheid became diluted through the decades, benefits were gradually extended to other race groups and benefit levels were unified. Some of that growth was generated through the creation of the homelands and the tricameral parliament, some by the belated attempt to redesign social assistance schemes to be non-racial:

> (t)he social pensions and grants which were set up to protect the white population have gradually expanded their eligibility rules to include all South Africans. This makes it . . . an unusually comprehensive system compared with that found in other developing countries . . . (Lund 1993:22).

By this quirk of history, the social security system changed dramatically in terms of the relative size of the two components, with the formerly less important social grants becoming the major part of the social security system, reaching far more people than occupational insurance.

The South African social security system uses primarily social insurance to protect those in formal employment, while social assistance (also called social grants or social transfers) is meant to protect those poor left unprotected by social insurance. In addition, private provision against certain contingencies is both encouraged and common in certain areas (e.g. retirement and life insurance). The following section deals with social insurance, and the subsequent section with social grants.

Social insurance

South Africa's large insurance industry plays a crucial role in mobilising contractual savings for investment, much of it as occupational retirement insurance. Assets of retirement funds alone amounted to 73% of GDP in 1993 (Smith Committee 1995·D2.16). Occupational pensions are mainly responsible for the fact that the elderly are on average somewhat better off than the working-age population (Mouton Committee 1992:62). In 1992, total benefits of R17,2 billion were paid out by occupational retirement funds, of which R3,3 billion were resignation and withdrawal benefits, leaving retirement benefits of R13,9 billion, compared to the R4,8 billion paid as social old-age pensions (Smith Committee 1995:D2.1, 2.2 & 2.6).

Aided by agreements between employers and employees, occupational retirement has expanded its coverage to most industries. It is usually mandatory for employees in most industries or firms to join their pension or provident fund. Coverage is still low in agriculture, in trade, catering and accommodation (mainly employees of small traders and shopkeepers) and in domestic service. Coverage amongst men is probably much higher than amongst women, who are disproportionately present in services, including both trade and domestic service. Insofar as agreements and convention have made occupational insurance for retirement the norm in the formal sector, occupational insurance can be regarded as social insurance, despite the absence of legal compulsion to provide such insurance. However, as the 'taxes' imposed on employers and employees do not flow through state coffers, fiscal comparisons understate social security provision in South Africa. But although coverage of the *formally employed* by occupational pensions schemes for retirement – even after allowing for some double counting – is high, at about 73% (Mouton Committee 1992:490, Smith Committee 1995:D2.11), the large extent of unemployment means that only some 40% of the *labour force* is covered (Kruger 1992:215, Smith Committee 1995:D.2.11). According to the Smith Committee (1995:D2.8), retirement fund benefits were paid to only 44,5% of the elderly in 1993, as against 78,7% receiving social old-age pensions.

Workers and employers typically each contribute 7,5% of the monthly wage to a retirement fund. Workers can then claim benefits upon retirement. The Pension Funds Act of 1956 lays down the rules for the 16 000 retirement funds, so as to safeguard the interests of their members (Sephton *et al.* 1990:1). Retirement funds also provide withdrawal benefits to employees who resign or are dismissed, and retrenchment benefits and sometimes insured benefits to employees who are disabled or to the dependants of employees who die (Sephton *et al.* 1990). Benefits are generally not portable, that is, they cannot be transferred from one fund to another. Consequently, most workers who change jobs get a certain share of the accumulated benefits paid out to them and do not transfer retirement benefits to their new employer's fund. It has been estimated that 90% of pension fund members are expected to change jobs before retirement (Munro 1991).

Typically, an African worker outside the primary sectors accumulates a retirement income of about R40 per month (2% of final salary) for every year that he/she belongs to a retirement fund, thus he/she would need to work 13 years to accumulate retirement benefits greater than the full social pension. If the individual changes jobs and withdraws from the fund after ten years, R400 retirement pension per month – which is less than the social pension of R500 per month – is forfeited. Moreover, upon withdrawal, workers get back at least their own accumulated contribution and some interest. Furthermore, the social pension, unlike the occupational pension, can be expected roughly to keep pace with inflation.

Occupational retirement insurance is vital for many South Africans, but cannot cater to those outside paid employment, nor for some parts of the employed population presently not covered. Of particular concern is that the interaction with the means test for social old-age pensions could discourage private retirement provision for many low-income workers, an issue we shall return to.

Unemployment insurance only applies for certain workers covered by the Unemployment Insurance Fund (UIF). Agricultural and domestic workers, certain public sector employees, seasonal workers and those whose incomes exceed a certain level are excluded (Kruger 1992:198). Until the late 1970s, the UIF usually did not cover African workers (Mouton Committee 1992:153–4). In 1993, legislation was enacted to extend coverage to agricultural workers.

Workers and their employers each contribute 1% of the wage to the UIF, which is publicly administered and to which the government also commits funds from time to time. When a worker is unemployed or ill, UIF benefits of 45% of the weekly wage are paid for one week out of every six weeks the worker contributed, but not exceeding 26 weeks. Maternity benefits and benefits to the dependants of deceased workers are of a similar magnitude, although the former was a major contentious issue in the debate about the Basic Conditions of Employment Bill. At best, such benefits can be a way of sheltering the presently unemployed against temporary job loss. In 1993, 6,3 million workers were covered, up from 1,7 million in 1970, a growth rate of 5,9% for more than two decades. But despite its rapid growth, UIF coverage still extended to less than half of the labour force. In 1990, the average payment per unemployed beneficiary amounted to only R1 270 per annum. The unemployed beneficiaries of the UIF stood at about 538 000 in 1991 (Mouton Committee 1992:513, D3.5), i.e. only about 6% of those without formal jobs. Benefits paid of R1,6 billion in 1994 represented 0,5% of total remuneration (Van der Merwe 1996:386–8).

The UIF's financial position has been seriously eroded by large-scale retrenchments over the past decade. This makes it difficult to improve the level of benefits it offers. Until the labour surplus situation in South Africa has effectively been overcome (which could take decades), unemployment insurance can only cover a small part of the labour force for a short period against the scourge of unemployment.

Worker's compensation, instituted in 1941, requires employers to make risk-related contributions to the Accident Fund (Kruger 1992:198), and is paid to employed workers below a threshold income who are temporarily or permanently disabled as a result of injuries or industrial diseases sustained at work. In this case also, growth of coverage was fairly rapid, from 3,9 million in 1971 to 5,2 million in 1988 (Statistics South Africa 1992:6.8). In 1988, a total of R320 million was paid from the fund. There was some concern that the criteria for such compensation were sometimes too strictly applied, which disqualified some from receiving these benefits and sometimes made them an effective burden on the state if they had to draw disability pensions. Mineworkers fell under separate legislation (the Occupational Diseases in Mines and Works Act), which in addition to occupational injuries covered them against certain occupational diseases, mainly respiratory, prevalent in the industry (Lund 1993:8). Beneficiaries received lump sum payments rather than pensions. It is estimated that coverage had improved to 5,2 million people by 1990. In 1994, new legislation was introduced in the form of the Compensation for Industrial Injuries and Diseases Act, which replaced both previous Acts, provided much improved coverage and removed racial discrimination. Benefits relate to medical aid, compensation for temporary disability and lump sum payments or pensions for permanent disability. A fuller treatment of this topic is given by Lund (1994).

Health insurance is similarly common amongst better-paid workers in the private sector. Others fall back on subsidised public health services, usually means-tested to ensure that subsidies target the poor. While these medical aid funds have recently increased their coverage of lower-income workers, cost containment problems arising *inter alia* from the usual moral hazard problems associated with such insurance have slowed down this expansion, despite concerns about the quality of public health services.

Social assistance

Table 7.4 summarises the available information on the various social pensions and allowances for the last years in which racially based data were still provided (all the homelands included).

Numerically, the most important social transfers were social old-age pensions, covering about three-fifths of all recipients or some one and a half million people, followed by disability pensions (another fifth) and child maintenance grants. Other categories were much smaller. Although this effectively targets many of the poor (Ardington & Lund 1995; Case & Deaton 1996), not all the poor could be reached in this way. The table also shows that by that time coloureds and Asians benefited more in per capita terms from social assistance transfers than whites, who had larger incomes and thus qualified less frequently.

TABLE 7.4

Social pensions and grants paid by category and race (1990 and 1993)[a]

	White	Coloured	Asian	African	Total
Number of grants (thousands) (1993)					
Old age	122,9	129,6	34,3	1 227,1	1 513,6
War veterans	8,9	4,8	0,1	3,7	17,5
Disability	38,8	102,5	22,8	335,1	499,2
Blind	0,8	1,6	0,4	16,0	18,7
Special care	0,0	0	0,1	2,0	2,1
Parent allowances	9,6	64,2	14,9	29,4	118,2
Child maintenance	25,7	167,0	26,6	92,4	311,7
Foster parent	5,9	22,9	2,0	16,8	47,6
Single parent	3,2	0,8	0	0,0	4,0
Total	**215,5**	**493,3**	**101,3**	**1 722,5**	**2 532,7**
Value of grants (millions of rands) (1990)					
Old age (including war veterans)	490,8	289,9	69,0	1 753,1	2 602,8
Disability (including blind)	115,6	201,2	51,6	459,4	827,8
Family (including child grants)	103,6	210,5	55,0	46,4	415,5
Relief	7,8	23,2	1,3	5,8	38,1
Total	**717,8**	**724,8**	**176,9**	**2 264,7**	**3 884,2**
Population (thousands)	**5 068**	**3 286**	**987**	**28 780**	**38 121**
Per capita spending	**R142**	**R221**	**R179**	**R79**	**R102**
Proportion of income	**0,8%**	**6,6%**	**3,0%**	**5,3%**	**2,5%**

[a] Calculated from figures obtained from Department of National Health and Population Development and from Lund, 1993, Table 1 and accompanying text. For the TBVC states, equal numbers of recipients were assumed pro rata as in the other homelands.

Table 7.5 shows more recent data on the distribution of social security spending across different social assistance programs and the administration of social security. It is evident that the old-age pension still dominates, though it has declined somewhat as a proportion of the total. Disability grants, in contrast, have grown from 22 to 26% of total spending on social assistance. Interesting, too, is the still-low cost of administering social assistance, although this has grown in relative terms in an effort to combat inefficiency in delivery and fraud in the system.

TABLE 7.5

Composition of social assistance expenditure by field of service[a]

	Expenditure		Percentage of total		Average annual growth over period
	1995–96 Actual	1998–99 Voted	1995–96	1998–99	
	(R '000s)	(R '000s)			
Administration	32 470	32 470	0,3%	3,0%	149,2%
Child and family care	1 427 736	1 427 736	11,6%	11,2%	9,8%
Old-age pensions[b]	8 138 280	8 138 280	66,1%	59,3%	7,0%
Disability grants[c]	2 699 979	2 699 979	21,9%	26,0%	17,4%
Relief	12 354	12 354	0,1%	0,4%	76,0%
Total social security	**12 310 819**	**12 310 819**	**100%**	**100%**	**10,9%**

[a] South Africa 1998b:29, Table 5.
[b] Including war veterans' grants.
[c] Including pensions for the blind.

Table 7.6 shows data on the social security budget by province. There are wide differences in per capita allocations to different provinces, but these result not so much from inequality in allocations as from differences in demographic structure and take-up rates in different provinces, the latter partly determined by the means test and historical factors. Thus the richest province, Gauteng, has the lowest spending per capita on social transfers due to a smaller proportion of its elderly population qualifying under the means test for social old-age pensions. High take-up rates, especially of the old child and family grants that are being replaced by the new child support grants, have kept social assistance spending in the Northern Cape inordinately high. Unfortunately, spending on disability grants is rather difficult to express relative to the target population, as the numbers of disabled are very uncertain.

Social old-age pensions are paid to men from 65 years of age and to women from age 60. Below the lower threshold (60% of annual benefit), applicants qualify for the full pension. Above this level, every R2 increase in pre-pension income reduces the benefit by R1 until the benefit is zero. For married applicants, only half the combined income of the applicant and spouse is taken into consideration. The marginal 'tax' rate or clawback of 50% creates a typical poverty trap and has severe implications for the behaviour of low-income workers, as referred to earlier. In the past, the absence of adequate occupational retirement insurance left most people of pensionable age few income sources to fall back on other than social old-age pensions. Interestingly, social old-age pensions are paid to more than three-quarters of all people of pensionable age; thus the means test is largely a way of excluding the rich rather than targeting the poor.

Disability grants are the second most important form of social assistance. The state provides disability grants to the disabled (including the blind) from age sixteen up to retirement age, subject to medical eligibility criteria and the same means test as for old-age pensions. In 1993,

TABLE 7.6

Budgeted per capita spending by province (1998–99)[a]

	All social assistance spending per capita	Child, family care spending per child	Old-age pensions per elderly person
Eastern Cape	R596	R124	R6 945
Free State	R413	R233	R4 178
North West	R387	R46	R5 984
Northern Province	R386	R118	R4 784
Mpumalanga	R357	R100	R5 631
Northern Cape	R651	R358	R6 051
KwaZulu-Natal	R470	R153	R5 597
Western Cape	R444	R220	R3 275
Gauteng	R254	R 72	R2 815
Total	**R422**	**R133**	**R4 826**

[a] South Africa 1998b:32, Table 1.

disability grants went to thirteen out of every thousand South Africans: only to eight per thousand whites and twelve per thousand Africans. However, the figures for coloureds (31 per thousand) and Asians (23) were extremely high, and may indicate some abuse of the system, particularly in the apartheid dispensation where different administrations applied eligibility rules differently. Considering the extent of unemployment, take-up of such benefits will be as great as administrative leniency allows.

Child maintenance benefits actually comprise two types of grants: parent allowances and child allowances. These are paid mainly to single mothers (including widows, divorcees, women abandoned by their spouses and those never married) and their children who had no other means of support. In the past, it was largely not extended to Africans. When the social assistance system was deracialised, it became apparent that the cost of these grants could become astronomical, that there were potentially perverse incentive effects associated with them, and that other equally poor children in intact families may not have qualified for such support. Thus, following the Lund Committee recommendations, the Cabinet approved the phasing out of the old child and parent allowances, the institution of a new flat-rate child support grant of R100 per month to caregivers of the poorest children under seven years of age, and a means test aimed at identifying the 30% of children in this age group who are most vulnerable. This should add to the flow of social transfers into poor communities, and particularly reach households in the bottom two quintiles of the income distribution. If we consider the mean annual household income in the quintile of R2 406 in 1993, annual flows of R1 200 or R2 400 to recipient households (assuming either one or two children in the relevant age category) may have a considerable impact, even allowing for inflation. Overall spending allocated for this purpose will total R2,7 billion per annum once it is fully operational. However, this constitutes little more than 10% of the income of the bottom two quintiles. Moreover, even under optimistic circumstances there would be some leakage to the non-poor, and some of the present R1,3 billion spent on the old grants also reaches the poorest. Thus such a programme, though important, would not have nearly the same impact on the conditions of the poor as an acceleration in employment would have.

Coverage against risk: the adequacy of social security

To understand the impact of the South African social security system, it is useful to consider how it reaches people in different income classes with diverging educational and skill levels. Ideally, such an analysis should consider education, employment, wages, income, living standards, life cycles and contingencies, uncovered risks, and opportunities for class mobility through education, rural–urban migration or marriage.

For convenience, we identify four income class types, which we shall call, not fully accurately:

- the affluent (largely Quintile 5);
- the stable urban working class (Quintile 4);
- the insecure formal sector (Quintile 3);
- outsiders (Quintiles 1 and 2, the poor).

Despite its many limitations, such a typology is useful for focusing on the contingencies that interest us.

- *The affluent (Quintile 5)*: Under apartheid, the affluent have long been mainly white, but in the past two decades their ranks have been joined by members of other race groups. By 1993, only about two-thirds of the richest income quintile were white, and by 1995 whites may even have declined to only about half of households in this class (South Africa 1997:Fig. 36). This group exhibits high levels of education, and wage and per capita income levels three times the national average. Moreover, almost all children enrol for secondary education and a substantial proportion goes on to tertiary education. Thus this income class reproduces itself. Lifestyles reflect the suburban nature of this group (though perhaps less so amongst recent African converts to their ranks): spacious homes (two rooms per person, on average), universal access to electricity, commuting to work by private means and general satisfaction with their quality of life.

  Contingencies amongst this group approximate those in industrial societies, and most risks are well covered by occupational insurance (or private insurance for self-employed professionals). Although coverage against cyclical unemployment is weak (the upper income groups are excluded from compulsory unemployment insurance), they are least affected by

TABLE 7.7

Socioeconomic situation of different income classes (1993)[a, b]

| | Income–consumption quintiles | | | | | Total |
| | Poorest | | | | Richest | |
	Q1	Q2	Q3	Q4	Q5	
Per capita income	R390	R1 056	R1 974	R4 158	R20 478	R5 611
Household income	R2 406	R6 372	R11 550	R22 458	R82 536	R30 630
Household monthly wage[c]	R287	R546	R930	R1 611	R4 689	R1 598
Unemployed	53%	43%	30%	17%	4%	30%
No education	24%	18%	13%	7%	6%	15%
Less than full primary education	54%	42%	33%	21%	9%	35%
Completed secondary education	4%	8%	13%	23%	62%	19%
Completed tertiary education	0%	0%	0,2%	0,6%	10,3%	1,8%
Primary enrolment (net)	85%	87%	88%	89%	90%	87%
Secondary enrolment (net)	46%	57%	67%	78%	83%	60%
Tertiary enrolment (net)	4%	5%	8%	20%	38%	11%
Remittances/income	27%	14%	6%	2%	1%	3%
Regular wage/income	23%	44%	67%	79%	65%	65%
Regular wage main income source (% of households)	19%	41%	65%	84%	84%	59%
Households rural	76%	68%	46%	33%	15%	47%
Households metropolitan	10%	14%	29%	40%	58%	30%
Households in other urban areas	14%	18%	25%	27%	27%	23%
Households African	96%	93%	82%	68%	25%	73%
Households white	1%	1%	3%	16%	66%	17%
Household size	6,3	6,0	5,9	5,4	4,2	5,5
Persons per room	2,3	1,7	1,4	1,0	0,5	1,4
Households in shacks or traditional dwellings	39%	32%	25%	15%	2%	23%
Households with electricity	15%	28%	49%	77%	98%	53%
Commute to work by car/motorcycle	7%	7%	10%	26%	77%	30%
Treated by private doctor	23%	31%	41%	53%	73%	44%
Stunting of children under 5	38%	27%	23%	18%	6%	27%
Satisfied with quality of life	17%	22%	29%	39%	70%	35%
Government food aid a major issue	34%	27%	17%	14%	11%	20%

[a] World Bank/RDP Office 1995; SALDRU 1994; Janisch 1996; Klasen 1996.

[b] Figures not fully comparable across dimensions, as criteria for division into quintiles differed (e.g. income–consumption group, quintile of households/individuals, etc.).

[c] Including casual labour.

cyclical downswings, and their skills and education limit the risk of long-term structural unemployment.

- *Stable urban working class (Quintile 4)*: In this largely urban income class, Africans already dominate in numerical terms, but Asians and coloureds are disproportionately represented, while lower middle class to working-class whites typically also fall into this category. The striking feature of this group is their access to relatively well-paid urban employment; unemployment occurs mainly amongst women or other secondary earners. This group is characterised by above-average educational levels (though appreciably less than those of the affluent), but more particularly by high levels of enrolment of children in secondary and tertiary education: this is an upwardly mobile group.

  This group faces some risk of falling victim to unemployment because of lower education and skill levels, which may pull them down the income distribution ladder once unemployment insurance benefits have been exhausted. Younger members of this group are accumulating adequate occupational insurance benefits before retirement to be potentially independent of the social old-age pension, but this group is most affected by rules relating to the withdrawal of benefits when they change jobs and by the means test for old-age pensions. Though coverage is for many of them still of recent origin, this group looks mainly to occupational insurance rather than to social assistance for their social security.

- *The insecure formal sector (Quintile 3)*: This group is most mixed in terms of employment status and geographic origin. Where the affluent are clearly urban and engaged in long-term formal jobs, this group includes many better-paid farm workers and a large proportion of migrant 'men of two worlds', who may have families and assets in rural areas but who are economically dependent on urban areas. Their access to jobs, however, is tenuous, as they usually have limited skills and low educational levels. As a result, many live in crowded housing or squatter shacks in the cities, while housing for farm workers is only as secure as their jobs.

  High risks of unemployment subject many in this group to fluctuating fortunes which depend on cyclical factors and uncertain prospects of finding new employment. When the duration of unemployment is appreciable and households have no other employed earner, many slip down the income ladder. On the other hand, those with some skills and education who do obtain regular employment may graduate to the second quintile. Life-cycle factors may be particularly important for this group; youths who do find employment could add dramatically to the household's fortunes.

  Social insurance has a limited role amongst this group, although many of them are nominally covered by it. They prefer provident rather than pension funds for occupational retirement provision, as taking lump sum retirement benefits may still allow them to qualify under the means test for the full social old-age pension. If they are disabled (and physical disabilities are common for both this group and the outsiders), workmen's compensation helps those injured on the job, while disability grants or social pensions are generous enough to maintain smaller households in this income class.

- *Outsiders (Quintiles 1 and 2, the poor)*: This group consists predominantly of rural Africans who are poorly educated (78% of household heads in the bottom quintile have not even completed primary education [World Bank 1995:27]). In this poorest group, social stress is evident in high rates of absenteeism from rural areas of able-bodied males who work in the cities. Extremely high unemployment rates plus low wages – often in casual jobs – result in less than one in four of these households having a regular wage as the main source of income. A permanent job or a social pension may sometimes move such households up the income ladder, but that partly depends on the burden of dependants. Household size is typically large, despite the absence of many workers from rural areas, whose remittances are a crucial but often very uncertain source of income (remittances contribute more than a regular wage to household incomes). Such broken households are also one of the factors that account for the higher proportion of women than men in poverty (World Bank 1995:13). The poor nutritional status of children is shown by stunting rates of one in three children under five, as against only 6% amongst the affluent. Small wonder this group places a high premium on government food aid and is extremely dissatisfied with their quality of life.

Social assistance is vital for this group. For one in four individuals, social assistance is the main source of income, compared to only 5% amongst other households (World Bank 1995:15). Without such flows of funds to pensioners and the disabled, the nutritional and social situation of the beneficiaries and their extended families would be much worse. It has been convincingly shown that such social transfers reach communities who have otherwise been poorly provided with social services such as education or health (Ardington & Lund 1995; Case & Deaton 1996).

Social security policy

The challenge for South Africa is to offer a safety net for the poor, who are still numerous mainly due to the lack of remunerated employment, while insuring those in employment against major contingencies (loss of employment, old age, ill health, disability). It has been shown in an earlier chapter that social transfers contribute more towards reducing poverty than to increasing incomes, an indication that indeed they are relatively well targeted. But although the social security system is relatively well targeted and has developed to almost unprecedented levels for a semi-industrial country, the preceding section showed that there are still major gaps. However, the resources from state general revenue devoted to social security (as opposed to enforced social security taxes) are already generous, and competing demands on fiscal resources at a time of political transition leave little scope for additional resources for social security.

Another growing problem is the HIV/AIDS epidemic, which is likely to have a major impact on the welfare of many South Africans. The number of projected deaths is worrying, but the many orphans are also likely to have a profound impact on social support structures. In this respect, the demand for social security may grow sharply.

The major contingency against which no proper protection is given is unemployment. This has been extensively discussed in other chapters, and is strongly linked to poverty. At best, occupational insurance can reach only half of the labour force, leaving the most vulnerable dependent upon various forms of social assistance. As living standards depend largely on access to remunerative employment, their poor education and skills imply that the rural African population will be worst affected.

A second major deficiency of the social security system is that its impact on the poorest — those uncovered by social insurance — is almost exclusively tied to the presence of elderly or disabled members in households. There is naturally a life-cycle component to this, as families may materially benefit at different stages from such a presence. However, at any particular time there are many poor families without such support. Social assistance for the elderly is a necessary, but insufficient, condition for reaching most poor households. Social old-age pensions may have affected family structures by encouraging poor families to retain older members in the household, thus enhancing the status of old people in rural society and making them the main 'bread-winners' in many extended families (see Case & Deaton 1996:11). However, those households without access to employment, and with no elderly or disabled members, have become the poorest. Thus many children and young families are especially vulnerable, as are older workers who cannot effectively compete for manual work but are as yet too young to qualify for pensions. If the prevention or amelioration of poverty is one of the major roles of the social security net, then there is still considerable need for targeting of such households.

The options in this regard are limited, given the large resource transfers required and the potential perverse incentive effects associated with certain possible targeting devices. For instance, substantial social transfers targeted at the unemployed may have perverse impacts on job search, labour input or even educational attendance. One possible approach is low-wage public employment schemes as self-targeting mechanisms in rural areas, but efforts to this end have run into union opposition, capacity constraints and limited enthusiasm in government, *inter alia,* because of the lack of a 'powerful interest group to fight for the programme' (Breslin *et al.* 1997:34). One major reason for this is the persistent view that social transfers are handouts and therefore to be avoided. It is thus unclear what measures could or would be taken in this regard, though improvements to unemployment insurance for those in employment are almost certain to take place in the next few years and would improve the situation of those who lose their jobs. They are, however, a small proportion of the unemployed. Of more importance is an expansion in the provision of low-wage programmes that could reach large segments of the very poor.

International experience has shown that it is essential that such programmes offer relatively low wages in order to attract only the poorest and not those already engaged in productive activities in the informal sector.

A continuing concern is the interaction between social insurance and social assistance, especially for retirement provision. The crucial issue is how the means test interacts with occupational or private insurance and with the tax system. As more and more cohorts of Africans who retire have accumulated some occupational pension claims, the operation of the means test becomes more difficult. Improved targeting may seem one option, but does not reduce the negative aspects of the means test, that is, the poverty trap and associated perverse incentive effects on saving behaviour, the propensity to lie about private income and the difficulty of administration. The National Consultative Retirement Forum, set up by the government in 1997, expressed some support for a universal grant for the elderly, though it noted the fiscal constraints. A universal grant would remove the perverse incentives flowing from the present means test for withdrawal of retirement benefits, private retirement insurance for informal sector participants and domestic servants, the choice between lump sum retirement benefits and pensions, and the form in which assets are held. Abolishing the means test should encourage private retirement provision. Moreover, the means test encourages dishonesty and withholding of information and is difficult to administer. It would become even more difficult to apply when more people who retire receive some occupational retirement benefits.

The fiscal consequences of a universal old-age grant could partly be reduced by clawing back some spending through higher income tax, both by removing the old-age rebate and by the normal operation of the income tax scales. Thus net fiscal costs may appear manageable. However, more rapid aging of the South African population means that the numbers in the higher age categories are presently growing more rapidly than the aggregate population and, indeed, as rapidly as the economy. Thus, just to maintain real benefit levels, fiscal expenditures for old-age pensions would have to grow as rapidly as the economy. Unless economic growth accelerates markedly, such a universal grant is fiscally unrealistic. This point is underlined by the fact that the tax system — which is supposed to claw back some of the cost — is still operating inefficiently and is being confronted by rapid expansion of potential numbers in the income tax-paying brackets.

As long as the lurking menace of unemployment remains, the outsiders in South African society cannot be fully drawn into the economic and social mainstream, either by social security or by other means. Social assistance programmes can, at best, alleviate the plight of the rural poor, in itself an important enough objective. But for the moment, improved benefit levels for existing programmes are also unlikely, for that is not now the main priority. Increased employment is the only thing that will allow social security needs to be contained to levels commensurate with the fiscal capacity of the economy. Only then will South Africa be able to make further progress on the road to an advanced social security system.

The major gap in income security thus remains the large-scale unemployment that so plagues South Africa. An extension of the unemployment insurance system offers little hope, for this cannot reach those who have never been employed. A more promising avenue is the provision of low-wage public works programmes. These have the benefit of self-targeting: only the really poor are willing to work at very low wages. Attempts to expand such programmes in South Africa have thus far come up against opposition from trade unions, either because of the low wages, or because they see such programmes as undercutting unionised work. Within government, too, there has been little acceptance of such programmes as low-wage income support schemes rather than permanent job-creation or training schemes. Moreover, fiscal costs and managerial capacity within government pose further constraints on the massive expansion of such programmes, so that it appears that a moderate growth over time is the most that can be expected at this stage. The impact on the poor is thus likely to remain small.

Conclusion

Government policies have already shifted substantially towards poverty alleviation, and there is limited scope for further initiatives to improve the position of the poor without major additional outlay of resources. In the policy field, the discussion above suggests three areas for increased government attention in order to reduce poverty over the medium to long term, supplementing those policies already in place. These are:

- improving the quality of education, *inter alia,* through better information systems on cognitive achievement levels in education;
- expanding low-wage public works programmes as a form of self-targeted poverty relief for those who cannot get access to jobs;
- government intervention in the capital market to ensure enhanced access to capital by the poor, particularly for entrepreneurial purposes (though education would probably also benefit from this). This policy area did not fall within the ambit of this chapter.

These policies, by themselves, cannot reduce poverty drastically. However, as everywhere in the world, sustained economic growth is the best alleviator of poverty – especially if such growth is employment-creating. To some extent, the policy thrusts suggested above may contribute to such an outcome, but they also need to be underpinned by viable macroeconomic policies that would create the necessary climate for attracting international capital. For this reason the government's macroeconomic growth strategy, GEAR, will have to be continued and consolidated. If poverty-ameliorating policies such as those suggested above complement a successful growth strategy, poverty alleviation may be quite rapid. As in Latin America, where the turning point in inequality may have been reached, South African racial inequalities are also now being reduced in the new political dispensation. If economic growth is added to the mix, both poverty and racial inequality may be strongly reduced, and the trend towards increased inequality within racial groups may be arrested.

Notes

1. The South African data is based on expenditures, not income, and the situation with regard to incomes may show even greater inequality.

2. In discussing Chen's conclusion that the pattern of household formation is the major factor explaining increasing household inequality in the 1980s and 1990s in Taiwan, Kanbur remarks that this factor is 'missing from nearly all studies in the 'Kuznetsian' tradition' (Kanbur, 1998:14). In South Africa, too, this is still a far too neglected field.

3. If logarithm of earnings of worker i is

   $$\log y_i = \alpha + \beta S_i + u_i$$

   (y_i is earnings, S_i schooling, u_i residual uncorrelated with schooling),

   then $V(\log y_i) = \beta^2 V(S_i) + V(u_i)$.

   Thus earnings inequality (log-variance) is a linear function of variance in schooling.

   If schooling inequality is measured by the coefficient of variation $CV = s/m$ (standard deviation divided by mean), which is mean-invariant, then greater earnings inequality is possible despite reduced schooling inequality. Lam (1999) shows that the standard deviation for schooling rose less than the mean for Brazilian cohorts born 1925 to 1950; thus the coefficient of variation declined. But lower schooling inequality did not also reduce high earnings inequality, as variance of schooling rose.

4. De Villiers (1996:288–9) reports that more than 90% of teachers will not receive more than one promotion in a lifetime of teaching.

5. This part of the chapter is largely based on the author's previous work, particularly that published as Van der Berg (1997).

6. In conjunction with universal health care for those who cannot afford private health care. Health is not usually regarded as part of social security in South Africa, not even in the case of health insurance, so that this issue will not be explored further here.

7. Under apartheid, a large number of administrations were created (10 homelands, 4 provincial administrations covering Africans outside the homelands and a separate administration under the tricameral parliament for each of the other three groups), each of which had some leeway to set rules and administrative procedures; however, funding levels were essentially determined by the white central government. The major way in which the homelands deviated from the practice set in South Africa was by not implementing certain types of grants at all, or by reducing real benefit levels.

8

Contemporary Labour Market Policy and Poverty in South Africa

Muzi Maziya

Amongst the major challenges that faced the new ANC-led government in 1994 was the extent of poverty and inequality, which was largely a legacy of apartheid and past race-based policies. A household survey conducted in late 1993 to assist the new government by providing an empirical basis for its policies found that 53% of the population lived in poor households, and among the poor 95% were African (RDP 1995) The survey also found that South Africa had one of the worst records in terms of social indicators (health, education, safe water and fertility) and income inequality, even when compared to countries at lower levels of development.

Not surprisingly, the advent of the ANC-led government led to the adoption of policies that were intended to help eradicate poverty and reduce inequality, as part of the Reconstruction and Development Programme (RDP). The RDP included policies that aimed to foster macroeconomic stability, meet the basic needs of the population, create jobs, develop human resources and provide a social safety net.

One of the important factors determining the extent and character of poverty and inequality in South Africa is the labour market. Indeed, the strongest evidence in this book is that labour market participation (and non-participation) by members of the household explains a significant amount of household poverty and inequality. These results are hardly surprising, but they elevate the importance of labour market policy and policies that impact on the functioning of the labour market, as potential tools in efforts to reduce poverty and inequality.

Since 1994, the government has embarked upon a series of labour market reforms which it claimed had efficiency and equity objectives. The aim of this chapter is to examine these reforms more closely, focusing on their potential impact on poverty and inequality.

The chapter first presents an outline of recent labour market reforms, followed by a discussion of conceptual frameworks that can help us to assess the role of labour market policy in poverty alleviation. We then move on to use these frameworks to assess the impact of recent labour reforms on household poverty and to consider the potential impact of these reforms on the position of low-paid workers. Finally, we present some policy recommendations.

Labour market reforms and institutions in post-apartheid South Africa[1]

The newly elected ANC government inherited a fragmented body of labour laws and an industrial relations system characterised by a high degree of antagonism between employers and worker representatives. Legislation that governed collective bargaining via the industrial councils excluded sectors such as mining and agriculture. In the early 1990s, less than 20% of workers were part of these industrial councils (MERG 1993).

Labour legislation aimed at protecting workers, where there was no collective bargaining, also did not cover all sectors or all areas. Until the early 1990s, agricultural and domestic workers were excluded from the 1983 Basic Conditions of Employment Act, whilst the entire system of wage and working conditions determination (falling under the 1957 Wages Act) was largely discredited. Indeed, it was described by the ILO country review as 'a haphazard process, with almost arbitrary selective coverage, low wage minima, infrequent revisions and poor conditions of employment attached to them' (Standing, Sender & Weeks 1996).

Following the recommendations of a tripartite Labour Market Commission, the new government's labour market policy response has consisted essentially of two approaches: the promotion of 'voice' regulation and 'regulated flexibility'.

Voice regulation essentially commits the government to strengthening the role of its social partners, business and labour. Since 1993, the number of registered unions and employer organisations has increased (see Table 8.1), and a national-level bargaining forum, NEDLAC (National Economic Development and Labour Council), has been established. This forum deliberates on socioeconomic and development policies, and consists of representatives from employers, workers, government and community organisations.

Union membership has grown more than 50% since 1994, whilst the number of registered unions has also increased from 201 in 1993 to 463 in 1998. This trend can be attributed to the adoption of 'union-friendly' policies and legislation. Surprisingly, the number of registered employer organisations declined in 1995 and in 1998, despite an overall increase since 1994. The changes in the number of bargaining councils also largely reflect a rationalisation and consolidation consistent with the demands of the new laws.

TABLE 8.1

Registered trade unions, employers' organisations and bargaining councils (1993–98)[a]

Year	1993	1994	1995	1996	1997	1998
Unions	201	213	248	334	417	463
Union membership	2 890 174	2 470 481	2 690 727	3 016 933	3 412 645	3 801 388
Employers' organisations	195	191	188	196	258	241
Bargaining councils	68	86	80	77	73	76

[a] Department of Labour Annual Report 1999.

The government's macroeconomic policy document, GEAR, describes the policy of 'regulated flexibility' as a strategy 'to extend the protection and stability afforded by existing labour market regulations to an increased number of workers' (South Africa, 1996a:17). At the same time, the aim is to make sure that the labour market is regulated in manner 'that allows for flexible collective bargaining structures, variable application of employment standards, and voice regulation'.

Four major pieces of labour legislation have been enacted since 1994. These are the Labour Relations Act (1995), the Basic Conditions of Employment Act (1997), the Employment Equity Act (1998) and the Skills Development Act (1998).[2] Table 8.2 presents the main features of these pieces of legislation.

The Labour Relations Act (LRA) was the first major piece of labour legislation to be adopted by the new government, and it provides the framework for collective bargaining. The Basic Conditions of Employment Act (BCEA) sets up minimum conditions of work, and is particularly aimed at protecting workers who fall outside collective bargaining. The Employment Equity Act attempts to provide incentives for firms to redress past imbalances in the labour market. It abolishes discrimination in the workplace and provides for the implementation of affirmative action by firms, and for the monitoring and reduction of wage differentials. The Skills Development Act (1998) was the last major piece of labour legislation adopted during the presidency of Nelson Mandela, and it provides for the setting-up of mechanisms to finance and promote skills development in the workplace.

Labour market policy and poverty: a review of tools for analysis

The aim of this section is to discuss different conceptual frameworks or tools for analysing the link between labour markets and poverty, and how they can be used to assess the effectiveness or relevance of labour market policies in poverty alleviation strategies.

Despite international evidence that suggests that poor households depend heavily on labour incomes (Lipton & Ravallion 1995:2591), the literature exploring the labour market–poverty nexus is fairly limited. A major weakness of the existing studies is that they tend to view the impact of the labour market only through the lenses of employment and unemployment effects, whilst only a minority of the studies consider the overall impact on household poverty.

Partial and general equilibrium analyses are among the tools that have been used to explore the link between labour markets and poverty (Rama 1998). However, these approaches often fail to provide insights on the determinants of poverty at the household level and how these determinants interact with the labour market to produce certain economic outcomes.

TABLE 8.2

The new labour laws (1994–99)

Name of Act	Key aims	Coverage	Institutional implications	Key provisions
Labour Relations Act, 1995	• Promote orderly collective bargaining, workplace democracy and effective resolution of labour disputes	• All workers excluding the defence force, secret services and essential services	• New dispute resolution institutions include the Labour Court and the Commission for Conciliation, Mediation, and Arbitration (CCMA)	• Voluntary centralised industry-level collective bargaining through the setting up of bargaining, and statutory councils • Extension of bargaining council agreements to non-parties, and provision for exemptions • The establishment of workplace forums • Regulations on unfair dismissals
Basic Conditions of Employment Act, 1997	• Extend an improved 'floor' of rights to all workers • Improve enforcement mechanisms	• All workers excluding defence force and secret services (including part-time and casual workers)	• Replacement of Wage Board by an Employment Conditions Commission (ECC) • Labour inspectorate to be improved and given responsibility for monitoring and enforcement	• Introduction of a 45-hour week (goal of 40-hour week) • Increase in overtime payment, 21 days' annual leave, 4 months' maternity leave, and family responsibility leave • Changes to notice provisions, and new regulations on termination of employment • Variation of Act allowed through collective bargaining or by Minister • Sectoral determinations by Minister upon the advice of ECC
Employment Equity Act, 1998	• Eliminate unfair discrimination • Ensure the implementation of affirmative action	• Employees in 'designated companies'	• Commission for Employment Equity (CEE) will be responsible for advising the Minister on codes of good practice	• Prohibition of unfair discrimination • Designated employers draw up employment equity plans that will be submitted to the Department of Labour • Every designated employer must take measures to reduce *wage differentials* subject to such guidance as may be given by the Minister of Labour (upon advice of CEE)
Skills Development Act, 1998[a]	• Provide an institutional framework to devise and implement national, sector, and workplace strategies to improve the skills of the South African workforce	• Designated employers and sectors	• National Skills Authority • National Skills Fund • Sector Education and Training Authorities (can be established for any economic sector) • A skills development planning unit within the Department of Labour	• Establishment of a National Skills Fund to be financed through the levies and state provision • Sector Education and Training Authorities (SETAs) will develop sector skills plans and implement them by establishing *learnerships* • *Learnerships* are to consist of a structured learning component and practical working experience. They will lead to a qualification tied to an occupation and recognised by the National Qualifications Framework (NQF)

[a] This law is accompanied by the Skills Development Levies Act (1999), which provides for a 1% payroll levy.

Another way of examining the link between the labour market and poverty is to isolate those labour market factors and household characteristics that determine the level of poverty within a household.

Barros and Camargo (1995) have developed a simple framework for understanding the interaction between the labour market and poverty in the household. Based on a set of identities, where per capita family income (y) is used as an indicator of the poverty status of a household, they arrive at an equation where poverty at the household level is dependent upon one or a combination of the following factors:

- the unemployment rate of household members;
- the dependency ratio within the household;
- the bargaining power of working household members;
- the skills of the average household's working member; and
- the quality of the job (ie how far workers can realise their potential qualification in a job).

The important assumptions of the framework are that the household is the relevant unit to analyse poverty, income inside the family is equally distributed, there is a direct relation between income and basic need satisfaction and, as already mentioned above, per capita income is a useful indicator of poverty. Income transfers are also not considered.

The per capita income of a household with n members can be expressed in terms of average income for working members of the household (w) and the rate of unemployment and the dependency ratio (d). Therefore:

$$y = w\,(l - u)/(l + d) \tag{1}$$

where l = the number of working members in a household.

The framework can be developed further by examining the determinants of the average income of the household's working members. It is assumed that the earnings received depend on the value of the marginal productivity of the workers (v) and their bargaining power (b). Where bargaining power of the workers is defined as a ratio between average earnings of the household's working members (w) and the value of the marginal productivity, it is possible to substitute, and the poverty status of a household becomes:

$$y = b.v.\,(l - u)/(l + d) \tag{2}^3$$

The factors that contribute to the marginal value of productivity are considered in more detail when Barros and Camargo introduce firm-level characteristics, such as the capital stock ($g(k)$) and the quality of labour supplied by the average household working member (q). Where k represents the capital/labour ratio, the average marginal value of productivity (v) can be expressed as follows:

$$v = g\,(k).q \tag{3}$$

The final equation is arrived at through substitution in (2), where the quality of a household's working members (q) is determined by the effort workers put into the job (e) and the extent to which they can realise their potential qualification in the jobs (p). Thus, we can write formally:

$$y = [\, (l–u)/(l + d)].[b.g(k)].[e.p] \tag{4}$$

The final equation (4) helps us to understand that the determinants of household poverty include household demographic factors and labour market factors such as unemployment, bargaining power of workers, the quality of the workforce and the quality of the job. Past household surveys in South Africa have shown the importance of some of these factors in the characteristics of the poor. The poor often have higher dependency ratios, higher household unemployment rates and poor quality of jobs (RDP 1995). Amongst the employed, the overwhelming majority of the working poor is not unionised, as reflected in Chapter 4, a fact which further confirms the importance of bargaining power as a labour market determinant of poverty.

The advantage of this framework is that it can identify the multiple causes of poverty at both the household level and in the labour market. The potential role of labour market policies and the mechanisms through which they can impact on a household's poverty status are clearly established.

While this framework is useful, it nevertheless has important limitations. The most important of these is that the framework is descriptive and static, and therefore does not allow for adequate recognition of the interrelationships between individual factors. For example, it does not consider the trade-offs that can exist between bargaining power and unemployment rates. In addition, for the last two decades the South African experience has generally been one in which changes in the capital stock have generally been associated with employment shedding and increased unemployment. However, the framework appears sufficiently flexible to be expanded and improved upon. The introduction of household endowments, such as household assets, access to infrastructure and social capital could be done and would make it a potentially more powerful tool.

Labour reforms and household poverty in South Africa: an assessment

The Barros and Camargo framework presented above has advantages and disadvantages. So it is important to justify its use in exploring the possible impacts of labour market reforms on poverty in South Africa.

There is little doubt that more econometrically sophisticated methods would be attractive, but these would be inadequate because the reforms are fairly new. Reforms have also been implemented at different stages, so that it is still too soon to set up models to explore their overall impact. In addition, there is a clear lack of adequate household statistics. The Labour Relations

Act of 1996, which came into effect earlier than the other laws, can still not be properly evaluated due to the unavailability of household survey statistics for the period 1996 to 1998.[4]

Our approach in the following section is to evaluate the likely impact of each piece of legislation on the 'variable' presented in the Barros and Camargo framework. In presenting the likely impact of the legislation, we do not use any empirical methods, due to the data and other problems identified above. Instead, we refer to the relevant theoretical considerations, international experience and any South African evidence that is available.

Whilst this approach can be characterised as speculative and over-reliant on international experience, we can draw comfort from the fact that other, more influential assessments of recent labour laws have tended to be weaker. When not ideologically driven, these assessments have been *ad hoc* and not based on a coherent framework. Their failure to draw on insights from economic theory and international experience has also been a major shortcoming.[5]

Employment creation

The decline in formal employment has been particularly pronounced since 1996, as reflected in Table 8.3. There is a consensus amongst analysts that unemployment, and the failure of the economy to generate sufficient employment opportunities, are among the major policy challenges that face the country. However, there is also considerable debate over the factors that underlie the lack of job creation, particularly the role of the recent labour market reforms.

In perfectly competitive models of the labour market, where all individuals can get a job at a wage equal to value of their marginal product, and labour markets determine the Pareto-efficient levels of working conditions and training, labour market regulations will lead to inefficiencies and increased unemployment.

However, as we all know, most labour markets do not function like those in competitive models. Firms do possess some monopsony power because, in most cases, labour supply is not perfectly elastic. As a result, labour market regulation – which, for example, leads to a rise in wages – need not necessarily jeopardise employment (Gregg & Manning 1997:413).

TABLE 8.3

Employment, productivity and earnings in South Africa (% change)[a]

	1994	1995	1996	1997	1998
Formal employment (private sector)	−0,9	0,5	−2,6	−2,5	−6,0
Formal employment (public)	0,5	−4,2	3,4	−0,3	−1,4
Remuneration per worker[b]	4,8	1,7	2,7	2,4	7,6
Labour productivity	3,2	5,3	4,0	4,2	5,3
Nominal unit labour costs	10,8	6,1	7,1	6,3	9,9

[a] South African Reserve Bank, *Quarterly Economic Bulletin* (various years).
[b] At constant prices.

It is important also to note the argument which suggests that labour market regulations may not result in significant efficiency losses in developing countries because (a) the regulations may not be binding at the market equilibrium, or (b) even if binding, the relevant elasticities of demand and supply may be small, and (c) even if binding and the elasticities sizable, compliance may be low (Squire & Suthiwart-Narueput 1997:119).

The recent labour reforms have contributed to employer perceptions that the South African labour market is inflexible (COSATU 1999). Standard economic analysis, as presented above, and where labour market regulation is viewed as distortionary, suggests that they may contribute significantly to employment losses by increasing labour costs (and hence reduce incentives for employers to hire labour). However, there are some important features of the new legislative set-up that are sources of 'flexibility'. Such aspects need to be strengthened and could in the long run improve the economy's performance with regards to job creation. These include the LRA's considerations for small enterprises and firms facing economic hardships, and the variation mechanisms in the BCEA.

In terms of the literature on collective bargaining, the Labour Relations Act could negatively affect employment by leading to a wage structure that deviates from 'competitive' levels. The union–non-union wage has been shown to be relatively high (Moll 1995), and unions are associated with lower returns to education and post-schooling experience (Mwabu & Schultz 1993). Reduction of pay differentials, job protection regulations and restrictive working practices (e.g. job-grading systems and working-time arrangements) are also features of centralised collective bargaining, such as that envisaged under the LRA, which could negatively affect employment (Marsden 1995). The LRA's provisions for the stronger 'voice' for small and medium enterprises (section 30) in bargaining councils, and clear guidelines for 'exemptions' from bargaining agreements for companies facing economic hardships, are sources of flexibility that have largely been ignored in the discussions.[6] In addition, the setting-up of workplace forums should lead to improved productivity and competitiveness, if taken seriously by both employers and trade unions. The literature on industrial relations systems suggests that where management and employees can jointly manage important areas of employee relations and foster workplace cooperation, as is the case with the workplace forums, there is a potential for increased firm competitiveness and, indirectly, employment creation (Marsden 1995).

The Basic Conditions of Employment Act (BCEA) has improved and extended minimum working conditions to all workers, including previously uncovered workers such as those in agriculture, domestic work and atypical forms of employment (i.e. part-time, casual and home workers). It includes provisions on employment protection, labour utilisation and sectoral determinations.

The dominant view is that the BCEA has made the labour market less conducive to employment creation. As the influential business magazine, *Financial Mail*, commented during the passage of the law, 'all the evidence shows that the government is destroying jobs'.[7]

Whilst there is little doubt that employer perceptions of the labour market have been affected, the impact of the BCEA's employment protection regulations on labour demand and jobs will depend on the extra costs of hiring labour (particularly in the formerly uncovered sectors) and the relevant elasticities of labour demand in the various sectors. It is possible that some of the potential job losses could be diluted by transitional mechanisms set up to help employers in certain sectors to adjust over time, or by the time taken by the Department of Labour to improve its enforcement capabilities.

Undoubtedly the most controversial (and topical) regulations in the BCEA are those that relate to sectoral determinations and the powers given to the Minister of Labour to establish minimum terms and conditions of employment, including minimum wages.

Traditional economic analysis would suggest that an effective minimum wage reduces employment (Freeman 1993). However, empirical evidence from a number of developing countries also suggests that, when the enforced minimum wage is set at relatively low levels, the impact is mostly on the composition, rather than the levels, of employment (Inter-American Development Bank 1998).

It has been argued that the Employment Equity Act and the Skills Development Act will negatively affect employment by leading to increased 'non-wage' costs of labour (Schlemmer & Levitz 1998). The magnitude of this impact should be small because of the sufficient warning provided for firms with respect to the implementation of both Acts. In addition, the two laws are aimed at improving the quality of labour and the optimal use of human resources. The longer-term benefits are expected to be substantial.

The Employment Equity Act also attempts to encourage a reduction of the wage differential within firms. The Commission for Employment Equity still has to set out benchmarks for the appropriate wage differential. But there is likelihood that raising the price of less skilled workers relative to that of skilled workers could lead to job losses amongst the less skilled in sectors where the demand for their labour is fairly elastic.

Improving the quality of the job

In the present policy environment, interventions designed to improve the 'quality' of the job by upgrading informal sector and small enterprise activity largely fall within the domain of macroeconomic and industrial policies. More than a million workers are involved in the informal sector, whilst small businesses were responsible for 44% of total employment in 1995 (NEPA 1997). The Department of Trade and Industry coordinates a supporting package of policies that includes both financial and non-financial support for small business.

The new labour regulations can be assessed in terms of how supportive they are for the state of small business and the informal sector. Many commentators expect that the new labour laws, such as the BCEA, will adversely affect these businesses and lead to deterioration in the quality of the job by raising labour costs substantially. However, a task team set up to investigate the impact of the BCEA on small enterprises found that its impact might not be so severe (ILO 1999). It is also important to realise that small business is affected more by problems such as access to credit, high interest rates, lack of adequate training and issues related to marketing, rather than labour costs (COSATU 1999).

Developing the skills of the workforce

The incoming ANC-led government found in place a training system that was racially segregated, 'market-led and employer-dominated', and made up of fragmented training institutions and qualifications (ILO 1996). The Skills Development Act should change this significantly because it provides for improved coordination for skill development and training among the workforce.

A number of key institutions are to be set up, such as the National Skills Authority, Sector Education and Training Authorities (SETAs), a National Skills Fund and a Skills Development Planning Unit in the Department of Labour.

The Skills Development Levies Act (1999) provides for skills development levies to be collected from employers.[8] Department of Labour officials indicate that at least 20% of the funds in the National Skills Fund will be used for training projects for the unemployed and those in the labour market but who fall outside SETAs.[9]

The concept of learnerships is one of the innovations in the Act. Learnerships essentially combine structured learning and work experience and lead to nationally recognised qualifications which signify job readiness. A minimum of 4 000 people will have successfully completed learnerships by the year 2001 (Department of Labour 1999).

If properly implemented, the whole Act should contribute towards an improved skills profile within the workforce. It is generally argued that, in the past, the private sector underinvested in skills development, especially when South Africa is compared to other countries (COSATU 1999). Through the imposition of the levy and the setting-up of a national skills authority, all existing training schemes will be assessed and skills gaps identified. A recent company survey has found that 76% of companies felt that they did not have adequate skilled personnel (Grawitzky 1999). The Act attempts to address these concerns through public–private sector partnerships to upgrade the skills among the workforce.

The bargaining power of the working members of a household

There is widespread consensus among analysts that the new labour market regulatory regime, particularly through the BCEA and the LRA, has greatly increased the bargaining power of workers relative to employers. A framework that provides for voluntary centralised bargaining, with strong employer and worker organisations, now covers all workers. Workers who fall into sectors or areas that are not covered by collective bargaining are protected by regulations on minimum conditions of work.

Union membership has increased over time, although its share of the labour force has declined (see Table 8.4). However, this is a regional trend, and it is also possible that the demise of apartheid could lead to slower mobilisation and growth of unions. In addition, there are still some sectors where unions are still relatively absent, such as agriculture and domestic work.

TABLE 8.4

Trade union membership (1990–95)[a]

Country	Number of central unions	Number of national unions	Total membership (thousands)		Membership as % of labour force	
			1990	1995	1990	1995
South Africa	3	213	2 900	3 154	23	19
Botswana	1	25	53	45	12	7
Zambia	1	21	477	274	18	7

[a] Fashoyin 1998.

The overall assessment of the recent reforms, in terms of the criteria developed earlier in this chapter, is that they are likely to contribute to a reduction in household poverty. However, the only weak area is in terms of their impact on employment creation and the dependency ratio in the household. In our discussion of the impact of the reforms on employment, we have sought to highlight aspects of the legislation that may be harmful to job creation whilst recognising the importance of equity in the labour market. The Presidential Job Summit held in late 1998 and reviews of the various pieces of legislation point to a realisation that access to the labour market is an important mechanism for reducing household poverty levels.

Labour reforms and the 'working poor'

The framework developed earlier in this chapter allows us to examine the impact of the labour market and labour market policy on household poverty. In addition, we are also interested in the likely impact on low-paid workers, particularly the so-called 'working poor'. The following evaluation of the reforms is less dependent on a coherent framework but draws insight from the theoretical and empirical literature and available information on the position of low-paid workers in the South African labour market.

The nature and characteristics of South Africa's working poor are sensitive to the definition used for 'low pay'. Chapter 4 provided an analysis of recent household survey data, in which low pay is measured with respect to two 'absolute' standards — R293 and R650 per month — which generates an interesting and largely similar picture of the working poor.[10]

At least a quarter of all employed workers earn less than R650 per month, whilst the proportion is reduced to less than 10% if the R293 per month standard is used. Since our concern centres on reducing poverty at both the household and individual level, the R650 per month standard is appropriate, as it is the wage required to meet the household poverty line.

The majority of the working poor are African (82%) and coloured (15%). They are mostly men, but women (particularly African women) tend to be overrepresented among them. Using educational attainment as a proxy for skill levels, we find that the incidence of low pay is higher for unskilled workers. At least two-thirds of the working poor have only primary schooling or less.

The agricultural sector has the highest share of low-paid workers (37%), closely followed by domestic work (34%). The fast-growing retail, wholesale trade and accommodation services sector also has a considerable share of the low-paid workers (14%). Not surprisingly, white-collar occupations are relatively high-paid, with the majority of the low-paid falling among agricultural labourers (31%) and domestic workers (23%). The incidence of low pay is also much higher in non-unionised as compared to unionised sectors. Whilst the data is not available, we would expect a majority of the working poor to be found in small enterprises as compared to larger ones.

Low-paid workers are unlikely to benefit from the new LRA, at least in the short to medium term, because an overwhelming majority of them are to be found in non-unionised sectors — whatever standard we set for low pay.[11]

Historically, it has proved difficult to organise effective worker organisations in the agricultural sector or among domestic workers. Whilst setting up collective bargaining mechanisms would be impractical in the domestic sector (i.e. in the absence of employer organisations), it is certainly feasible in the case of the agricultural sector. However, the LRA fails unions in this sector, and the working poor, because it does not regulate for situations where worker representatives can have access to workers and use the employer's facilities without first having to become representative. Hence, many a farmer can stifle union growth and collective bargaining in this sector by hindering the access that is necessary to become representative (LAPC 1997).

The LRA also excludes many of the working poor from the benefits of workplace forums by insisting on such forums only where there are more than 100 employees. This has been shown to effectively exclude 98% of farms and more than 60% of firms in the wholesale and retail trade sector.[12] At the same time, the LRA has been praised for its accompanying dispute-resolution mechanisms, such as the CCMA. There is considerable anecdotal evidence that domestic and other vulnerable workers, particularly in Gauteng, have made use of these mechanisms.

By far the most important piece of labour legislation for the working poor is the BCEA. To the extent that it is effectively enforced, the BCEA will vastly improve working conditions for low-paid workers through its regulations on employment protection, labour utilisation (ie working time and leave) and sectoral determinations. Some concerns have been raised about the potentially negative effects of the BCEA's employment protection legislation on workers in agriculture and the domestic sector (Fallon & Lucas 1997). By raising labour costs, it is argued, such regulation could lead to employment losses, and increasing levels of poverty among workers. Indeed, a recently completed study on labour demand trends in South Africa seems to support this contention. This work indicates very clearly that formal employment patterns over the last 25 years have shifted strongly away from unskilled workers toward skilled employees (Bhorat & Hodge 1999). For example, the authors show that the demand for professionals grew by 265% over the period 1970–95, while the figure for unskilled workers was as low as −54% (Bhorat & Hodge 1999:362). In this environment, the BCEA, in protecting the most marginalised amongst the employed, needs to avoid large rises in labour costs to firms, as these employees will clearly bear the primary brunt of the cost adjustment. With high attrition rates at the bottom end likely to continue, the implementation of certain clauses of the BCEA will need to be approached with care.

There is extensive evidence nationally to suggest that employment protection legislation, such as that put in place by the BCEA, may not have a significant impact on employment but rather tend to dramatically affect the *composition of employment*.[13] However, the changing composition of employment is often not in favour of low-paid and unskilled workers. Empirical studies for OECD countries have shown that the elasticity of employment with respect to labour costs is higher for 'low-skilled' workers than for high-skilled ones (OECD 1997). It is quite realistic, then, to expect the working poor in South Africa to suffer, through employment losses, as a result of these particular regulations in the BCEA.

The minimum wage provisions of the BCEA, and future sectoral determinations, are also likely to affect the working poor by reducing the demand for their labour. However, there is also evidence to suggest that, if set at reasonable levels, the minimum wage could actually be beneficial for the working poor. In a survey of recent studies on the minimum wage, the Inter-American Development Bank concludes that:

> Overall evidence on the impact of minimum wages on income distribution points to some positive but small declines in inequality and somewhat larger positive effects on poverty (IADB 1998).

An empirical study of thirty developing countries has also found that increases in the minimum wage may be associated with declining poverty levels (Lustig & Mcleod 1996). Whilst acknowledging that minimum wages may negatively affect employment and thus contribute to poverty amongst workers in the long term, it concludes that 'eliminating or reducing minimum wages in developing countries may hurt the poor'. If the Minister of Labour does go through with modest sectoral determinations for agriculture and the domestic sectors, it can be expected that a greater proportion of the working poor will be lifted out of poverty.

The Skills Development Act provides for the establishment of sectoral education and training authorities that should develop skills among the workforce. The working poor are unlikely to benefit from this aspect of the law unless authorities go out of their way to set up a SETA for the agricultural and retail sectors. This is because these sectors do not have strong unions or a history of tripartism. However, the educational attainment level among these workers is very low, and they are definitely in need of mechanisms to equip themselves for the globalised economy and its uncertainties.

The National Skills Fund will allocate funds for the development of skills programmes not only for the unemployed and workers in rural areas but also for domestic workers and service-sector workers. However, the details of this process have not been mapped out clearly so far.

The Employment Equity Act, as it stands, is unlikely to benefit the working poor. The working poor are to be found in non-unionised and small enterprises. The success of this legislation is largely dependent on effective worker organisation and mechanisms such as the workplace forums through which employment equity plans can be discussed and monitored. However, the Act is definitely irrelevant for most employees in agriculture and domestic work.

In summary, we can note that the new labour market regulatory framework – through the BCEA and LRA – will improve the working conditions for the majority of low-paid workers and the working poor. The proposed sectoral determinations, if set at appropriate levels, are likely to significantly reduce poverty amongst workers. However, it is also to be expected that the working poor will experience employment losses due to a reduced demand for their labour. By excluding the working poor from the focus of the Skills Development Act, and the Employment Equity Act, the new labour laws have also meant that low-paid and unskilled workers will face the burden of these changes alone.

Policy recommendations: the labour market as a tool for poverty alleviation

The centrality of the labour market in the determination of poverty and inequality among house-holds necessitates that we consider labour market policy to be a potentially powerful tool in the battle to eradicate poverty and inequality. A careful reading of the ANC-led government's policy documents, including GEAR, would tend to suggest that it has adopted a particular vision of the desirable labour market, ie as one characterised by equity and efficiency. This vision of the labour market implies that inequalities, in terms of opportunities, working conditions and incomes, need to be reduced. By promoting 'flexibility', and improved labour productivity, the aim is to strategically position South Africa in an increasingly interdependent world economy. This approach reflects the historical objective, within the ranks of the democratic movement, to address the legacy of apartheid. At the same time, it reflects the strength of the Congress of South African Trade Unions (COSATU) within the ANC–SACP–COSATU alliance.

However, there are costs associated with implementing this vision. Our earlier assessment of the potential impact of new labour laws on household poverty and the working poor can direct us to policies that could minimise some of these costs, particularly as they disproportionately affect the poorest workers.

Employment creation

It is generally acknowledged that the determinants of employment are not only to be found in the functioning of the labour market and labour market institutions. Macroeconomic and industrial policies are also important. Nevertheless, as a tool against poverty in this country, labour market policy can be used to facilitate increased labour absorption.[14]

The employment impacts of the recently introduced labour reforms need to be monitored closely, and the new laws continuously reviewed. In terms of collective bargaining under the LRA, more emphasis (and promotion) of the 'flexibility' mechanisms and aspects that can improve productivity (such as workplace forums) can dilute some of the disemployment effects. The proposed sectoral determinations (BCEA) need to be effective but cautious.

The regulations in the Employment Equity Act concerning the reduction of wage differentials need to be reviewed because of their likely impact on unskilled workers whose wages may rise artificially whilst their employment declines.

The links between the Department of Labour and small-scale traders, farmers and the informal sector could be improved, with the aim being to assist them to comply with the labour laws (where applicable) and to assess the skills needs of these sectors and the impact of labour laws.

If the employment losses take place mainly in sectors where the working poor are to be found, and, due to their weak skills profile, they are unable to obtain jobs in newly growing sectors, it may be necessary for government to adopt targeted employment subsidies to stimulate demand for unskilled labour. These subsidies could be targeted to particular sectors where low-paid workers face the greatest hardships.

Training for the unskilled and 'working poor'

The poverty- and inequality-reducing objectives of recent labour reforms will come to naught if no support is provided for workers in previously 'uncovered' sectors, who are likely to face employment losses, and the working poor. Training and retraining can improve the employability of these workers and their job mobility, thus reducing potentially negative social impacts.

In terms of training, the present institutional framework appears to be fairly weak to address the needs of these workers. It remains to be seen whether the new Skills Development Act will be able to cover the gaps. However, the targets being set thus far by the Department of Labour appear to be rather small and not explicitly aimed at the most needy groups.

Social safety net

The existing social security system is presently under review and it is hoped that an immediate outcome of the new system will be improved social protection for workers. The present Unemployment Insurance Fund (UIF) does not cover all workers, especially the working poor such as domestic workers, farm workers and workers in the informal sector. An improved social safety net system (such as a basic income grant) should not only promote job mobility but also reduce social costs associated with employment losses.[15]

Conclusion

Poverty and inequality are among the major challenges that face South Africa today. The ending of apartheid and racial domination has been accompanied by the implementation of labour market policies that are generally aimed at addressing apartheid-induced imbalances in the labour market. Such policies are also potential tools in the battle against poverty and inequality, and the lives of low-paid workers will improve in the presence of the LRA and BCEA.

However, we have argued that the implementation of these labour laws should take into account the potential loss of jobs and the fact that the most vulnerable workers are likely to feel the biggest brunt of employment losses. Apart from adopting policies to increase job creation, the government has a duty to ensure that the working poor do not pay the costs of change on their own. The costs of future employment losses should be socialised, such that the state can consider policies to encourage greater employment creation for low-paid workers, or prepare them to deal with these changes by improving their skills, and through adequate social safety net mechanisms. We believe that such an approach will not only ensure that the overall vision of the labour market is maintained but will contribute to reductions in both poverty and inequality.

Notes

1. The primary agency responsible for labour market policy in South Africa is the Department of Labour. This chapter focuses on its legislative initiatives since 1994. However, there are other government departments whose work also directly affects the labour market but which will not be discussed in any detail. These include the Departments of Education (education policy), Finance (macroeconomic policies), Trade and Industry (trade liberalisation and support for small and medium enterprises), Land Affairs and Agriculture (land reform and agricultural policies) and Public Works (national and community-based public works programmes).

2. The government and its social partners are currently reviewing the labour legislation in order to make it more market-friendly. Several legislative proposals were released for public comment in July 2000 but it is unlikely that significant revisions of the laws will take place for some time.

3. This is possible because *v* represents the average marginal productivity, and following the earlier assumption, then $w = b.v$.

4. This lack of adequate household data gives support to those who only evaluate labour laws on the basis of their impact on employment. However, South African employment statistics have also been the subject of much debate. See Standing, Sender and Weeks (1996).

5. For examples, see Fallon and Lucas (1996).

6. The applications for exemptions are to be decided upon by an independent body set up by the bargaining council. The Labour Relations Amendment Bill (1998) changes this body to one of appeal that should expedite the processing of applications for exemption (Department of Labour, 1998:63)

7. *Financial Mail* 4 July 1997, cited in Schlemmer and Levitz (1998)

8. The excluded employers are those whose total annual wage bill is less than R250 000, or those not required to register for employee's tax purposes. From April 12 000, the levy was set at 0,5% of the employer's payroll per month, increasing to 1% from April 2001.

9. Telephone conversation with Adrian Bird, Chief Director Human Resource Division, Department of Labour, Pretoria.

10. The two standards are the per capita adult equivalent (R293 per month) and the wage required to meet the household poverty line, given the mean number of employed workers in a household (R650 per month). It should be noted that these standards are significantly less than the relative poverty lines, such as the 25th percentile of all wages of the employed (R800 per month).

11. However, it is useful to note that the share of the working poor in unionised sectors does increase slightly when low pay is defined as R650 per month, as compared to R293 per month.

12. LAPC (1997), and own calculations based on NEPA (1997).

13. See Inter-American Development Bank (1998), and Di Tella and MacCulloch (1998), for some of the evidence from various countries.

14. The Presidential Job Summit held in October 1998, included agreements on projects for employment creation. These included the special employment programmes, youth brigades and promotion of small businesses. Our focus is largely on labour market policy.

15. It is commendable that parties to the Job Summit Declaration committed themselves to 'achieving the implementation of an effective comprehensive social security system'. Unfortunately, no time frames were set for the implementation of the new system.

TABLE A-1

Comparison of distribution measures[a, b]

Measure	Between component	Within component	Residual	Total
Theil-T	0,340 (48,2)	0,365 (51,8)		0,705
Theil-L	0,293 (40,8)	0,425 (59,2)		0,718
Atkinson $e = 0,5$	0,149 (50,0)	0,148 (49,7)	0,001 (0,3)	0,299
Atkinson $e = 1,5$	0,322 (46,0)	0,373 (53,2)	0,006 (0,8)	0,701
Atkinson $e = 2,5$	0,393 (41,0)	0,566 (59,0)	0,0001 (0,01)	0,959

[a] The figures in brackets show the percentage contribution to total inequality.

[b] The PSLSD data set includes 33 households (0,4%) with zero income. For technical reasons, the Theil-L measure cannot be calculated for a sample that includes households with zero income. Consequently, all three measures in tables A-1 and A-2 are calculated after dropping these 33 households. It is easily shown that this does not influence the results.

TABLE A-2

Within-race contribution to overall inequality

Measure	African	Coloured	Asian	White
Theil-T	0,414 [0,159] (22,6)	0,276 [0,023] (3,3)	0,491 [0,028] (4,0)	0,326 [0,156] (22,1)
Theil-L	0,463 [0,345] (48,1)	0,325 [0,025] (3,5)	0,390 [0,011] (1,5)	0,295 [0,045] (6,3)

Notes:

1. The first row of figures show the measure when considering only the particular race group.
2. The figures in square brackets show the absolute contribution to total inequality.
3. The figures in round brackets show the percentage contribution to total inequality.
4. Atkinson's index is *generally* but not *additively* decomposable, hence we cannot apportion the within contribution amongst the race groups.

TABLE A-3

Decomposition of total national income by income sources

Income source	Proportion of households receiving income source	Mean income from source	Share in total income	Gini for income source for households receiving such income	Gini for income source for all households	Gini correlation with total income rankings	Contribution to Gini coefficient of total income	Percentage share in overall Gini	Effect on overall Gini of a 1% change in income component
	(P_k)		(S_k)	(G_A)	(G_k)	(R_k)	$(S_kG_kR_k)$		
Remittances	0,27	R68,07	0,03	0,52	0,88	−0,08	0,00	−0,40	−0,021
Wage income	0,66	R1 427,94	0,69	0,53	0,69	0,92	0,44	73,50	0,021
Capital income	0,67	R285,55	0,13	0,82	0,87	0,81	0,09	15,20	0,015
State transfers	0,23	R97,38	0,05	0,26	0,83	0,00	0,00	0,00	−0,029
Agriculture	0,18	R79,68	0,04	0,92	0,99	0,79	0,03	4,70	0,008
Self-employment	0,11	R123,47	0,06	0,75	0,97	0,97	0,04	7,00	0,006
Total		R2 082,04	1,00				0,60	100,00	

Notes:
1. G_A is the Gini for the income source when we only consider households with positive income from that source.
2. G_h is for the Gini of the income source when we consider all households. Lerman and Yitzhaki (1994) show that
$$G_k = P_k \times G_A + (1 - P_k).$$

TABLE A-4

Decomposition of total national income by income sources, below and above the poverty line (PSLSD)

Income source	Proportion of households receiving income source (P_k)	Mean income from source	Share in total income (S_k)	Gini for income source for households receiving such income (G_A)	Gini for income source for all households (G_k)	Gini correlation with total income rankings (R_k)	Contribution to Gini coefficient of total income ($S_kG_kR_k$)	Percentage share in overall Gini	Effect on overall Gini of a 1% change in income component
(a) Below the poverty line									
Remittances	0,42	R80,62	0,18	0,44	0,75	0,19	0,03	6,71	−0,044
Wage income	0,35	R171,56	0,38	0,36	0,76	0,69	0,20	51,57	0,051
Capital income	0,72	R32,53	0,07	0,67	0,75	0,42	0,02	5,84	−0,005
State transfers	0,30	R119,78	0,27	0,21	0,75	0,55	0,11	28,42	0,006
Agriculture	0,31	R18,19	0,04	0,61	0,87	0,34	0,01	3,08	−0,004
Self-employment	0,11	R23,97	0,05	0,50	0,94	0,34	0,02	4,39	−0,004
Total		R446,65	1,00				0,39	100,00	
(b) Above the poverty line									
Remittances	0,16	R57,42	0,02	0,52	0,92	−0,11	0,00	-0,41	−0,012
Wage income	0,83	R2 049,90	0,72	0,48	0,57	0,88	0,36	70,70	−0,006
Capital income	0,63	R379,86	0,13	0,75	0,84	0,75	0,08	16,61	0,017
State transfers	0,19	R88,85	0,03	0,29	0,87	−0,11	0,00	-0,60	−0,019
Agriculture	0,12	R101,45	0,04	0,94	0,99	0,86	0,03	5,92	0,012
Self-employment	0,11	R173,22	0,06	0,72	0,97	0,68	0,04	7,82	0,009
Total		R2 850,71	1,00				0,51	100,00	

TABLE A-5

Narrow definition of unemployment[a]

Household type (number of unemployed)	0	1	2	3+	Total	Column shares
A General						
ALL	85,5	10,4	2,7	1,4	8 801 992	100,0
African	82,8	12,0	3,4	1,9	5 950 904	67,6
Coloured	81,4	14,0	3,3	1,3	747 530	8,5
Asian	86,0	11,3	2,3	0,4	245 661	2,8
White	96,0	3,6	0,4	0,0	1 857 897	21,1
Rural	87,0	9,0	2,7	1,3	3 483 220	39,6
Urban	84,6	11,3	2,7	1,5	5 318 772	60,4
B Other demographics						
Average age	30,9	26,9	27,2	27,8	30,4	
Average size	4,1	5,1	6,6	8,1	4,3	
Average number of children	1,4	1,8	2,1	2,2	1,5	
Average number of adults	2,6	3,3	4,4	5,8	2,8	
Average number of labour market participants	1,2	1,9	2,8	4,3	1,4	
Average adult years of education	6,8	6,4	5,9	6,1	6,7	
C Labour market						
% of total unemployment	0	48,9	26,2	24,9	100	
% of total self-employment	88,5	8,1	2,2	1,2	100	
% of total formal employment	87,7	9,1	2,1	1,1	100	
Average household unemployment rate	0	63,9	78,9	84,4	13,1	
Average unemployment rate	0	51,7	71,0	81,4	16,4	
Average self-employment rate	14,6	6,3	4,3	2,9	12,1	
Average formal employment rate	85,2	41,9	24,7	15,6	71,3	
D Poverty and inequality						
Average household income per annum (standard deviation)	37 979 (71 717)	24 752 (38 952)	20 206 (24 867)	19 592 (16 230)	35 770 (67 662)	
Average household expenditure per annum (standard deviation)	36 664 (70 172)	24 837 (36 324)	19 766 (24 432)	20 049 (16 489)	34 658 (66 073)	
Theil-T (% contributions to overall inequality)	91,3	5,6	0,9	0,3	98,2	
Poverty shares:						
$FGT(P_0)$	78,5	13,5	4,9	3,1	100,0	
$FGT(P_1)$	77,8	13,5	5,4	3,3	100,0	
$FGT(P_2)$	77,3	13,3	5,8	3,6	100,0	

[a] The figures sum to 98,2%, the remaining 1,8% is the 'between group' inequality.

TABLE A-6

Earnings profile by occupation and race

	African		White		Coloured		Asian	
	Median	H index (%)	Median	H index (%)	Median	H index (%)	Median	H index (%)
(a) Male employees								
Armed forces	1 887	0	na	na	na	na	na	na
Managers	2 940	0	7 254	0	2 845	0	3 500	0
Professionals	3 500	0	7 254	0	4 500	0	5 120	0
Technicians	2 800	0	5 500	0	3 611	0	3 772	0
Clerks	1 738	1	3 379	0	1 718	0	2 700	0
Service and shop workers	1 500	1	3 333	1	1 500	1	1 666	0
Skilled agricultural workers	700	15	3 999	0	1 346	7	na	na
Craft workers	1 250	2	4 460	0	1 400	1	2 200	1
Machine operators	1 317	3	3 379	0	1 288	1	1 917	0
Domestic helpers	1 115	2	na	na	900	3	na	na
Agricultural labourers	430	24	na	na	507	12	na	na
Mining/construction labourers	919	2	na	na	800	8	na	na
Manufacturing labourers	1 076	3	na	na	1 000	2	na	na
Transport labourers	1 152	2	na	na	950	5	na	na
Other labourers	1 115	3	3 379	0	1 000	3	na	na
Various 'informal' occupations	na	na			na	na	na	na
(b) Female employees								
Managers	2 167	3	3 379	0	2 177	0	na	
Professionals	3 200	0	4 230	0	3 400	0	4 692	0
Technicians	2 500	0	3 379	0	2 708	0	3 068	0
Clerks	1 465	1	2 400	0	1 472	2	1 500	0
Service and shop workers	1 000	7	1 642	0	1 000	4	1 450	3
Skilled agricultural workers	na	na	na	na	na	na	na	na
Craft workers	848	8	1 938	4	950	4	1 200	0
Machine operators	1 000	3	na	na	1 115	1	1 200	0
Domestic helpers	850	8	na	na	750	9	na	na
Agricultural labourers	300	46	na	na	340	30	na	na
Mining/construction labourers	700	16	na	na	na		na	na
Manufacturing labourers	800	6	na	na	848	3	na	na
Transport labourers	na	na	na	na	na		na	na
Other labourers	900	9	1 383	0	1 115	2	na	na

TABLE A-7

Earnings profile by occupation and race

	African		White		Coloured		Asian	
	Median	H index (%)	Median	H index (%)	Median	H index (%)	Median	H index (%)
(a) Self-employed males **Registered activities**								
Managers	13 000	3	12 500	0	7 000	0	15 400	0
Professionals	na	na	18 137	0	na	na	12 000	0
Technicians	na	na	8 000	0	na	na	na	na
Skilled agricultural workers	na	na	11 249	0	na	na	na	na
Craft workers	na	na	5 000	0	na	na	na	na
Various 'informal' occupations	4 392	0	na	na	na	na	na	na
Unregistered activities								
Managers	2 596	4	5 000	0	na	na	na	na
Technicians	1 600	11	na	na	na	na	na	na
Craft workers	1 192	4	4 649	0	1 200	6	na	na
Domestic workers	431	29	na	na	na	na	na	na
Other labourers	1 083	7	na	na	na	na	na	na
Various 'informal' occupations	2 760	4	na	na	na	na	na	na
(b) Self-employed females **Registered activities**								
Managers	na	na	7 991	0	na	na	na	na
Skilled agricultural workers	na	na	4 649	4	na	na	na	na
Unregistered activities								
Technicians	800	4	1 378	2	na	na	na	na
Craft workers	500	14	1 300	5	na	na	na	na
Domestic workers	377	38	na	na	360	37	na	na
Other labourers	660	15	na	na	na	na	na	na
Various 'informal' occupations	1 336	5	na	na	na	na	na	na

TABLE A-8

The participation patterns of male adults

	Participation		In labour force			Employed	Self-employed		Hybrid	
	% In labour force	% Out of labour force	% Employed	% Unemployed, searching	% Unemployed, not searching	% Wage employee	% Registered business	% Unregistered business	% Registered business	% Unregistered business
Education										
None	69	31	78	8	14	94	1	6	0	1
Literate (more than 8 years)	69	31	73	13	14	94	1	5	0	1
Incomplete secondary (8–10 years)	54	46	75	14	11	91	3	6	0	2
Matriculated (10 years)	78	22	81	11	8	89	7	3	0	1
Diploma (11–12 years)	86	14	95	4	2	88	9	1	1	1
Degree (more than 12 years)	85	15	93	3	4	80	14	3	2	2
Presence of young children										
Mean number of young children	0,52	0,55	0,50	0,55	0,61	0,50	0,36	0,62	0,48	0,56
1 or more children under 6 years	68	32	77	12	12	91	3	5	0	2
No children under 6 years	68	32	79	11	10	91	5	4	0	1
Age of individual										
16–25	33	67	57	22	21	98	1	2	0	1
25–55	88	12	82	9	9	91	4	4	0	1
55–65	49	51	91	4	5	83	10	10	0	1
Potential experience										
5 or less years	17	83	60	25	16	98	2	2	1	2
6–10 years	48	52	62	20	18	95	3	2	0	1
11–20 years	87	13	77	12	11	92	4	3	0	2
20+ years	82	18	85	7	8	89	5	6	0	1
Location										
Urban	74	26	81	11	8	91	5	4	0	2
Rural	60	40	73	11	16	92	4	4	0	1

TABLE A-9

Urban African male and female labour participation equations for expanded and narrow definitions of unemployment

	Urban male				Urban female			
	Expanded		Narrow		Expanded		Narrow	
	Marginal effects	x-bar	Marginal effects	x-bar	Marginal effects	x-bar	Marginal effects	x bar
None–Grade 3	0,00416*	5,057	0,00770*	5,05754	0,008409*	5,05748	0,00715**	5,057
Grade 4–8	0,00675*	1,857	0,01722*	1,85798	0,03802*	1,8025	0,06277*	1,8026
Tertiary	−0,0012	0,1366	0,00080	0,136614	−0,012424	0,14637	0,012587**	0,1463
26–35	0,04769*	0,3700	0,1295*	0,370018	0,11867*	0,37385	0,17698*	0,3738
36–45	0,05944*	0,2720	0,1759*	0,272077	0,12216*	0,26495	0,24484*	0,2649
46–55	0,04078*	0,1420	0,14104*	0,142091	0,071356	0,14082	0,22022*	0,1408
56–65	0,02572*	0,0484	0,12731*	0,04884	0,01957	0,04308	0,19905*	0,0430
No. of children under 7 years	0,00653	0,6804	0,0138*	0,680472	−0,01264*	0,93524	−0,02184*	0,9352
No. of children aged 8–15	0,00137	0,7273	−0,0025	0,727369	0,00071	0,94158	−0,00553	0,9415
No. of males aged 16–59	−0,00198	1,989	−0,0231*	1,98956	−0,00872	1,3584	−0,01304**	1,358
No. of females aged 16–59	−0,01114*	1,461	−0,0256*	1,46165	0,0211*	2,12692	0,01154**	2,126
No. of adults over 60 years	−0,02709*	0,2766	−0,06931*	0,276624	0,00075	0,28785	−0,01897*	0,2878
Other household income	−4,05e − 07*	22 205,2	3,63e − 07	22 205,2	−2,12e − 06*	26 645	−1,96e − 06*	26 645
Other household income squared	7,98e − 13	1,5e + 09	1,80e − 12	1,5e + 09	2,33e − 12*	2,8e + 09	2,15e − 12*	2,8e + 09
Observed probability	0,9367		0,8243		0,7925		0,6377	
Predicted probability (at x-bar)	0,9519		0,8540		0,8105		0,6508	
Number observed	6 521		6 521		7 707		7 707	
Chi²	328,2*		908,61*		548,9*		785,33*	
Pseudo R²	0,098		0,1386		0,0665		0,076	

* Significant at the 1% level.
** Significant at the 5% level.

TABLE A-10

Urban African male and female employment equations for expanded and narrow definitions of unemployment

| | Urban male | | | | Urban female | | | |
| | Expanded | | Narrow | | Expanded | | Narrow*** | |
	Marginal effects	x-bar	Marginal effects	x-bar	Marginal effects	x-bar	Marginal effects	x-bar
None–Grade 3	–0,01593*	5,085	–0,01438*	5,108	–0,00227	5,1671		
Grade 4–8	0,01392**	1,883	0,00231	1,914	0,06397*	1,9462		
Tertiary	0,03879*	0,1395	0,042044*	0,1470	0,11611*	0,16291		
26–35	0,05078*	0,3749	–0,02919	0,3745	0,28184*	0,39632		
36–45	0,12273*	0,2817	–0,01835	0,2987	0,42543*	0,27488		
46–55	0,16620*	0,1437	0,03033	0,1512	0,39832*	0,13170		
56–65	0,23943*	0,0461	0,08335*	0,0499	0,39031*	0,03621		
Eastern Cape	–0,02294	0,0938	0,06925*	0,0862	–0,06509**	0,13070		
Northern Cape	–0,05055	0,0124	0,00093	0,0119	–0,10312**	0,01186		
Free State	–0,02629	0,0841	0,10175*	0,0768	–0,07232**	0,10782		
KwaZulu-Natal	0,01830	0,1522	0,02675	0,1534	–0,00886	0,1727		
North West	0,07827**	0,0809	0,06247*	0,0828	0,02066	0,06899		
Gauteng	0,0513**	0,4459	0,06451*	46 052	–0,00559	0,38568		
Mpumalanga	0,03884	0,0391	0,07693*	0,0362	–0,15908*	0,0366		
Northern Province	0,04587	0,0258	0,1129*	0,0242	–0,11747*	0,02743		
Lambda	–1,3549*	0,1206	–0,56492*	0,2726	0,18644*	0,33571		
Observed probability	0,7329		0,8328		0,6061			
Predicted probability (at x-bar)	0,7576		0,8610		0,6248			
Number observed	6 056		5 206		5 957			
Chi²	1 082,7*		681,4*		1 148,7*			
Pseudo R²	0,1481		0,1407		0,1427			

* Significant at the 1% level.
** Significant at the 5% level.
*** There were too few narrowly unemployed females for this equation to be estimated.

TABLE A-11

Urban African male and female earnings equations for expanded and narrow definitions of unemployment

	Urban male		Urban female	
	Expanded unemployment	Narrow unemployment	Expanded unemployment	Narrow unemployment
None–Grade 3	0,04804*	0,0499*	0,0426*	0,0448*
Grade 4–10	0,1071*	0,1052*	0,0741*	0,0924*
Tertiary	0,05094	0,0447	0,0343	0,0485
Eastern Cape	–0,03586	–0,0455	–0,1482*	–0,1700*
Northern Cape	–0,0574	–0,0407	–0,2584*	–0,2725*
Free State	–0,21795*	–0,2336*	–0,3370*	–0,3707*
KwaZulu-Natal	0,0883	0,0893**	–0,0624	–0,0609
North West	0,1077	0,1017	–0,1258*	–0,129**
Gauteng	0,1599*	0,1581*	0,1697*	0,1629*
Mpumalanga	0,08287	0,079	0,1065	0,0643
Northern Province	0,32880*	0,3037*	0,0759	0,0555
Mining	0,1661762*	–0,1603029*	0,4207	0,4217
Manufacturing	0,2845617*	0,2828365*	0,2309	0,2262
Electricity	0,5899361*	0,5866131*	0,533	0,5350
Construction	0,1137356	0,1129959	0,3380	0,3297
Wholesale trade	0,1247791	0,1256877	0,1888	0,1848
Transport	0,372437*	0,3683933*	0,4944*	0,4952**
Finance	0,3085486*	0,3042547*	0,4715**	0,4702**
Commercial services	0,3275005*	0,3256818*	0,3941**	0,3899
Other	0,227513	0,020014	0,1066	0,1224
Armed forces	0,8778821*	0,8646148*	0,7430	0,7425
Managers	1,112009*	1,114832*	0,929*	0,9507*
Professionals	0,9747265*	0,9663315*	0,9155*	0,9360*
Technicians	0,7456466*	0,7399523*	0,7825*	0,7989*
Clerks	0,5202852*	0,5163703*	0,5080*	0,5249*
Services and sales	0,4786886*	0,4743847*	0,2533	0,2686
Skilled agricultural workers	–0,073708	–0,0684681	0,6278	0,6321
Craft workers	0,4804153*	0,4768006*	0,0935	0,1083
Machine operators	0,470309*	0,4668909*	0,2986**	0,3162**
Unspecified	0,3251987*	0,3239393*	0,4489*	0,4670*
Domestic helpers	0,2419549	0,2379359	0,0871	0,1027
Mining labourers	0,2490426	0,2472353	–0,0440	–0,0381
Manufacturing labourers	0,3638321*	0,3604891*	0,2534	0,2663
Transport labourers	0,2505165	0,2492946	–0,1385	–0,1355
Domestic workers	–0,4324948*	–0,4373609*	–0,4373**	–0,4223
Union membership	0,163868*	0,1641*	0,1741*	0,1768*
Experience	0,02947*	0,0282*	0,0122*	0,0174*
Experience squared	–0,00032*	–0,0003*	–0,0001*	–0,0001*
Log of hours per month	0,1803*	0,1736*	0,1623*	0,1629*
Constant	4,8883*	4,969*	5,065*	4,809*
Lambda	–0,1288*	–0,2411*	–0,2774*	–0,1604
Number observed	6 018	5 185	5 922	4 689
Model Chi^2	1 142,33*	755,44*	1 185,7*	737,16

* Significant at the 1% level.
** Significant at the 5% level.

TABLE A-12

Rural African male and female labour participation equations for expanded and narrow definitions of unemployment

	Rural male				Rural female			
	Expanded		Narrow		Expanded		Narrow	
	Marginal effects	x-bar	Marginal effects	x-bar	Marginal effects	x-bar	Marginal effects	x-bar
None–Grade 3	0,00339**	3,794	0,00461	3,794	–0,00147	3,664	0,00169	3,664
Grade 4–8	0,00298	1,017	0,0146*	1,017	0,05909*	0,9386	0,05025*	0,9386
Tertiary	0,00721	0,0745	0,03130**	0,0745	–0,03539**	0,0762	0,00267**	0,0762
26–35	0,06557*	0,3282	0,15007*	0,3282	0,07492*	0,3224	0,09867*	0,3224
36–45	0,08092*	0,2248	0,19841*	0,2248	0,03958*	0,2442	0,13210**	0,2442
46–55	0,05995*	0,1442	0,17883*	0,1442	–0,07081*	0,1543	0,07275*	0,154
56–65	0,00657	0,0580	0,15387*	0,0580	–0,21457*	0,0547	–0,01019*	0,0547
Number of children < 7	–0,00131	0,8929	0,0026	0,8929	–0,02523*	1,228	–0,02566*	1,228
Number of children 8–15	–0,0022	1,032	–0,01241*	1,032	–0,01393*	1,271	–0,01911*	1,271
Number of males 16–59	–0,01229*	1,938	–0,0295*	1,938	–0,01024	1,323	–0,01518	1,323
Number of females 16–59	–0,00456**	1,568	0,01966*	1,568	0,03333*	2,166	0,01238*	2,166
Number of adults > 60	–0,03176*	0,3625	–0,10120*	0,3625	–0,00143	0,3831	–0,03698	0,3831
Other household income	–2,19e – 06*	12 414	–5,10e – 06*	12 414	–1,94e – 06*	17 180	–4,14e – 07	17 180
Other household income squared	1,96e – 11*	7,1e + 08	5,18e – 11*	7,1e + 08	1,98e – 12*	1,6e + 09	8,38e – 14	1,6e + 09
Observed probability	0,8862		0,7255		0,5723927		0,3895	
Predicted probability (at x-bar)	0,9230		0,7774		0,5775		0,3849	
Number observed	9 137		9 137		11 841		11 841	
Chi^2	842,47		1 777,8*		1 009,3*		832,2	
Pseudo R^2	0,1344		0,1686		0,0626		0,0523	

* Significant at the 1% level.
** Significant at the 5% level.

TABLE A-13

Rural African male and female employment equations for expanded and narrow definitions of unemployment

	Rural male				Rural female			
	Expanded		Narrow		Expanded		Narrow	
	Marginal effects	x-bar	Marginal effects	x-bar	Marginal effects	x-bar	Marginal effects	x-bar
None–Grade 3	−0,00724*	3,8013	−0,00365	3,7785	0,0025	3,8942	0,00586	3,9199
Grade 4–8	0,0059	1,0072	−0,00543	1,0055	0,00363	1,1610	−0,0602*	1,2250
Tertiary	0,0519*	0,0751	0,0341**	0,08079	0,15577*	0,09371	0,18805*	0,11438
26–35	0,02973	0,33754	0,01835	0,33751	0,17383*	0,36172	0,05610*	0,35061
36–45	0,06921*	0,24030	0,03011	0,25760	0,31589*	0,24621	0,10424*	0,26615
46–55	0,12879*	0,14988	0,04884*	0,16165	0,40319*	0,12676	0,21521*	0,14366
56–65	0,26790*	0,05208	0,09339*	0,05849	0,44982*	0,03099	0,24965*	0,03773
Eastern Cape	−0,36825*	0,15302	−0,09449	0,1333	−0,34332*	0,19162	0,06836	0,1821
Northern Cape	−0,00751	0,0087	−0,12155	0,01068	0,11547	0,00297	0,10189	0,00417
Free State	−0,12948	0,09123	−0,00748	0,10507	−0,07559	0,07263	−0,02837	0,08728
KwaZulu-Natal	−0,20595**	0,23660	−0,08260	0,23725	−0,26387*	0,26490	0,0877	0,27169
North West	−0,31503*	0,15361	−0,07203	0,15270	−0,28464*	0,12382	0,09488	0,11817
Gauteng	0,0149	0,03873	−0,00889	0,04601	−0,00525	0,0234	−0,03883	0,03088
Mpumalanga	−0,27706*	0,15002	−0,02809	0,15217	−0,28012*	0,1170	0,06296	0,11361
Northern Province	−0,17699	0,15103	−0,01851	0,14237	−0,34838*	0,19861	0,10333	0,18577
Lambda	−1,1393*	0,18971	−0,31876*	0,38249	−0,14034	0,64426	−0,65184*	0,93297
Observed probability	0,7005		0,8556		0,4926		0,7239	
Predicted probability (at x-bar)	0,7357		0,8946		0,4953		0,7524	
Number observed	8 147		6 725		6 853		4 721	
Chi²	1 838,6*		986,15*		978,65		678,4*	
Pseudo R²	0,1882		0,1840		0,1030		0,1236	

* Significant at the 1% level.
** Significant at the 5% level.

TABLE A-14

Rural African male and female earnings equations for expanded and narrow definitions of unemployment

	Rural male		Rural female	
	Expanded unemployment	*Narrow unemployment*	*Expanded unemployment*	*Narrow unemployment*
None–Grade 3	0,0262*	0,0273*	0,0478*	0,0488*
Grade 4–8	0,1004*	0,1013*	0,0890*	0,0922*
Tertiary	0,0114	0,0102	0,0371	0,0048
Eastern Cape	–0,4011*	–0,4103*	–0,0656	–0,0444
Northern Cape	–0,4151*	–0,4085*	–0,1938	–0,1476
Free State	–0,5753*	–0,5771*	–0,7315*	–0,715*
KwaZulu-Natal	–0,2224*	–0,2248*	0,1796	0,2003
North West	–0,3300*	–0,3336*	–0,0327	–0,0311
Gauteng	–0,3541*	–0,3568*	–0,0183	0,0089
Mpumalanga	–0,3225*	–0,3338*	0,1668	0,1804
Northern Province	–0,2000*	–0,2089*	0,2416	0,2591**
Mining	0,7579127*	0,7570094*	0,2203	0,2244
Manufacturing	0,6252782*	0,6272172*	0,2482**	0,2595*
Electricity	0,8139617*	0,8148491*	0,5340	0,5443**
Construction	0,5345509*	0,536156*	0,4242**	0,4268*
Wholesale trade	0,5716519*	0,5738369*	0,1798	0,1843**
Transport	0,7709761*	0,7735797*	0,5935*	0,5932*
Finance	0,5965777*	0,5997498*	0,4253*	0,4230*
Commercial services	0,7018911*	0,7037523*	0,3021*	0,3087*
Other	–0,3265729*	–0,32589*	0,3742*	0,3783*
Armed forces	0,49524*	0,493589*	(dropped)	(dropped)
Managers	0,6469359*	0,6474902*	0,8197*	0,8297*
Professionals	0,9065049*	0,9038113*	1,104*	1,097*
Technicians	0,5282483*	0,5276259*	1,022*	1,020*
Clerks	0,2504032*	0,2509869*	0,6078*	0,6127*
Services and sales	0,141053*	0,1413896*	0,3725*	0,3735*
Skilled agricultural workers	0,3405803*	0,3402449*	–0,0404	–0,0176
Craft workers	0,1922901*	0,1922264*	0,2898*	0,2979*
Machine operators	0,1111536*	0,1112566*	0,2742**	0,2817**
Unspecified	–0,0562722	–0,0549814	–0,0151	–0,0055
Domestic helpers	–0,0486589	–0,0478983	0,2741*	0,2729*
Mining labourers	–0,1081574**	–0,106682**	0,2514	0,2532
Manufacturing labourers	–0,2533656*	–0,2527708*	0,1950	0,1891
Transport labourers	–0,0079984	–0,0101031	–0,6912	–0,6433
Domestic workers	–0,8721786*	–0,8712416*	–0,2885*	–0,2936*
Union membership	0,2366*	0,2359*	0,2969*	0,2947*
Experience	0,0397*	0,0392*	0,0272*	0,0243*
Experience squared	–0,0005*	–0,0005*	–0,0003*	–0,0003*
Log of hours per month	0,0324	0,0307	0,1035*	0,1012*
Constant	6,172*	6,179*	4,695*	4,752*
Lambda	–0,0889**	–0,1321*	–0,1706*	–0,3425*
Number observed	8 106	6 701	6 801	4 704
Model Chi^2	1 927,80*	995,55*	1 026,9*	708,2*

* Significant at the 1% level.
** Significant at the 5% level.

BIBLIOGRAPHY

Anand, S. 1983. *Inequality and Poverty in Malaysia: Measurement and Decomposition*. New York: Oxford University Press.

Abromovitz, M. 1989. *Thinking about Growth, and other Essays on Economic Growth and Welfare*. Cambridge: Cambridge University Press.

Adler, T. 1989. 'The problem with pensions'. *Institute for Personnel Management Journal*. 8(3): 20–22.

Alber, J. 1982. *Vom Armenhaus zum Wohlfahrtsstaat – Analysen zur Entwicklung der Sozialversicherung in Westeuropa*. Frankfurt: Campus Verlag.

Andersson, P. (undated). 'Labour Market Structure in a Controlled Economy: The Case of Zambia'. *Ekonomiska Studier Utgivna av Nationalekonomiska Institutionen Handelshoqskolan vid Gotemborgs Universitet No. 37*.

Ardington, E. & Lund, F. 1995. 'Pensions and development: How the social security system can complement programmes of reconstruction and development'. *Development Paper 61*. Midrand: Development Bank of Southern Africa.

Atkinson, A.B. 1977. *The Economics of Inequality*. Oxford: Clarendon Press.

Atkinson, A.B. 1987. 'On the measurement of poverty'. *Econometrica*. 55(4): 749–64.

Barro, R.J. 1999. 'Inequality, growth and investment'. *NBER Working Paper 7038*. Cambridge, Mass.: National Bureau of Economic Research.

Barros, T. & Camargo, S. 1995. 'Labour market policy and poverty'. Figueiredo, J. & Shaheed, Z. (eds). *Reducing Poverty through Labour Market Policies*. Geneva: International Institute of Labour Studies/ILO.

Basson, D. 1987. 'Debat oor voorsorgfondse kry momentum'. *Finansies & Tegniek*. 27 November.

Baumol, W., Africanman, S. & Wolff, E. 1989. 'International convergence: The comparative US productivity lag'. *Productivity and American Leadership: The Long View*. Cambridge, Mass.: MIT Press. Chap. 5: 85–113.

Bausch, R. 1996. 'Neglected trade-offs in poverty measurement'. *IDS Bulletin*. 27: 1. Sussex: University of Sussex.

Beckerman, W. 1984. 'Measuring poverty in rich and poor countries'. *Carnegie Conference Paper No. 3*. Cape Town: South African Labour and Development Research Unit (SALDRU).

Bhorat, H., Leibbrandt, M. & Woolard, I. 1995. 'Towards an understanding of South Africa's inequality'. *Paper presented at the African Economic Research Consortium Conference*. Johannesburg. December.

Bhorat, H. 1995. 'The South African social security net: past present and future'. *Development Southern Africa*. 12(4): 595–604.

Bhorat, H. 1996. 'Inequality in the South African labour market'. Unpublished MA dissertation. Stellenbosch: University of Stellenbosch.

Bhorat, H. 1999b. 'Distinguishing between individual- and household-level poverty'. *Development Southern Africa*. 16(1): 157–62.

Bhorat, H. 1999a. 'Public expenditure and poverty alleviation in the South African labour market'. *DPRU Working Paper No. 99/26*. Development Policy Research Unit. University of Cape Town.

Bhorat, H. 1999c. 'The October Household Survey, unemployment and the informal sector: a note' *South African Journal of Economics*. 67(2): 320–6.

Bhorat, H. & Hertz, T. 1995. 'A statistical overview of the South African labour market'. *Input paper for the Presidential Labour Market Commission*.

Bhorat, H. & Hodge, J. 1999. 'Decomposing shifts in labour demand in South Africa'. *South African Journal of Economics*. 67(3): 348–80.

Bhorat, H. & Leibbrandt, M. 1996. 'Understanding unemployment'. Baskin, J. (ed.) *Against the Current: Labour and Economic Policy in South Africa*. Randburg: Ravan Press.

Bhorat, H. & Leibbrandt, M. 1998. 'Poverty amongst the self-employed'. *Studies in Economics and Econometrics*. 22(3): 25–41.

Bhorat, H. & Leibbrandt, M. 1999a. 'Correlates of vulnerability in the South African labour market'. *DPRU Working Paper No. 99/27*. Development Policy Research Unit. University of Cape Town.

Bhorat, H. & Leibbrandt, M. 1999b. 'Modelling vulnerability and low earnings in the South African labour market'. *DPRU Working Paper No. 99/32*. Development Policy Research Unit. University of Cape Town.

Bhorat, H. & Van der Berg, S. 1999. 'The present as a legacy of the past: the labour market, inequality, and poverty in South Africa'. *DPRU Working Paper No. 99/29*. Development Policy Research Unit. University of Cape Town.

Bourguignon, F., Fournier, M. & Gurgand, M. 1998. 'Distribution, development and education: Taiwan 1979–1992'. Mimeo. Paris: Delta.

Breen, R. 1996. *Regression Models: Censored, Sample-Selected, or Truncated Data*. Thousand Oaks, California: Sage Publications.

Breslin, E.D., Delius, P. & Madrid, C. 1997. 'Strengthening institutional safety nets in South Africa: sharing Operation Hunger's insights and experiences'. *Development Southern Africa* 14(1): 21–41.

Bromberger, N. 1982. 'Government policies affecting the distribution of income, 1940–1980'. Schrire, R. (ed.) 1982. *South Africa: Public Policy Perspectives*. Cape Town: Juta.

Callan, T. & Nolan, B. 1991. 'Concepts of poverty and the poverty line'. *Journal of Economic Surveys*, 5(3): 243–61.

Card, D. & Krueger, A. 1994. 'A living wage? The effects of a minimum wage on the distribution of wages, the distribution of family earnings, and poverty'. *Working Paper No. 333*. Princeton: Industrial Relations Section, Princeton University.

Case, A. & Deaton, A. 1996. 'Large cash transfers to the elderly in South Africa.' *Discussion Paper 176*. Princeton: Research Program in Development Studies.

Case, A. & Deaton, A. 1998. 'Large cash transfers to the elderly in South Africa'. *Economic Journal*. 108(450): 1330–61.

Case, A. & Deaton, A. 1999. 'School inputs and educational outcomes in South Africa'. *Quarterly Journal of Economics*. 114(3): 1047–84.

Chambers, R. 1988. 'Poverty in India: concepts, research and reality'. *Discussion Paper 241*. Institute of Development Studies, University of Sussex.

COSATU. 1999. 'COSATU submission on labour market policy in the era of transformation'. On website www.cosatu.org.za/docs/1999/labr-mkt.htm. Retrieved on 5 August 1999.

Cowell, F. 1995. *Measuring Inequality*. (2nd edn). London: Prentice Hall.

Deaton, A. 1997. *The Analysis of Household Surveys: A Microeconometric Approach to Development Policy*. Baltimore: Johns Hopkins Press.

Deaton, A. & Case, A. 1988. 'Analysis of household expenditures'. *Living Standards Measurement Study Working Paper 28*. Washington, D.C.: World Bank.

Deaton, A. & Muellbauer, J. 1980. *Economics and Consumer Behaviour*. New York: Cambridge University Press.

De Haan, A., Lipton, M., Darbellay, E., O'Brien, D. & Samman, E. 1997. *The Role of Government and Public Policy in Poverty Alleviation in Sub-Saharan Africa*. Review of the literature prepared for the African Economic Research Consortium's collaborative project on poverty, income distribution and labour markets. Mimeo. Sussex: Poverty Research Unit.

De Villiers, A.P. 1996. 'Effektiwiteit van Suid-Afrika se onderwysstelsel: 'n ekonomiese analise.' *Unpublished PhD thesis*. Stellenbosch: University of Stellenbosch.

De Wulf, L. 1975. 'Fiscal incidence studies in developing countries: survey and critique.' *IMF Staff Working Papers*. 22(1). March.

Deininger, K. & Squire, L. 1996. 'A new data set measuring income inequality'. *World Bank Economic Review*. 10(3): 565–91.

Department of Finance. 1996. *Growth, Employment, and Redistribution: A Macroeconomic Strategy*. Pretoria: Government Printer.

Department of Finance. 1998a. *1998 Medium term Expenditure Review: Education*. Pretoria: Department of Finance

Department of Finance. 1998b. *1998 Medium Term Expenditure Review: Welfare*. Pretoria: Department of Finance.

Department of Labour. 1996. *Labour Relations Act*. Pretoria: Government Printer.

Department of Labour. 1997. *Basic Conditions of Employment Act*. Pretoria: Government Printer.

Department of Labour. 1998a. *1997 Annual Report*. Pretoria: Government Printer.

Department of Labour. 1998b. *Employment Equity Act*. Pretoria: Government Printer.

Department of Labour. 1998c. *Skills Development Act*. Pretoria: Government Printer.

Department of Labour. 1999. *1998 Annual Report*. Pretoria: Government Printer.

Department of Statistics. 1960. *Union Statistics for 50 years, 1910–1960*. Pretoria: Government Printer.

Di Tella, R. & MacCulloch, R. 1998. 'The consequences of labour market flexibility: panel evidence on survey data'. *Unpublished paper*. Harvard Business School.

Donaldson, A. 1992. 'Restructuring the social services'. Howe, G. & Le Roux, P. (eds) *Transforming the Economy: Policy Options for South Africa*. Durban: Indicator South Africa.

Donaldson, A. 1993. 'Basic needs and social policy: The role of the state in education, health and welfare'. Lipton, M. & Simkins, C. (eds) *State and Market in Post-Apartheid South Africa.* Johannesburg: University of the Witwatersrand Press.

Edusource. 1999. *Edusource Data News 24.* Johannesburg: Education Foundation. March.

Fagerberg, J. 1994. 'Technology and international differences in growth rates'. *Journal of Economic Literature.* 32(3): 1147–75.

Fallon, P. 1992. 'An analysis of employment and wage behaviour in South Africa'. *Informal Discussion Paper No. 3 on aspects of the economy of South Africa.* Unpublished paper. Washington, D.C.: World Bank.

Fallon, P. & Lucas, R. 1996. 'South African labour markets: adjustment and inequalities'. *Informal Discussion Paper No. 12 on aspects of the economy of South Africa.* Washington, D.C.: World Bank.

Fashoyin, T. 1998. 'Industrial relations in Southern Africa: the challenge of change'. *ILO/SAMAT Policy Paper No. 5.* Harare: ILO/SAMAT.

Ferreira, F.H.G. & Litchfield, J.A. 1999. 'Calm after the storms: income distribution in Chile, 1987–1994'. *World Bank Policy Discussion Paper 1960.* Washington, D.C.: World Bank. 49.

Field, W. 1991. 'Employees' pension and provident fund rights: a renewed interest develops'. *Industrial Law Journal.* 12: 965–83.

Fields, G.S. 1980. *Poverty, Inequality, and Development.* Cambridge: Cambridge University Press.

Fields, G. 1998. 'Accounting for income inequality and its change'. *Unpublished paper.* Ithaca, NY: Cornell University.

Filmer, D. & Pritchett, L. 1998. 'The effect of household wealth on educational attainment around the world: demographic and health survey evidence'. *World Bank Policy Research Paper 1980.* Washington, D.C.: World Bank.

Fiszbein, A. & Psacharopoulos, G. 1995. 'Income inequality trends in Latin America in the 1980s'. Lustig, N. (ed.) *Coping with Austerity: Poverty and Inequality in Latin America.* Washington, D.C.: The Brookings Institution.

Foster, J.E., Greer, J. & Thorbecke, E. 1984. 'A class of decomposable poverty measures'. *Econometrica.* 52 (3): 761–6.

Foster, J.E. & Shorrocks, A.F. 1988. 'Poverty orderings'. *Econometrica.* 56: 173–7.

Freeman, R.B. 1993. 'Labour market institutions and policies: help or hindrance to economic?'. *Proceedings of the World Bank Annual Conference on Development Economics 1992.* Washington: World Bank.

Fuchs, M. 1985. *Soziale Sicherheit in der Dritten Welt: Zugleich eine Fallstudie Kenias.* Baden-Baden: Nomos Verlagsgesellschaft.

Fuller, B., Pillay, P. & Sirur, N. 1995. *Literacy Trends in South Africa: Expanding Education while Reinforcing Unequal Achievement?* Mimeo. Cape Town: SALDRU. University of Cape Town.

Glewwe, P. 1988. 'The distribution of welfare in Côte d'Ivoire in 1985'. *Living Standards Measurement Study Working Paper 29.* Washington, D.C.: World Bank.

Glewwe, P. 'Investigating the determinants of household welfare in Côte d'Ivoire'. *Journal of Development Economics.* 35(2): 307–37.

Glick, P. & Sahn, D. 1997. 'Gender and education impacts on employment and earnings in West Africa: evidence from Guinea'. *Economic Development and Cultural Change.* 22: 95–125.

Gohan, T. & Robinson, J. 1998. 'What model for the South African labour market? Lessons from the OECD and LDCs'. *Paper presented at a conference on 'Politics of Economic Reform'*. University of Cape Town. 16–18 January 1998.

Goldin, C. & Katz, L.F. 1999. 'The returns to skills in the United States across the twentieth century'. *NBER Working Paper 7126*. Cambridge, Mass.: National Bureau of Economic Research.

Grawitzky, R. 1999. 'Researchers forecast poor jobs growth'. *Business Day*. 26 August.

Gregg, P. & Manning, A. 1997. 'Labour market regulation and unemployment'. Snower, D.J. & de la Dehesa, G. (eds). *Unemployment Policy: Government Options for the Labour Market*. Cambridge: Cambridge University Press.

Gruat, J.V. 1984. 'The extension of social protection in the Gabonese Republic: consolidating the development process'. *International Labour Review*. 123(4): 457–71.

Greenberg, S. 1980. *Race and State in Capitalist Development*. Johannesburg: Ravan Press.

Greene, W.H. 1993. *Econometric Analysis*. (2nd edn). New York: Macmillan Publishing Company.

Gupta, S., Verhoeven, M. & Tiongson, E. 1999. 'Does higher government spending buy better results in education and health care?' *IMF Working Paper*. Washington, D.C.: International Monetary Fund.

Haddad, L. & Kanbur, R. 1990. 'How serious is the neglect of intra-household inequality?'. *The Economic Journal*. 100(402):866–81. September.

Heckman, J. 1979. 'Sample selection bias as a specification error'. *Econometrica*. 47: 153–61.

Heckman, J. & Hotz, J. 1986. 'The sources of inequality for males in Panama's labour market'. *The Journal of Human Resources*. 21(4): 507–42.

Hentschel, J. & Lanjouw, P. 1996. 'Constructing an indicator of consumption for the analysis of poverty. Principles and illustrations with reference to Ecuador'. *Living Standards Measurement Study Working Paper 124*. Washington D.C.: World Bank.

Hertz, T. 1995. 'Jobs, farms, discrimination and education in South Africa: simulations and regressions on household survey data'. *Unpublished paper*. Department of Economics. University of Massachusetts at Amherst.

Hindson, D. & Crankshaw, O. 1990. 'New jobs, new skills, new divisions: the changing structure of South Africa's workforce'. *South African Labour Bulletin* 15(1): 23–31.

Hofmeyr, J.F. 1990. 'Black wages: The post-war experience'. Nattrass, N. & Ardington, E. (eds) *The Political Economy of South Africa*. Cape Town: Oxford University Press.

Hofmeyr, J.F. 1999. 'Segmentation in the South African labour market.' *SANER Working Paper* (in preparation). Cape Town: South African Network for Economic Research.

Hofmeyr, J. & Lucas, R. 1998. 'The rise in union wage premia in South Africa'. *IED Discussion Paper Series No. 83*. Boston, Mass.: Institute for Economic Development, Boston University.

Huppi, M. & Ravallion, M. 1991. 'The sectoral structure of poverty during an adjustment period: evidence from Indonesia in the mid-1980s'. *World Development*. 19(12): 1653–78.

Iliffe, J. 1987. *The African Poor: A History*. Cambridge: Cambridge University Press.

Institute of Race Relations. (various years). *Race Relations Survey/South Africa Survey*. Johannesburg: South African Institute of Race Relations.

Inter-American Development Bank. 1998. *Economic and Social Progress Report, 1998–1999.* Washington D.C: Johns Hopkins University Press.

International Labour Office. 1996. *Restructuring the Labour Market: The South African Challenge.* Geneva: ILO Publication Office.

ILO. 1999. *Studies on the Social Dimensions of Globalization: South Africa.* Geneva: ILO (final draft).

Janisch, C. 1996. 'An analysis of the burdens and benefits of taxes and government expenditure in the South African economy for the year 1993/94'. *Unpublished MA dissertation.* Pietermaritzburg: University of Natal.

Johnson, D. 1996. 'Poverty lines and the measurement of poverty'. *Australian Economic Review.* 1: 110–26.

Kanbur, R. 1985. 'Inequality, poverty and development with an application to Fiji'. *Unpublished manuscript.* University of Essex.

Kanbur, R. 1987. 'Measurement and alleviation of poverty'. *IMF Staff Papers.* Vol. 34(1).

Kanbur, R. 1998. 'Income distribution and development'. *World Bank Working Paper WP98-13.* Mimeo. Washington, D.C.: World Bank.

Klasen, S. 1996. *Poverty and Inequality in South Africa.* Mimeo. Cambridge: Centre for History and Economics, King's College.

Klasen, S. 1997. 'Poverty, inequality and deprivation in South Africa'. *Social Indicator Research.*

Klasen, S. & Woolard, I. 1998. 'Unemployment, household formation, poverty and nutrition in South Africa.' *Unpublished paper.* Port Elizabeth: University of Port Elizabeth.

Kruger, J.J. 1992. 'State provision of social security: some theoretical, comparative and historical perspectives with reference to South Africa.' *Unpublished MA thesis.* Stellenbosch: University of Stellenbosch.

Lachman, D. & Bercuson, K. (eds) 1992. 'Economic policies for a new South Africa'. *IMF Occasional Paper (91).* Washington, D.C.: International Monetary Fund.

Lam, D. 1999. *Generating Extreme Inequality: Schooling, Earnings, and Intergenerational Transmission of Human Capital in South Africa and Brazil.* Mimeo. Ann Arbor: University of Michigan.

Lanjouw, P. & Ravallion, M. 1995. 'Poverty and household size'. *The Economic Journal.* 105(433): 1415–34.

LAPC. 1997. 'A policy study of agricultural employment'. *Unpublished study commissioned by the Department of Labour.*

Lee, J. & Barro, R.J. 1997. 'Schooling quality in a cross section of countries'. *NBER Working Paper 6198.* Cambridge, Mass.: National Bureau of Economic Research.

Leibbrandt, M. & Woolard, I. 1999. 'Household incomes, poverty and inequality in a multivariate framework'. *DPRU Working Paper No. 99/31.* Development Policy Research Unit. University of Cape Town.

Leibbrandt, M. & Woolard, I. 1999. 'Measuring poverty in South Africa'. *DPRU Working Paper No. 99/33.* Development Policy Research Unit. University of Cape Town.

Leibbrandt, M. & Woolard, I. 1999. 'A comparison of poverty in South Africa's nine provinces'. *Development Southern Africa.* 16(1): 37–54.

Leibbrandt, M. & Woolard, I. 1996. 'Rural labour markets, migrant labour and rural poverty in South Africa'. *Report for the International Labour Office*.

Leibbrandt, M., Bhorat, H. & Woolard, I. 1999. 'Understanding contemporary household inequality in South Africa', *DPRU Working Paper No. 99/25*. Development Policy Research Unit. University of Cape Town.

Leibbrandt, M., Woolard, C. & Woolard, I. 1996. 'The contribution of income components to income inequality in South Africa'. *LSMS Working Paper 125*. Washington, D.C.: World Bank.

Leistner, G.M.E. 1968. Table insert. *Africa Institute Bulletin* VI. No. 6: 175–7.

Lerman, R.I. & S. Yitzhaki. 1994. 'Effect of marginal changes in income sources on U.S. income inequality'. *Public Finance Quarterly*, 22(4): 403–16.

Le Roux, P. 1978. 'The poor white problem – an economist's perspective'. *Social Work*, 14(1 & 2). March & June.

Le Roux, P. 1994. 'Parental care and family structure: some interesting findings from the South African Living Standards Survey'. *Unpublished manuscript*. Cape Town: University of the Western Cape.

Leser, C.E.V. 1963. 'Forms of Engel functions'. *Econometrica*. 31(14): 694–703.

Levine, R. & Renelt, D. 1992. 'A sensitivity analysis of cross-country growth regressions'. *American Economic Review* 82(4): 942–63.

Lipton, M. 1986. *Capitalism and Apartheid: South Africa, 1910–1984*. Second revised printing. Aldershot: Gower.

Lipton, M & Ravallion, M. 1995. 'Poverty and policy'. Behrman, J. & Srinivasan, T.N. (eds) 1995. *Handbook of Development Economics*, Vol. III. Amsterdam: North Holland. 2551–657.

Lipton, M., de Klerk, M. & Lipton, M. 1996. *Land, Labour and Livelihoods in Rural South Africa*. Vol. I. Indicator Press. Durban.

Londoño, J.L. 1996. *Poverty, Inequality, and Human Capital Development in Latin America, 1950–2025*. World Bank Latin American and Caribbean Studies: Viewpoints. Washington, D.C.: World Bank.

Lund, F.J. 1993. 'State social benefits in South Africa'. *International Social Security Review* 46(1): 5–25.

Lund, F.J. 1994. *Social Security for Disabled People in South Africa: Challenges Facing the New Society*. Mimeo. Durban: University of Natal.

Lundahl, M. & Moritz, L. 1994. 'The quest for equity in South Africa – redistribution and growth'. Odén, B. & Ohlson, T. (eds) 1994. *The South African Tripod: Studies on Economics, Politics and Conflict*. Uppsala: Scandinavian Institute of African Studies.

Lustig, N. & McCleod, J. 1996. 'Minimum wages and poverty in developing countries: some empirical evidence'. *Brookings Discussion Papers in International Economics*. Washington D.C.: The Brookings Institution.

Marks, S. & Rathbone, R. (eds) 1982. *Industrialisation and Social Change in South Africa: African Class Formation, Culture, and Consciousness, 1870–1930*. New York: Longman.

Marsden, D. 1995. 'The impact of industrial relations practices on employment and unemployment'. *The OECD Jobs Study Working Paper No. 3*. Paris: OECD.

May, J. 1998. *Experiences and Perceptions of Poverty in South Africa*. Durban: Praxis Publishing.

May, J., Carter, M. & Posel, D. 1995. 'The composition and persistence of poverty in rural South Africa: an entitlements approach'. *Land and Agriculture Policy Centre Policy Paper No. 15*. Land and Agriculture Policy Centre.

McGrath, M. 1983. 'The distribution of personal income in South Africa in selected years over the period from 1945 to 1980'. *Unpublished doctoral thesis*. Durban: University of Natal.

McGrath, M. 1990. 'Income redistribution: the economic challenge of the 1990s'. Schrire, R. (ed.). *Critical Choices for South Africa: An Agenda for the 1990s*. Cape Town: Oxford University Press.

McGrath, M. & Whiteford, A. 1994. 'Inequality and the size distribution of income in South Africa'. *Occasional Paper No. 10*. Stellenbosch Economic Project.

MERG. 1993. *Making Democracy Work*. Cape Town: Center for Development Studies.

Moll, P. 1995. 'Wage developments in South Africa in the 1990s'. *Unpublished paper*.

Moll, P. 1998. 'Discrimination is declining in South Africa but inequality is not'. *SANER Working Paper 5*. Cape Town: South African Network for Economic Research.

Moser, C. 1996. 'Confronting crisis: a comparative study of household responses to poverty and vulnerability in four poor urban communities'. *Environmentally Sustainable Development Studies and Monographs Series No. 8*. World Bank.

Mouton Committee. 1992. *Report of the Committee of Investigation into a Retirement Provision System for South Africa*. 2 vols. Johannesburg: Government Printer.

Munro, R. 1991. 'Beware those "golden handcuffs"'. *Sunday Times*. 14 July.

Murphy, K.M. & Welch, F. 1994. 'Industrial change and the rising importance of skills'. Danziger, S. & Gottschalk, P. (eds). 1994. *Uneven Tides: Rising Inequality in America*. New York: Russel Sage Foundation. 101–32.

Mwabu, G. & Schultz, T. 1996a. 'Wage premia for education and location by gender and race in South Africa'. Unpublished paper. New Haven, Conn.: Yale University.

Mwabu, G. & Schultz, T. 1996b. 'Education returns across quantiles of the wage function: alternative explanations for the returns to education by race in South Africa'. *American Economic Review*. 86(2): 335–39.

Mwabu, G. & Schultz, T. 1998. 'Labour unions and the distribution of wages and employment in South Africa'. *Industrial and Labour Review*. 51(4): 680–703.

Native Economic Commission. 1932. *Report of the Native Economic Commission 1930–32*. Pretoria: Government Printer.

Nattrass, N. & Seekings, J. 1998. 'Changing patterns of inequality in the South African labour market'. Petersson, L. (ed.). *Post Apartheid Southern Africa*. London: Routledge.

Ncube, D. 1985. *Black Trade Unions in South Africa*. Johannesburg: Skotaville.

Nelson, J.A. 1988. 'Household economies of scale in consumption: theory and evidence'. *Econometrica*. 56(16): 1301–14.

NEPA. 1997. *The State of Small Business in South Africa*, Pretoria: NEPA.

Neumark, D. & Wascher, W. 1997. 'Do minimum wages fight poverty?' *Working Paper 6127*. NBER.

Ng, K. 1981. 'Welfarism: a defence against Sen's attack'. *The Economic Journal*. 91(362): 527–30.

Nicholson, J.L. 1976. 'Appraisal of different methods of estimating equivalence scales and their results'. *Review of Income and Wealth*. 22: 1–11.

Nolan, B. & Whelan, C.T. 1996. 'The relationship between income and deprivation: a dynamic perspective'. *Revue Economique*. 47(3): 709–17.

Nygard, F. & Sandstrom, A. 1981. *Measuring Income Inequality*. Stockholm: Almquist and Wicksell.

OECD. 1997. *Policies for Low-paid Workers and Unskilled Job Seekers*. Paris: OECD.

Patel, L. 1992. *Restructuring Social Welfare: Options for South Africa*. Johannesburg: Ravan Press.

Potgieter, J.F. 1993 and 1995. *The Household Subsistence Level in the Major Urban Centres of the Republic of South Africa*. Port Elizabeth: University of Port Elizabeth.

Poverty and Inequality Report. 1998. *Poverty and Inequality in South Africa*. Report prepared for the Office of the Executive Deputy President and the Inter-Ministerial Committee for Poverty and Inequality. Pretoria: Government Printer.

Presidential Commission. 1996. *Restructuring the South African Labour Market: Report of the Presidential Commission to Investigate Labour Market Policy*. Pretoria: Government Printer.

Rama, M. 1998. 'Poverty alleviation and the labour market'. *Draft unpublished paper*. Washington, D.C.: World Bank.

Ravallion, M. 1992. 'Poverty comparisons: a guide to concepts and methods'. *Living Standards Measurement Study Working Paper 88*. Washington D.C.: World Bank.

Ravallion, M. 1994 *Poverty Comparisons*. Switzerland: Harwood Academic Publishers.

Ravallion, M. 1996. 'Poor areas'. Giles, D. & Ullah, A (edn). *The Handbook of Applied Economic Statistics*. New York: Marcel Dekkar.

Ravallion, M. 1998. 'Poverty lines in theory and practice'. *AERC Working Papers CR2-2*.

Ravallion, M. & Sen, B. 1996. 'When method matters: monitoring poverty in Bangladesh'. *Economic Development and Cultural Change*.

RDP Office. 1995. *Key Indicators of Poverty in South Africa*. Pretoria: RDP Office.

Rousseeuw, P. & Leroy, A. 1987. *Robust Regression and Outlier Detection*. New York: John Wiley and Sons.

Roy, A. 1951. 'Some thoughts on the distribution of earnings'. *Oxford Economic Papers*. 3: 135–146.

Rumney, R. 1988. 'Saving pensions'. *Finance Week*. 5–11 May: 35–6.

Sadie, J.L. ca. 1982. 'The performance of labour in South Africa during the sixties and seventies.' Stellenbosch. *Unpublished report to the National Manpower Commission*. Stellenbosch.

Sadie, J.L. 1991. 'The South African labour force, 1960–2005'. *BMR Report 178*. Pretoria: Unisa, Bureau of Market Research.

SALDRU. 1989. *Wage Determinations in South Africa, Vol.II: 1978–1988*. Cape Town: SALDRU.

SALDRU. 1991. *Directory of South African Trade Unions*. (5th edn). Cape Town: SALDRU.

SALDRU. 1994. *South Africans Rich and Poor: Baseline Household Statistics*. Cape Town: SALDRU.

Schlemmer, L. & Levitz, S. 1998. *Unemployment in South Africa: The Facts, Prospects and an Exploration of Solutions*. Johannesburg: South African Institute of Race Relations.

Sen, A. 1976. 'Poverty: an ordinal approach to measurement' *Econometrica*. 44(2): 219–31.

Sen, A. 1987. *The Standard of Living*. Cambridge: Cambridge University Press.

Sen, A. 1992. *Inequality Re-examined.* Cambridge: Harvard University Press.

Sephton, B., Cooper, D. & Thomson, C. 1990. *A Guide to Pension and Provident Funds: Legal and Policy Considerations.* Cape Town: University of Cape Town, Labour Law Unit.

Shorrocks, A. 1983. 'The impact of income components on the distribution of family income'. *Quarterly Journal of Economics.* 98(2): 311–26.

Simkins, C. 1998. *On the Durability of South African Inequality.* Macarthur Foundation Working Paper. Princeton: Macarthur Network on Inequality and Poverty.

Simkins, C. & Hindson, D. 1979. 'The division of labour in South Africa, 1969–1977'. *Social Dynamics* 5.

Smith Committee. 1995. *Report of the Committee on Strategy and Policy Review of Retirement Provision in South Africa.* Pretoria: Department of Finance.

Social Security Committee. 1944. *Report of the Committee on Social Security.* Pretoria: Government Printer.

South Africa 1998e. *Declaration of the Presidential Jobs Summit: 30 October 1998,* mimeo.

South African Reserve Bank (various years). *Quarterly Economic Bulletin.* Pretoria: South African Reserve Bank.

Spandau, A. 1971. *Income Distribution and Economic Growth in South Africa.* PhD. Pretoria: University of South Africa.

Squire, L. & Suthiwart-Narueput, S. 1997. 'The impact of labour market regulation'. *World Bank Economic Review.* 11: 119–41. January.

Stadler, A. 1987. *The Political Economy of Modern South Africa.* Cape Town: David Philip.

Standing, G., Sender, J. & Weeks, 1996. *Restructuring the Labour Market: The South African Challenge.* Geneva: ILO Publication Office.

Stark, O., Taylor, J. & Yitzhaki, S. 1986. 'Remittances and inequality'. *Economic Journal.* 96: 722–40.

StataCorp. 1997. *Stata Reference Manual (Release 5).* College Station: Stata Press.

Statistics South Africa. 1992. *South African Statistics 1992.* Pretoria: Statistics South Africa.

Statistics South Africa. 1994. *The October Household Survey 1993.* Pretoria: Government Printer.

Statistics South Africa. 1995. *The October Household Survey 1994.* Pretoria: Government Printer.

Statistics South Africa. 1996a. *October Household Survey 1995.* Statistical Release P0317. Pretoria: Statistics South Africa.

Statistics South Africa. 1996b. *Living in South Africa: Selected Findings of the 1995 October Household Survey.* Pretoria: Statistics South Africa.

Statistics South Africa. 1997. *Earning and Spending in South Africa. Selected Findings of the 1995 Income and Expenditure Survey.* Pretoria: Statistics South Africa.

Statistics South Africa. 1998. *Living in South Africa: Selected Findings of the 1995 October Household Survey.* Pretoria: Statistics South Africa.

Statistics South Africa. Various years. *South African Labour Statistics.* Pretoria: Government Printer.

Statistics South Africa. Various years. *South African Statistics.* Pretoria: Government Printer.

Streeten, P. 1994. 'Poverty concepts and measures'. *Poverty Monitoring: An International Concern.* London: St Martin's Press.

Tarsitano, A. 1990. 'The Bonferroni Index of Income Inequality'. Dagum, C. & Zenga, M. (eds). *Studies in Contemporary Economics: Income and Wealth Distribution, Inequality and Poverty.* Heidelberg: Springer-Verlag.

Terreblanche, S. 1978. 'Moontlike fiskale strukture in 'n alternatiewe konstitusionele model in Suid-Afrika'. Benyon, J. (ed.). *Constitutional change in South Africa.* Pietermaritzburg: University of Natal: 190–224.

Terreblanche, S. 1977. *Gemeenskapsarmoede: Perspektief op chroniese armoede in the Kleurlinggemeenskap na aanleiding van die Theron verslag.* Cape Town: Tafelberg.

Terreblanche, S. & Nattrass, N. 1990. 'A periodisation of the political economy from 1910'. Nattrass, N. & Ardington, E. (eds). *The Political Economy of South Africa.* Cape Town: Oxford University Press.

Theron Commission. 1976. *Verslag van die Kommissie van Ondersoek na Aangeleenthede rakende die Kleurlingbevolkingsgroep.* RP38/1976. Pretoria: Government Printer.

Tomlinson Commission. 1955. *Summary of the Report of the Commission for the Socio-Economic Development of the Bantu Areas within the Union of South Africa.* UG61/1955. Pretoria: Government Printer.

Van den Bosch, K., De Lathouwer, L. & Deleeck, H. 1997. 'Poverty and social security transfers – results for seven countries and regions in the EC'. Ott, N. & Wagner, G.G. (eds). *Income Inequality and Poverty in Eastern and Western Europe.* Heidelberg: Physica Verlag. 53–67.

Van der Berg, S. 1987. 'Die verband tussen die aard en omvang van ekonomiese groei en die bevrediging van basiese behoeftes in Suid-Afrika'. *Unpublished PhD thesis.* Stellenbosch. University of Stellenbosch.

Van der Berg, S. 1989. 'Long term economic trends and development prospects in South Africa'. *African Affairs.*

Van der Berg, S. 1992a. 'Fiscal dilemmas over popular aspirations'. Howe, G. & Le Roux, P. (eds) *Transforming the Economy: Policy Options for South Africa.* Papers from the 1989 Lausanne Colloquium. Durban: Indicator Project South Africa.

Van der Berg, S. 1992b. 'Social reform and the reallocation of social expenditures'. Schrire, R. (ed). *Wealth or Poverty? Critical Choices for South Africa.* Cape Town: Oxford University Press.

Van der Berg, S. 1994. *Issues in South African Social Security.* Commissioned paper prepared for the World Bank. Mimeo. Washington, D.C.

Van der Berg, S. 1997. 'South African social security under apartheid and beyond'. *Development Southern Africa.* Vol. 14(4): 481–583.

Van der Berg, S. 1999. 'Social Policy to address Poverty'. *DPRU Working Paper No. 99/30.* Development Policy Research Unit, University of Cape Town.

Van der Merwe, T. 1996. *Bestaansbeveiliging: 'n Ekonomiese Perspektief.* DLitt et Phil Thesis. Pretoria: University of South Africa (UNISA).

Whiteford, A. & McGrath, M. 1994. 'Inequality in the size distribution of income in South Africa'. *Occasional Papers 10.* Stellenbosch: Stellenbosch Economic Project.

Whiteford, A., Posel, D. & Kelawang, T. 1995. *A Profile of Poverty, Inequality and Human Development.* Pretoria: Human Sciences Research Council.

Willis, R. 1987. 'Wage determinants: a survey'. Ashenfelter, O. & Layard, R. *Handbook of Labor Economics.* Amsterdam: North Holland. 525–602.

Wilson, F. & Ramphele, M. 1989. *Uprooting Poverty: The South African Challenge.* Cape Town & Johannesburg: David Philip.

Winter, C. 1998. 'Women workers in South Africa: participation, pay and prejudice in the formal labour market'. *Unpublished paper.* World Bank.

World Bank. 1990. *World Development Report.* New York: Oxford University Press.

World Bank. 1997. *World Development Report.* New York: Oxford University Press.

World Bank/RDP Office. 1995. *Key Indicators of Poverty in South Africa.* Prepared for the Reconstruction and Development Programme Office. Pretoria: Government Printer.

Working, H. 1943. 'Statistical laws of family expenditure'. *Journal of the American Statistical Association*, 38(221): 43–56.

INDEX

Page references in **bold** refer to tables and diagrams.